From 'SPAM' to BALONEY

Leonard O'Donnell

Cover Art Work
By Dennis Cox
www.clipartof.com
(used by permission)

FROM 'SPAM' TO BALONEY
Copyright © 2018 by Leonard O'Donnell

Library of Congress Control Number: 2018941707
ISBN-13: Paperback: 978-1-64151-717-1

All rights reserved. No part of this publication may be reproduced, distributed, or transmitted in any form or by any means, including photocopying, recording, or other electronic or mechanical methods, without the prior written permission of the publisher or author, except in the case of brief quotations embodied in critical reviews and certain other noncommercial uses permitted by copyright law.

Although every precaution has been taken to verify the accuracy of the information contained herein, the author and publisher assume no responsibility for any errors or omissions. No liability is assumed for damages that may result from the use of information contained within.

Printed in the United States of America

LitFire LLC
1-800-511-9787
www.litfirepublishing.com
order@litfirepublishing.com

Contents

Acknowledgements v
Chapter 1   Blonde Comedy 1
Chapter 2   Children Comedy 9
Chapter 3   Christian Comedy 19
Chapter 4   Christmas Comedy 27
Chapter 5   Church Comedy 41
Chapter 6   Florida Comedy 75
Chapter 7   Good ole days Comedy 81
Chapter 8   Jewish Comedy 87
Chapter 9   Married Comedy 93
Chapter 10   Military (Memories) 113
Chapter 11   One-liner Comedy 123
Chapter 12   Patriotic (Memories) 139
Chapter 13   Redneck Comedy 149
Chapter 14   School Comedy 163
Chapter 15   Senior Comedy 171
Chapter 16   Sports Comedy 187
Chapter 17   Travel Comedy 193
Chapter 18   Work Comedy 201
Chapter 19   Amazing facts 225
Chapter 20   Church' stories 233
Chapter 21   HOLIDAY stories 255
Chapter 22   Inspirational Stories 269
Chapter 23   Political stories 303
Chapter 24   Senior Stories 317
Chapter 25   Supernatural stories 323
Chapter 26   Testimonies 333

Index(Punch-Lines) 343

Acknowledgements

"Once I started, I couldn't stop!"

John D. Pantuso
Author, "Songs From My Heart"

"I read this one (over the phone) to my Dad and nephew… they found it hilarious…"

Kerri Trottier

"Leonard: what a great book to enjoy!"

Tina Martin

From the Author:

"I love to read, maybe too much. I hate to forget what I read. I have no idea where a lot of the statements in this book came from. (If anyone can help me in this area I will certainly take care of that in my re-print)."

"I have acknowledged the sources that I can remember, but where I have not, it is because I did not know. Is that OK? My apologies for being so careless, but come to think of it, everything I do know, I guess I read it somewhere. Is that the way it is with you too? OK. You do understand. Please forgive me."

Thanks to...

- My brother Harold O'Donnell, from New Brunswick, Canada, for reading and laughing and encouraging me.
- My good friend George Dennis, from upstate New York, for taking me trout fishing and reading my jokes back to me.
- My friend 'Bill' Young, guitar picker and Lawn Man, from WBCA in Brooksville, Florida and all the 'corny' jokes he throws at me.

I also had a lot of help from...

- Proofreading and editing from Diana S. O'Donnell Lyons, New Brunswick, Canada and from Florida, USA…

  John D. Pantuso,
  Kerri and Michael Trottier,
  Melissa Sexton and others…

- From the little church congregations; from music Jamboree fans (Including the 'New Wine Pickers' band)…you laughed anyway!

- And, from my wife Joyce, who gave me the 'thumbs-up' or the 'thumbs-down', but always with a smile – I knew what she meant.

"Is God good, or what?"*- Author: Leonard O'Donnell*

I got up from bed about 10:30 pm last night and started reading… However, I laughed so hard that I couldn't get to sleep until all hours…!!!

Be in touch soon…..Di

Chapter 1

Blonde Comedy

(1) There was a blonde who was sick of all the blonde jokes. One day, she decided to get a makeover, so she cut and dyed her hair. She went driving down a country road and came across a herd of sheep. She stopped and called the sheepherder over. "Tell you what. I have a proposition for you," said the woman. "If I can guess the exact number of sheep in your flock, can I take one home?"

"Sure," said the sheepherder. So, she sat up and looked at the herd for a second and then replied, "Three hundred eighty-two."

"Wow!" said the herder. "That is exactly right. Go ahead and pick out the sheep you want to take home." So the woman went and picked one out and put it in her car.

Then, the herder said, "Okay, now I have a proposition for you." "What is it?" queried the woman.

"If I can guess the real color of your hair, **can I have my dog back?**

(2) A blonde got lost in her car in a snowstorm. She remembered what her dad had once told her. "If you ever get stuck in a snow storm, wait for a snow plow and follow it." Pretty soon a snow plow came by, and she started to follow it.

She followed the plow for about forty-five minutes. Finally the driver of the truck got out and asked her what she was doing. She explained that her dad had told her if she ever got stuck in the snow, to follow a plow.

The driver nodded and said, "Well, I'm done with the Wal-Mart parking lot, now you can **follow me over to K-Mart.**"

• •

(3) A blonde pulled into a crowded parking lot and rolled down the car windows to make sure her dog had fresh air. Her dog was sitting in the back. And to make sure he stayed there, she walked backwards to the curb, pointing her finger at the car and saying, "Now you stay, you stay!"

The driver across the street, seeing what was going on, as he enjoyed watching the blonde, yell out to her, "Hey, lady, why don't you just put it in **park like the rest of us do**!"

• •

(4) Lisa, a 23-year-old blonde from California, was visiting her in-laws and was asked to run to the grocery store to pick up a few things. Several people noticed her sitting in her car in the parking lot with the windows rolled up and her eyes closed and she had both hands on the back of her head.

One passerby became concerned and approached her and shouted through the rolled up window asking her if she was OK. Without removing her hands or her head she yelled back that she had been shot in the back of the head and had been holding her brains in for over an hour now.

The man called the paramedics, who broke into her car and Lisa removed her hands from her head. The paramedics discovered that Lisa had a **wad of bread dough** on the back of her head where a Pillsbury biscuit canister had exploded from the heat, making a loud noise that sounded like a gun shot and a wad of dough hit her in the back of the head.

When she felt the dough she thought it was her brains and initially passed out but quickly recovered and thanks to a good Samaritan and the paramedics, she was able to drive back home safely!

· ·

(5) Two blondes living in Oklahoma were sitting on a bench talking, and one blonde says to the other, "Which do you think is **farther away... Florida or the moon**?" The other blonde turns and says "Hellooooooooooo, can you see Florida ?????"

· ·

(6) A ventriloquist was performing with his dummy on his lap. He was telling a dumb blonde joke when a young platinum haired beauty jumps to her feet. She yelled out, "what gives you the right to stereo-type us blondes that way? And what does hair color have to do with my worth as a human being?"

The ventriloquist became flustered and begins to stammer out an apology. The blonde, still infuriated yells back, "You stay out of this mister; I'm talking to that little **jerk sitting on your knee**."

· ·

(7) My sister is a blonde and one year at Thanksgiving, my mom went to my sister's house for the traditional feast. Knowing how

gullible my sister is, my mom decided to play a trick on her. She told my sister that she needed something from the store.

When my sister left, my mom took the turkey out of the oven, removed the stuffing, then stuffed the turkey with a Cornish hen; then re-stuffed the turkey. She then placed it all back in the oven.

When it was time for dinner, my sister pulled the turkey out of the oven and proceeded to remove the stuffing. When her serving spoon hit something, she reached in and pulled out the little bird.

With a look of total shock on her face, my mother exclaimed, "Patricia, you've **cooked a pregnant bird**." At the reality of this horrifying news, my sister started to cry.

It took the family two hours to convince her that turkeys don't have baby turkeys, they lay eggs! YEP...she's a blonde!

· ·

(8) An airplane was on its way to Montreal when a blonde in Economy Class gets up and moves to the First Class section and sits down. The Flight Attendant watches her do this and asks to see her ticket. She then tells the blonde that she paid for an Economy seat and that she will have to sit in the back. The blonde replies, "I'm blonde, and I'm beautiful and I'm going to stay in this seat."

The Flight attendant goes into the cockpit and tells the pilot and co-pilot that there is some blonde bimbo sitting in First Class that belongs at the back and won't move back to her assigned seat. The co-pilot goes back and tries to explain to her that she cannot sit in First Class. She says, "I'm blonde, and I'm beautiful and I'm going to stay in this seat."

The co-pilot suggests to the pilot that since the blonde will not listen to reason, they should probably have the police waiting at the terminal to arrest the blonde when she gets off the plane.

Then, the pilot says, "I'll handle this. I'm married to a blonde. I know what to do." So, this time the pilot goes and speaks to the blonde and without hesitation, the blonde moves to the back.

Well, the flight attendant and the co-pilot are certainly amazed and so they ask the pilot what he said to her that made her to quickly move from First Class to Economy without any fuss. The pilot simply said, "I told her that **First Class isn't going to Montreal!**"

....

(9) A blonde pushes her BMW into a gas station. She tells the mechanic it died. After he works on it for a few minutes, it is idling smoothly. She says, "What's the story?"

He replies, "**Just crap in the carburetor.**"

She asks, "How often do I have to do that?"

....

(10) A police officer stops a blonde for speeding and asks her very nicely if he could see her license. She replied in a huff, "I wish you guys would get your act together. Just yesterday **you take away my license** and then today you expect me to show it to you!"

....

(11) A highway patrolman pulled alongside a speeding car on the freeway. Glancing at the car, he was astounded to see that the blonde behind the wheel was knitting!

Realizing that she was oblivious to his flashing lights and siren, the trooper cranked down his window, turned on his bullhorn and yelled, "PULL OVER!"

"NO!" The blonde **yelled back, "IT'S A SCARF!"**

(12) A Russian, an American, and a blonde were talking one day.
   The Russian said, "We were the first in space!"
   The American said, "We were the first on the moon!"
   The blonde said, "So what? We're going to be **the first on the sun!**
   The Russian and the American looked at each other and shook their heads. "You can't land on the sun, you idiot! You'll burn up!" said the Russian.
   To which the blonde replied, "We're not stupid, you know. We're going at night!"

· ·

(13) A blonde was playing Trivial Pursuit one night... it was her turn. She rolled the dice and she landed on Science & Nature. Her question was, "If you are **in a vacuum and someone** calls your name, can you hear it?'
   She thought for a time and then asked, "Is it on or off?"

· ·

(14) A girl was visiting her blonde friend, who had acquired two new dogs, and asked her what their names were. The blonde responded by saying that one was named **Rolex and one was named Timex**. Her friend said, "Whoever heard of someone naming dogs like that?" "HELLLOOOOOOO," answered the blonde. "They're watch dogs."

· ·

(15) Two blondes were sipping their Starbucks coffee when a truck went past loaded with rolls of sod. One of the blondes said, "That's what I'm going to do when I win the lottery."
   The second blonde said, "Do what?" The first blonde replied, "I'm going to **send my lawn out to be mowed.**"

From 'SPAM' to BALONEY

(16) <u>The Grandmother of all blonde jokes</u>

This blonde decides one day that she is sick and tired of all these blond jokes and how all blondes are perceived stupid. So, she decides to show her husband that blondes really are smart.

While her husband is off at work, she decides that she is going to paint a couple of rooms in the house. The next day, right after her husband leaves for work; she gets down to the task at hand.

Her husband arrives home at 5:30 and smells the distinctive smell of paint. He walks into the living room and finds his wife lying on the floor in a pool of sweat.

He notices that she is wearing a heavy parka over her leather jacket. He goes over and asks her if she is OK. She replies "Yes." He then asks what she is doing and she replies that she wanted to prove to him that not all blonde women are dumb, and she wanted to do it by painting a couple of rooms in the house.

He then asks her why she has a parka over her leather jacket. She replies that she was reading the directions on the paint can and she said … (you'll love this) *"**For best results, put on two coats**!"*

. . . .

(17) A <u>blonde</u> was weed-a-whacking her yard and accidentally cut off the tail of her cat, who was hiding in the grass. She rushed her cat, along with the tail, over to WAL-MART! Why WAL-MART? HELLOOOOOOOOO! WALMART is the <u>largest</u> <u>Re-tailer in the world!</u>

7

Chapter 2

Children Comedy

(1) <u>Where God Ain't...</u>
   I watched a little boy as he sauntered down the street,
   He was coming home from Sunday school all dressed up so neat.
   He dug his shoe in a little hole and found a caterpillar,
   Then he picked a fluffy milkweed, and blew out all the filler.
   He looked up at a bird's nest, way up in a tree so high,
   Just looking at God's creatures with his little wondering eye.
   I hollered out to him as I stood there on my lawn,
   I asked him where he's been that day and what was going on.
   "I've been to Sunday School," he said as he scuffed a piece of sod,
   Then he picked up a wiggly worm and said, "I'm learning about God."

   "Well that's nice" I said, "but I don't like the way they jump and holler And if you can tell me where God is, I'll give you a brand new dollar." Quick as a flash, the boy replied, in a voice that was not faint, "I'll give you a dollar, Mister, if you can tell me where He ain't."

(2) A Sunday school teacher was telling her class the story of the Good Samaritan. She asked the class, "If you saw a person lying on the roadside, wounded and bleeding, what would you do?" A thoughtful little girl broke the hushed silence, "<u>I think I'd throw up</u>."

· ·

(3) <u>Things to think about</u>...
- You spend the first two years raising kids by teaching them to walk and talk; then you spend the next 16 years telling them to *"sit down and shut up!"*
- Mothers of teens now know why some animals eat their young.
- Children seldom misquote you; in fact, they usually repeat word for word what you shouldn't have said.
- We childproof our homes, but they still get in.
- If you have a lot of tension and you get a headache, do what it says on the Aspirin bottle, *"<u>Take two Aspirins and keep away from children.</u>"*

· ·

(4) Author and lecturer Leo Buscaglia once talked about a contest he was asked to judge. The purpose of the contest was to find the most caring child. The winner turned out to be a four year old whose next door neighbor was an elderly gentleman who had recently lost his wife.

Upon seeing the man cry, the little boy went into the old gentleman's yard, climbed up on his lap and just sat there. When his mother asked him what he had said to the neighbor, the little boy said, *"Oh, nothing, **<u>I just helped him cry</u>**."*

From 'SPAM' to BALONEY

(5) THE LORD IS MY SHEPHERD

A Sunday school teacher decided to have her young class memorize one of the most quoted passages in the Bible - Psalm 23. She gave the youngsters a month to learn the chapter. Little Rick was excited about the task - but he just couldn't remember the Psalm. After much practice, he could barely get past the first line.

On the day that the kids were scheduled to recite Psalm 23 in front of the congregation, Ricky was so nervous. When it was his turn, he stepped up to the microphone and said proudly, "The Lord is my Shepherd, and **that's all I need to know**".

· ·

(6) As the Scout-leader surveyed his troop he said, *"Well now, how did we spend the weekend; any good deed to enter in the Merit Book?"* The Scoutmaster

One lad said, "Yes sir, three boys from the troop and me helped a little old lady across the street."

"Mmm" said the **Scout-leader, *"And why did it take four of you?"***
The lad said, "Because she didn't want to go."

· ·

(7) The Sermon I think this Mom will never forget...

This particular Sunday sermon.... "Dear Lord," the minister began, with arms extended toward heaven and a rapturous look on his upturned face, "without you, we are but dust."

He would have continued but at that moment my very obedient daughter who was listening leaned over to me and asked quite audibly in her shrill little four year old voice.....

"**Mom, what is butt dust?**"

(8) <u>Great truths, according to children</u>
- No matter how hard you try, you can't baptize a cat.
- When your mom is mad at your dad, don't let her brush your hair.
- If your sister hits you, don't hit her back; they always catch the second person.
- Never ask a year old brother to hold a tomato.
- You can't trust dogs to watch your food.
- Don't sneeze when someone is cutting your hair.
- Never hold a dust-buster and a cat at the same time.
- You can't hide a piece of broccoli in a glass of milk.
- The best place to be when you are sad is on Grand-Pa's lap!

. . . .

(9) <u>Great truths, learned by adults</u>
- Raising Teenagers is like nailing Jell-O to a tree.
- Wrinkles don't hurt.
- Families are like fudge, mostly sweet but with a few nuts.
- Today's mighty oak is just yesterday's nut that held its ground.

. . . .

(10) A little boy wanted $100 badly and prayed for two weeks but nothing happened. Then he decided to write God a letter requesting the $100.

When the postal authorities received the letter simply addressed 'God, USA' they decided to send it to President Bush. The President was so impressed, touched and amused that he instructed his secretary to send the little boy a $5 bill.

President Bush thought this would appear to be a lot of money to a little boy.

The little boy was delighted with the $5 and sat down to write a thank you note to God, which read...

Dear God, thank you very much for sending the money. However, I noticed that for some reason you had sent it through Washington, D.C. and, as usual, **those crooks deducted $95.00-**

....

(11) Great truths, about growing old
- Growing old is mandatory; growing up is optional.
- When you fall down, you wonder what else you can do while you're down there.
- It's frustrating when you know all the answers but nobody bothers to ask you the questions.
- Time is a great healer but it's a lousy beautician.
- Wisdom comes with age but sometimes age comes all by itself.

....

(12) A woman once said to Evangelist Spurgeon, *"**I cannot understand** why God would say that he hated Esau,"* to which Mr. Spurgeon replied, *"That, dear one, is not difficult for me to understand. My difficulty is to understand how God could love Jacob."*

Their future was told to their mother while the children were yet in her womb, *"not having done anything good or bad."*

....

(13) A little girl walked to and from school every day. One morning, though, the weather was questionable and clouds were forming. She still made her daily trek to the elementary school, but as the day progressed, the wind whipped up along with thunder

and lightening. The girl's mother became concerned that her daughter would be frightened as she walked home from school, and she feared that the electrical storm might harm her child. So the mother quickly got into her car and drove along the route to her daughter's school.

Finally, up ahead she saw her little girl walking along, but with each flash of lightening, the child would stop, look up at the sky, and smile.

When the mother pulled the car alongside her daughter, the mother called her over to the car and asked, *"What are you doing?"*

The girl answered, *"I'm just walking home, but* **God keeps taking pictures of me!"**

· ·

(13) SAY A PRAYER

Little Johnny and his family were having Sunday dinner at his Grandmother's house. Everyone was seated around the table as the food was being served. When Little Johnny received his plate, he started eating right away. "Johnny! Please wait until we say our prayer," said his mother. "I don't need to," the boy replied.

"Of course, you do "his mother insisted. "We always say a prayer before eating at our house."

"That's at our house." Johnny explained. "But this is Grandma's house and she knows how to cook".

· ·

(14) Mary's Lamb

Mary had a little Lamb, His fleece was white as snow.
And everywhere that Mary went, the Lamb was sure to go.
He followed her to school each day, it wasn't against the rule
It made the children laugh and play, **to have the Lamb at school**.

And then the rules all changed one day. Illegal it became,
To bring the Lamb of God to school or even speak His name.
Every day got worse and worse, and days turned into years.
Instead of hearing children laugh, we heard gunshots and tears.
What must we do to stop the crime, that's in our schools today?
Let's let the Lamb come back to school, and teach our kids to pray!

It is said that 86% of Canadian, American and British people believe in God. Why don't we just tell the other 14% to shut up and sit down?

. . . .

(15) <u>A REDNECK LOVE POEM</u>
Susie Lee done fell in love, she planned to marry Joe.
She was so happy 'bout it all, she told her Pappy so.
Pappy told her Susie Gal, you'll have to find another.
I'd just as soon yo' Ma don't know, but Joe is yo' half brother.
So Susie put aside her Joe, and planned to marry Will.
But after telling Pappy this, he said, "there's trouble still,
You can't marry Will, my Gal, and please don't tell yo' Mother.
But Will and Joe, and several mo' I know is yo' half brother."
But Mama knew and said, "my child just do what makes yo' happy.
Marry Will or marry Joe, **you ain't no kin to Pappy**!"

. . . .

(16) A man left it in his will that he be **buried at sea**; four of his grandchildren drowned digging the grave!

(17) <u>Parents who drugged us</u>

The other day, someone at the store in our town read that a Meth Lab had been found in an old farmhouse in the adjoining county and he asked me a rhetorical question.

"Why didn't we have a drug problem when you and I were growing up?"
I replied; I had a problem when I was young:

- I was drug to church on Sunday morning, Sunday night and Wed. nights.
- I was drug to church for weddings and funerals.
- I was drug to family reunions and community socials no matter the weather.
- I was drug by my ears when I was disrespectful to adults.
- I was also drug to the woodshed when I disobeyed my parents, told a lie, brought home a bad report card, did not speak with respect, spoke ill of the teacher or the preacher, or if I didn't put forth my best effort in everything that was asked of me.
- I was drug to the kitchen sink to have my mouth washed out with soap if I uttered a profanity.

Those drugs are still in my veins and they affect my behavior in everything I do, say or think. They are stronger than cocaine, crack, or heroin; and if today's young people had this kind of a drug problem; this country would be a much better and safer place.

<u>*May God bless the parents who drugged us and may He raise up many more parents to do the same!*</u>

. . . .

(18) <u>Paul Harvey</u> tells about a 3-year-old boy who went to the grocery store with his mother. Before they entered the grocery store she said to him, *"Now you're not going to get any chocolate chip cookies; so don't even ask."*

She put him up in the cart and he sat in the little child's seat while she wheeled down the aisles. He was doing just fine until they came to the cookie section. He saw the chocolate chip cookies, and said, *"Mommy, can I have some chocolate chip cookies?"*

She said, *"I told you to not even ask! You're not going to get any at all."* So, he sat back down. They continued down the aisles, but ended up on the cookie aisle again. Again the 3-year-old pleaded, *"Mommy, can I have some chocolate chip cookies?"*

She said, *"Now, I told you before 'NO' so sit down and be quiet."* Finally, as they were approaching the check-out line, the little boy sensed that this might be his last chance. He stood up in his seat and yelled in his loudest voice, *"In the Name of Jesus, may I have some chocolate chip cookies?"*

Then everybody in line roared with laughter and some even applaudedd. According to Paul Harvey, and due to the generosity of the other shoppers, the little boy and his mother left the store that day with 23 boxes of **chocolate chip cookies**!

So, never underestimate the power in the Name of Jesus!

Chapter 3

Christian Comedy

Letter From Aunt Martha

(1) I got a letter from Aunt Martha the other day. She wrote...

    The other day I went to the local Christian bookstore and saw a 'Honk if you love Jesus' bumper sticker. I was feeling pretty sassy that day because I had just come from a thrilling choir performance, and an awesome prayer meeting. So I bought the bumper sticker, put it on and am I ever glad I did. What an uplifting experience it was that followed.

    I was stopped at a red light at a busy intersection, just lost in thought about the Lord and how good He is... and I didn't notice that the light had changed. It was a good thing that someone else loves Jesus because if he hadn't honked, I'd never have noticed.

    I found that lots of people love Jesus. While I was sitting there, the guy behind started honking like crazy, and then he leaned out of his window and screamed, "For the love of God, go! Go!" What an exuberant cheerleader he was for Jesus!

Then everyone started honking! I just leaned out my window and started waving and smiling at all these loving people. I even honked my own horn a few times to share in the love.

There must have been a man from Florida back there because I heard him yelling something about a "sunny beach." I saw another guy waving in a funny way with only one finger stuck up in the air. Then I asked my teenage son in the back seat what that meant. He said it was probably a <u>**Hawaiian good luck sign**</u> or something.

Well, I had never met anyone from Hawaii so I leaned out the window and gave him the good luck sign back. My son burst out laughing. It seemed he was even enjoying this religious experience!

A couple of people were so caught up in the joy of the moment that they got out of their cars and started walking towards me. I bet they wanted to pray or ask what church I attended, but then I noticed the light had changed.

Well, I just had time to wave at all my new-found brothers and sisters and drove on through the intersection. I did notice that I was the only car that got through the intersection before the light changed again and I felt kind of sad that I had to leave them after all the love we had shared, so I slowed the car down, leaned out the window one last time and gave them all the Hawaiian good luck sign again as I drove away!

<u>Praise the Lord for such wonderful folks!</u>

· ·

(2) Billy Graham had just finished a tour of the Florida East Coast and was taking a limousine to the airport. Having never driven a limo before, he asked the chauffeur if he could drive for awhile. Well, the chauffeur didn't have too much choice, so he got in the back of the limo and Billy took the wheel.

From 'SPAM' to BALONEY

Billy turned onto I-95 and accelerated to about 90 mph when he saw the blue lights of a police car in his rear-view mirror. When he pulled over and the trooper came up to the window and saw who the driver was, he called in to the chief.

He said over the radio, *"Chief, I don't know what to do. I've got this really important person stopped for speeding and I don't know if I should give him a ticket or not."*

The chief said, *"Who is it? It's not one of the Kennedy's again, is it?"* "No," said the officer, *"it's someone more important than that. He is sitting in the back of the limo and I don't recognize him."*

"Well," barked the chief, *"who do you think it might be?"*

"Well," said the officer, *"I don't know for sure, but it might be Jesus because **His chauffeur is Billy Graham**."*

• •

(3) <u>How A Christian Is Like A Pumpkin</u>

God picks you from the patch, brings you in, and washes the dirt off that you picked up from the other pumpkins. Then He cuts the top off and scoops out all the yucky stuff. He then removes the seeds of doubt, hate, greed etc. Then He carves you a new smiling face and puts His light inside you to shine for the entire world to see.

• •

(4) A young woman teacher explains to her class of children that she is an atheist. She asks her class if any of them are atheist. Not really knowing what an atheist is, but wanting to be like their teacher, their hands explode into the air. There is, however, one exception.

A girl named Sara has not gone along with the crowd. The teacher asks her why she has decided to be different. *"Because I am not an atheist"* says the student. *"Then what are you?"* asks the teacher.

"I'm Jewish" says the student. The teacher becomes a bit perturbed and embarrassed, and asks Sara why she is Jewish.

"Well," she says, "I was brought up knowing and loving God. My mom is Jewish and my dad is Jewish, so I'm Jewish." The teacher is now quite angry and says, "That's no reason. What if your mom was a moron? What would you be then?"

There was a pause and a smile on the little girl and she said, "Then, **_I guess I'd be an atheist!_**"

• •

(5) <u>KETCHUP</u>

A woman was trying hard to get the ketchup out of the jar.. During her struggle the phone rang so she asked her 4-year-old daughter to answer the phone.. 'Mommy can't come to the phone to talk to you right now; <u>she's hitting the bottle</u>.

<u>Never underestimate the power of prayer</u>...

• •

(6) The Reverend Dwight Nelson had a kitten that climbed up a tree in his backyard and then it was afraid to come down. The Reverend coaxed, offered warm milk, etc. but nothing worked.

The tree was not sturdy enough to climb. So the Reverend decided that if he tied a rope to his car bumper and drove away a few feet, the tree would bend down so he could reach up and get the kitten.

He did all this, checking his progress in the rearview mirror, then figured if he went just a little bit further, the tree would be bent sufficiently for him to reach the kitten.

Well, as he moved a little further forward, the rope broke. The tree went 'bo-ing' and the kitten went sailing aimlessly through the air; out of sight over the tree tops. The Reverend felt terrible and said a quick prayer for the poor little kitten.

The Reverend even walked all over the neighborhood and even into the next county, asking people if they had seen a stray kitten. No! Nobody had seen a stray kitten. So, he prayed, *"Lord, I just commit this kitten into Your safe keeping"* and then went on about his business.

A few days later, as he was at the grocery store, he ran into one of his church members. He happened to look into her shopping cart and was amazed to see cat food. Now, this woman was a cat-hater, and everybody knew it, so he said to her, *"Why are you buying cat food when you hate cats so much?"*

She replied, *"Reverend, you won't believe this, but my little girl had been begging for a cat for a long time, and wouldn't take no for an answer. So, last week, when my daughter brought up the subject again, I finally said to her, **"Honey, if God gives you a cat we'll keep it."***

The Reverend is now starting to figure this story out. The mother continues, *"I watched my child go out in the yard, get on her knees, and ask God for a cat. And really, Reverend, you won't believe this, but I saw it with my own eyes. A kitten suddenly came flying out of the clear blue sky, with its paws outspread and landed right in front of her!"*

Always remember, the power of prayer and what may appear to be breaking on one end is answering prayer on the other!

. . . .

(7) The Georgia town of Ringgold (pop. 2000) has decided to appease all beliefs and bring back *"good Christian values,"* reports the Atlanta Constitution. The Ten Commandments, the Lord's Prayer, and an empty picture frame are now displayed in the town's public buildings.

The empty frame is *"for **those who believe in nothing**,"* said a Councilman, who came up with the idea. He said, *"If you don't believe in the other two, you can go stand in front of it and believe anything you want."*

The ACLU is looking into a potential lawsuit against Ringgold.

(8) It was the end of the day when I parked my police van in front of the station. As I gathered my equipment, my K-9 partner, Jake, was barking, and I saw a little boy staring in at me.

'Is that a dog you got back there?' he asked. 'It sure is,' I replied.

Puzzled, the boy looked at me and then towards the back of the van. Finally he said, **'What'd he do?**

. . . .

(9) While working for an organization that delivers lunches to elderly shut-ins, I used to take my 4-year-old daughter on my afternoon rounds. She was unfailingly intrigued by the various appliances of old age, particularly the canes, walkers and wheelchairs.

One day I found her staring at a pair of false teeth soaking in a glass. As I braced myself for the inevitable barrage of questions, she merely turned and whispered, **'The tooth fairy will never believe this!'**

. . . .

(10) A WELL PLANNED LIFE????

Two women met for the first time since graduating from high school.
One asked the other, "You were always so organized in school, Did you manage to live a well planned life? "
"Yes," said her friend.
"My first marriage was to a millionaire;
my second marriage was to an actor;
my third marriage was to a preacher;
and now I'm married to an undertaker."

From 'SPAM' to BALONEY

Her friend asked,
"What do those marriages have to do with a well planned life?"
"One for the money,
two for the show,
three to get ready,
and four to go

Chapter 4

Christmas Comedy

(1) One woman said to another as they looked at the manger scene and stained glass windows in a downtown store window, "Hmm, look at that will ya! **Even the church is trying to horn in on Christmas.**

. . . .

(2) "Christmas is a weird time of the year. It's when fully grown adults love to sit and look at a dead tree & **eat candy out of a sock**!"

. . . .

(3) A redneck called the radio station and said, "would ya play *'**Grandma Got Run Over By A Reindeer**'* again….It just gets funnier and funnier every time I hear it!"

(4) A ten-year-old floored her grandmother by asking, "Which virgin was the mother of Jesus; the virgin Mary **or the King James virgin?**

. . . .

(5) It was Christmas and the judge was in a merry mood as he asked the prisoner, "What are you charged with?" The defendant replied, "Doing my Christmas shopping early."

"That's no offence", said the judge, "just how early were you doing this shopping?"

"**Before the store opened**," the prisoner replied.

. . . .

(6) Little Georgie received a new drum for Christmas. Shortly thereafter, his father came home from work and the mother told him, "*I don't think the man downstairs likes to hear Georgie play his new drum, but he's certainly subtle about it.*"

"Why do you say that?" asked the father.

"*Well,*" she said, "*this afternoon he gave Georgie a pocket knife and asked him if he knew **what was inside the drum**.*"

. . . .

(7) 'Twas the night of Christmas, and I couldn't sleep.
   I tried counting backwards, I tried counting sheep.
   The leftovers beckoned, the dark meat and white,
   But I fought the temptation with all of my might.
   Tossing and turning with anticipation,
   The thought of a snack became infatuation.
   So I raced to the kitchen, flung open the door;
   And gazed at the fridge full of goodies galore.
   I gobbled up turkey and buttered potatoes,
   Pickles and carrots, beans and tomatoes.

I felt myself swelling so plump and so round,
'till all of a sudden, I rose off the ground.
I crashed thru the ceiling, floated into the sky,
with a mouthful of pudding and a handful of pie.
But I managed to yell, as I soared past the trees,
"Happy eating to all**, pass the cranberries please**!"

. . . .

(8) **A lot of kneeling** will keep you in good standing.
   * He who kneels before God can stand before anyone.

   * To be almost saved is to be totally lost.

   * When praying, don't give God instructions, just report for duty.

. . . .

(9) A Nativity Scene was erected in a church yard. During the night the folks came across this scene. An abandoned dog was looking for a comfortable, protected place to sleep. He chose Baby Jesus as his comfort. No one had the heart to send him away so he was there all night.

We all should have the sense of this dog and curl up in Jesus' lap from time to time. But, no one seemed to notice that the breed of **the dog was a shepherd**!

. . . .

(10) The Supreme Court has ruled that there cannot be a Nativity Scene in the U.S. Capital this Christmas season. This isn't for religious reasons. They simply have not been able to find Three Wise Men in the Nation's Capital and a search for a virgin continues.

*However, there was no problem in **finding enough asses to fill the stable!***

(11) <u>Unearthed Biological Fact...</u>
- According to the Alaska Dept. of Fish and Game, while both male and female reindeer grow antlers in the summer each year, the male reindeer drop their antlers at the beginning of winter.
- But female reindeer retain their antlers till after they give birth in the spring.
- Therefore, according to every historical rendition depicting Santa's reindeer, every single one of them, from Rudolph to Blitzen **had to be a female reindeer**.
- But, we should have known that only a female would be able to drag a fat man in a velvet suit all around the world in one night and not get lost!

. . . .

(12) <u>The Christmas Pageant</u>

My husband and I had been happily married (most of the time) for five years but hadn't been blessed with a baby.

I decided to do some serious praying and promised God that if he would give us a child, I would be a perfect mother, love it with all my heart and raise it with His word as my guide.

God answered my prayers and blessed us with a son.

The next year God blessed us with another son. The following year, He blessed us with yet another son; the year after that we were blessed with a daughter.

My husband thought we'd been blessed right into poverty.

We now had four children, and the oldest was only four years old.

I learned never to ask God for anything unless I meant it.

As a minister once told me, "If you pray for rain make sure you carry an umbrella."

I began reading a few verses of the Bible to the children each day as they lay in their cribs. I was off to a good start.

From 'SPAM' to BALONEY

God had entrusted me with four children and I didn't want to disappoint Him.

I tried to be patient the day the children smashed two dozen eggs on the kitchen floor searching for baby chicks.

I tried to be understanding... when they started a hotel for homeless frogs in the spare bedroom, although it took me nearly two hours to catch all twenty-three frogs.

When my daughter poured ketchup all over herself and rolled up in a blanket to see how it felt to be a hot dog. I tried to see the humor rather than the mess.

In spite of changing over twenty-five thousand diapers, never eating a hot meal and never sleeping for more than thirty minutes at a time, I still thank God daily for my children.

While I couldn't keep my promise to be a perfect mother -

I didn't even come close... I did keep my promise to raise them in the Word of God.

I knew I was missing the mark just a little when I told my daughter we were going to church to worship God, and she wanted to bring a bar of soap along to "wash up" Jesus, too.

Something was lost in the translation when I explained that God gave us everlasting life, and my son thought it was generous of God to give us his "last wife."

My proudest moment came during the children's Christmas pageant. My daughter was playing Mary; two of my sons were shepherds, and my youngest son was a wise man. This was their moment to shine.

My five-year-old shepherd had practiced his line, "We found the babe wrapped in swaddling clothes." But he was nervous and said, "The baby was wrapped in wrinkled clothes." My four-year-old 'Mary' said, "That's not wrinkled clothes, silly. That's dirty, rotten clothes."

A wrestling match broke out between Mary and the shepherd and was stopped by an angel, who bent her halo and lost her left wing. I slouched a little lower in my seat when Mary dropped the doll representing Baby Jesus, and it bounced down the aisle crying, "Mama-mama."

Mary grabbed the doll, wrapped it back up and held it tightly as the wise men arrived. My other son stepped forward wearing a bathrobe and a paper crown, knelt at the manger and announced, "We are the three wise men, and we are bringing gifts of gold, common sense and fur."

The congregation dissolved into laughter, and the pageant got a standing ovation. "I've never enjoyed a Christmas program as much as this one," laughed the pastor, wiping tears from his eyes.

"For the rest of my life, I'll never hear the Christmas story without thinking of **gold, common sense and fur.**"

. . . .

(13) It was the night before Christmas, when all thru the abode,
    Only one was stirring, and she was cleaning the commode.
    The children were finally sleeping, all snug in their beds,
    While visions of Nintendos and Barbies, flipped thru their heads.

The dad was snoring in front of the TV,
With a half constructed bicycle on his knee.
So only the mom heard the reindeer hooves clatter;
Which made her sigh, *"Now what's the matter?"*

With toilet bowl brush still clutched in her hand,
She descended the stairs, and saw the old man.
He was covered with ashes, and soot fell with a shrug,
"Oh great," she muttered, *"Now I'll have to clean the rug."*

"Ho-ho-ho" cried Santa, *"I'm glad you're awake,*
Your gift was especially difficult to make."
"Thanks, Santa, but all I want is some time alone".
"Exactly," he chuckled, *"I've made you a clone."*

From 'SPAM' to BALONEY

"A clone?" she asked, "What good is that?
Run along, Santa, I've no time for chit-chat."
He made mom's twin, same hair, same eyes,
And the same double chin.

She'll do all the work, clean up every mess,
You relax, watch the 'Young & the Restless.'
"That's fantastic!" Mom cheered, "My dream come true!
I'll shop, I'll read; I'll sleep the whole night thru!"

From the room above, the youngest began to fret,
"Mommy, I'm scared, I'm tired and I'm wet."
The clone replied, "I'm coming sweetheart."
"Hey," the mom smiled, "I can handle that!"

The clone changed the baby while humming a tune,
And she wrapped the child in a blanket cocoon.
"You're the best mommy ever, I really love you."
The clone smiled and said, "And I love you too!"

The mom frowned and said, "Sorry, Santa, No deal,
That's my child's love, she's trying to steal."
Smiling wisely, Santa said, "To me it is clear,
Only one loving mother is needed here.

The mom kissed her child, and tucked her in bed,
"Thank you Santa, for clearing my head.
I sometimes forget, it won't be very long,
When they'll be too old, for my cradle-song."

The clock on the mantle began to chime,
Santa whispered to the clone, "It works every time."
With the clone by his side, Santa said, "Goodnight,
Merry Christmas Mom, you'll be alright!"

(14) <u>The Christmas Scout</u>

Thirteen-year-old Frank Wilson was not happy. He had received all the presents he wanted. He enjoyed the traditional Christmas Eve reunions, exchanging gifts and good wishes. But Frank was not happy because this was his first Christmas without his brother, Steve, who had been killed by a reckless driver.

Frank said goodbye to relatives and explained to his parents that he was leaving a little early to see a friend, and from there he could walk home. Frank put on his new red plaid jacket, his favorite gift and put all his other presents on his sled and started out.

As Frank hiked down the street towards home he caught a glimpse thru a window into a shabby room that had limp stockings hanging over an empty fireplace. He noticed a woman seated near and she seemed to be crying.

A sudden thought struck Frank that he had not done his 'good deed' for the day. And before he knew it, he knocked on the door and asked, *"May I come in?"*

"You very well may," the woman answered, as she saw his sled full of gifts. She assumed the boy was collecting for the poor and said she didn't know how she could give anything.

"That's not why I am here," Frank said, *"Please pick whatever presents you would like to have from my sled."*

"Why, God bless you," the amazed woman said gratefully. She picked out some candy, a game, and a couple of toys. When she reached for Frank's Boy Scout flashlight, Frank nearly cried, but soon she had her stockings filled.

"Please tell me your name," she said as he began to leave. He turned to the woman and said, *"Just call me the Christmas Scout,"* and he was gone.

Frank felt so good about what he had done he looked till he found others who were in need and did not get back home till he had given away all his presents. He even ended giving away his favorite red plaid jacket to a shivering boy on the street.

When he arrived home his mother said, *"But Frank, how could you be so impulsive? How will we explain to the relatives who bought those gifts for you?"*

Frank suddenly felt dreadfully discouraged and alone. He wondered if he would ever recapture joy in his life. Frank thought of how much he missed his brother as he sobbed himself to sleep.

The next morning he came downstairs to find his parents listening to Christmas music on the radio. Then he heard the announcer say, *"Merry Christmas everybody! The nicest Christmas story we have this morning comes from some very needy people in town. A crippled boy has a new sled this morning and another youngster has a fine red plaid jacket and several others reported receiving gifts from a teenage boy who simply called himself, 'the Christmas Scout.' No one seemed to be able to identify him, and some said he had to be one of Santa's elves, for sure!"*

The Christmas carols came over the air again filling the room with music... *"Praises sung to God the King, and peace to men on earth."* Yes, the "Christmas Scout's" sacrifice gives us a little peek into the sacrifice our Heavenly Father made when He gave His very best, His only begotten Son to be born to die for our sins on the cross. What gift can <u>you</u> give <u>Him</u>?

(15) <u>His Name at the top</u>...
> I had the nicest Christmas list, the longest one in town,
> Till Daddy looked it over and said, *"You'll have to cut it down."*
> I knew that what he said was true, beyond the faintest doubt;
> But was surprised to hear him say, *"You left your best Friend out."*
> And so I scanned my list, and said, *"That can't be true."*
> But Daddy said, *"His name's not there, the One who <u>died</u> for you."*
> And then I clearly understood 'twas Jesus that he meant.
> For he who should be first of all, I hadn't planned a cent.
> I'd made a Christmas birthday list and left the Savior out.
> But, oh, it didn't take me long to change the list about.
> And though I've had to drop some names of folks I like a lot.
> My Lord must have the most, and His Name must be on top!

. . . .

(16) <u>The Divorce</u>

A man in Phoenix calls his son in New York the day before Christmas and says, *"I hate to ruin your day, but I have to tell you that your mother and I are getting a divorce; forty-five years of misery is enough."*

"Pop, what are you talking about?" the son screams.

The dad says, *"We can't stand the sight of each other any longer. We're sick of each other, and I'm sick of talking about this, so you can call your sister in Chicago and tell her."*

In a panic, the son calls his sister who explodes over the phone. *"No way they're getting divorced,"* she shouts, *"I'll take care of this!"*

She calls Phoenix immediately and screams at her father, *"You are not getting divorced. Don't you do a single thing until I get there. I'm calling my brother back, and we'll both be there tomorrow. Until then, don't do a thing. Do you hear me?"* Then she hangs up.

The old man hangs up his phone and turns to his wife and says, *"O.K. they're coming for Christmas and they're **paying their own way!**"*

(17) _Bird For Christmas_ (as told by an old farmer)
"I got a nephew that I think a lot of and he works for the Shell Oil Company. About 4 years ago they moved him down to South America and we ain't seen him since. But, he still thinks of me and the Mrs.

"Every Christmas he sends us a nice present. This past Christmas he sent us a live bird; a big green bird, about 2 feet tall. He had little yella top feathers on his head, with some red on it and kind of a hooked beak. He sent it to us live from South America.

"I'll tell you somethin' that bird was delicious, yes sir, it really was! We had him for Christmas dinner. We fixed it up with some dressin' and cranberries and sweet paters.

Well, a week or so after Christmas, my nephew called and wanted to know if we got the bird. I said, *"Yea, we got 'em"*.

He wanted to know if we liked 'em and I said he was simply deli,cious. There was a brief pause on the line and then my nephew said, *"You don't mean that you ate the bird, do you?"*

And I said, *"Of course we did."*

Well, my nephew got al upset an just pitched a fit. He said "I paid a fortune for that bird." He said, *"Why that bird could speak two different languages."* Now I was silent for a spell, then I said, **"Well, he should-a said something!"**

. . . .

(18) A man dies and goes to heaven. Of course, St. Peter meets him at the 'Pearly Gate.' St. Peter says, "Here's how it works. You need **100 points to make it into heaven**. You tell me all the good things you've done, and I'll give you a certain number of points for each item, depending upon how good it was. When you reach 100 points, you can come in."

"O.K." says the man, *"I was married to the same woman for 50 years."* St. Peter says, *"That's wonderful. That's worth three points."*

The man says, *"Three points, is that all? Well, I attended church all my life, paid my tithe, and taught Sunday school."*

"That's terrific" says St. Peter, *"that's certainly worth a point."*

"Only one point? Man at that rate the only way I'll get into heaven is by the grace of God." St. Peter says, *"That's it. You're right. Come on in!"* Remember, like Christmas gifts, our eternal salvation is a <u>gift</u> from God that does not come through any ritual or rite, but through faith in Jesus alone!

· ·

(19) <u>A Christmas Gift</u>...

We were the only family in the restaurant. I sat Eric in the high chair and noticed that everyone was quietly eating and talking. Suddenly, Eric squealed with glee and said, *"Hi there."* His eyes crinkled in laughter.

I looked around and saw the source of his merriment. It was a man whose pants were baggy and his toes poked out of his would-be shoes. His shirt was dirty and his hair was uncombed and unwashed.

"Hi there, baby. Hi there, big boy. I see ya buster," the man said to Eric. My husband and I exchanged looks, *what do we do?* Eric continued to laugh and answer, *"Hi...Hi there!"*

Everyone in the restaurant noticed and looked at us and then at the man. The old geezer was creating a nuisance with my beautiful baby. Nobody thought the old man was cute. He was obviously drunk. My husband and I were embarrassed.

We finally finished our meal and headed towards the door. I prayed, *"Lord, just let me get out of here before he speaks to me or Eric."* But as I came closer to the man, I turned my back trying to sidestep him. Eric leaned over my arm and stretched with both arms in a "baby pick-me-up" position. Before I could stop him, Eric had propelled himself from my arms into the arms of this stranger. Suddenly, a very old smelly man and a very young baby consummated their love relationship. Eric, in an act of trust, love, and submission laid his sleepy head upon the man's ragged shoulder. The man's eyes closed and I saw tears hover beneath his lashes. His aged hands full of grime, pain, and hard labor, cradled my baby's bottom and stroked his back. No two beings have ever loved so deeply for so short a time. I stood there awestruck.

Finally, the old man pried Eric from his chest unwillingly, longingly, as though he were in pain. I received my baby and the man said, *"God bless you Ma'am, you've given me my Christmas gift."* I said nothing more than a muttered *'thanks.'* With Eric in my arms, I ran for the car. My husband was wondering why I was crying and holding Eric so tightly and why I was saying, *"My God, my God, please forgive me."*

You see, I had just witnessed Christ's love shown through the innocence of a tiny child, who saw no sin, who did not judge; a child who saw a soul and a mother who only saw a suit of clothes. I was a Christian who was blind, holding a child who was not. I felt it was God asking me, *"Are you willing to share your son for a moment? ... When He shared His for all eternity?"*

. . . .

(20) Merry Christmas - out on the ranch!

'Twas the night before Christmas and out on the ranch,
The pond was froze over & so was the branch.
The snow was piled up belly-deep to a mule,
The kids were all home, on vacation from school.
And happier young folks you never did see-
Just all sprawled around a-watchin' TV.
Then suddenly, some time around 8 o'clock,
There came a surprise that gave them a shock!
The power went off, the TV went dead,
Then Grandpa came in from out in the shed.

Leonard O'Donnell

With an armload of wood, the house was all dark.
"Just what I expected," they heard him remark.
"Them power line wires must be down from the snow.
Seems sorter like times on the ranch long ago."
"I'll hunt up some candles," said Mom, "With their light,
And the fireplace, I reckon we'll make out all right."
The teen-agers all seemed enveloped in gloom,
Then Grandpa came back from a trip to his room.
Uncased his old fiddle, & started to play,
That old Christmas song about bells on a sleigh.
Mom started to sing, & 1st thing they knew,
Both Pop & the kids were all singing it too.
They played some charades Mom recalled from her youth,
And Pop read a passage from God's Book of Truth.
They stayed up till midnight-and, would you believe,
The youngsters agreed 'twas a fine Christmas Eve.
Grandpa rose early, some time before dawn;
And when the kids wakened, the power was back on.
"The power company sure got the line repaired quick,"
Said Grandpa - & no one suspected his trick.
Last night, for the sake of some old-fashioned fun,
He had pulled the main switch - the old Son-of-a-Gun!

Chapter 5

Church Comedy

(1) It's so dry in Texas . . .
- that the Baptists are starting to baptize by sprinkling,
- the Methodists are using wet-wipes,
- the Presbyterians are giving out rain-checks,
- and the Catholics are praying for the wine to turn back into water. Now THAT'S Dry.

• •

(2) Sister Mary-Ann of the Catholic Parish works for a home health agency. She was out making her rounds when she ran out of gas. Fortunately, there was a gas service station just down the street.
   She walked to the station to borrow a gas can and buy some gas. The attendant told her that the only gas can had been loaned out, but she could wait until it came back. Since Sister Mary-Ann was on her way to see a patient she decided not to wait and walked back to her car.

As she was looking around for something in which to put the gas, she spotted the bedpan she was taking to the patient. "Great," she says to herself, "I'll use that!" So she carried the bedpan to the station, got it filled up with gas and carried it back to her car.

As she was pouring the gas into her tank, two Baptist guys watched from across the street. One guy turned to the other and said, "**If it starts, I'm turning Catholic!**"

. . . .

(3) The graveside service just barely finished when there was a massive clap of thunder followed by a tremendous bolt of lightning accompanied by even more thunder rumbling in the distance.

The little old woman looked at the preacher & calmly said, "**Well . . . he's there.**"

. . . .

(4) Ever since I was a little boy my mother knew I was going to be a preacher. She would watch me many times as I set the cat up on a little table and preach to him and Oh, did I ever preach!

One day my mom heard the cat scream and hollered out, "Son, what on earth are you doing?"

I said, "**I'm baptizing the cat**."

She said, "Stop that! Don't you know cats are afraid of water?"

I said, "Well, he should have thought about that before he joined my church."

. . . .

(5) **I hope I never get that way!**

An elderly Floridian called 911 on her cell phone to report that her car has been broken into.

From 'SPAM' to BALONEY

She was hysterical as she explained her situation to the dispatcher, "They've stolen the stereo, the steering wheel, the brake pedal and even the accelerator pedal!"

The dispatcher said, "Stay calm. An officer is on the way." In a few minutes the officer arrives and radios in. "Dispatcher," he says, "she got in the back seat by mistake! No charges necessary!"

I hope I never get that way!

. . . .

(6) <u>The Commode:</u>

From up north, a very proper retired lady was searching the internet trying to plan her first trip to Florida. She e-mailed a campground for reservations. She wanted to make sure the campground was fully equipped and modern, but couldn't bring herself to write the word 'toilet.'

She decided on the old-fashioned term, 'bathroom commode.' Once written down, even that phrase didn't seem appropriate. Finally, she decided on the abbreviation B.C.; so she wrote, "Does your campground have its own B.C.?"

When the campground owner got the message he couldn't figure out what the woman meant by B.C. but finally decided it must have meant Baptist Church. Soon he wrote back...

Dear Madam:

The B.C. is located 9 miles from the camp-ground ... in a beautiful grove of trees. I admit it is quite a distance if you are in the habit of going regularly. I'm sure you will be pleased to know that it will seat 300 people at one time and is open every Tuesday, Thursday and Sunday when there is organ accompaniment.

The acoustics are very good and everyone can hear even the quietest passages. It may interest you to know my daughter and her husband met there. They are now having a fund-raiser to purchase new seats, as the old seats have too many holes in them.

Unfortunately, my wife who is ill has not been able to go for about 6 months now. It pains her very much not to be able to go more often. As we grow older, it seems to be more of an effort, especially in cold weather. Perhaps I could accompany you the first time you go, sit with you, and introduce you to some of my friends there.

I look forward to your visit. We offer a very friendly campground and God Bless You...

. . . .

(7) <u>You know your church is a Redneck Church if...</u>
A member of the church requests to be buried in his 4-wheel drive truck because "It ain't ever been in a hole it couldn't get out of."

. . . .

(8) Three sons left home, went out on their own and prospered. Getting back together, they discussed the gifts that they were able to give to their elderly mother.

The first said, "I built a big house for our mother." The second said, "I sent her a big new car, with a driver."

The third smiled and said, "I've got you both beat. You know how mom enjoys the Bible and you know she can't see very well. I sent her a brown parrot that **<u>can recite the entire Bible</u>**. It took 20 monks in a monastery 12 years to teach him. I had to pledge $10,000 a year for the next 10 years but it was worth it! Mom just has to name the chapter and verse and the parrot will recite it."

Soon thereafter, Mom sent out her letters of thanks. She wrote the first son, "Milton, the house you built is so large I live in only one room so I don't have to clean the whole house."

She wrote the second son, "Marvin, I am too old to travel much so I stay home all the time so I never use the car you sent, and the driver is so rude."

She wrote the third son, "Dearest Melvin, you were the only son to have the good sense to know what your mother likes. The chicken was delicious! God bless you."

· ·

(9) CLOSING...

The next time you feel like God can't use you, just remember...

Noah was a drunk / Abraham was too old / Isaac was a daydreamer / Jacob was a liar / Leah was ugly / Joseph was abused / Moses had a stuttering problem.

Gideon was afraid / Samson was a womanizer / Rahab was a prostitute / Jeremiah and Timothy were too young / David had an affair and was a murderer / Elijah was suicidal /Jonah ran from God. Naomi was a widow / Job went bankrupt / John the Baptist ate bugs / Peter denied the Lord / Martha worried about everything / The Samaritan woman was divorced, more than once / Zaccheus was too small / Paul was too religious / Timothy had an ulcer...and... **Lazarus was dead**! Now, what's your excuse?

· ·

(10) A young boy had just gotten his driving permit. So, he asked his father, who was a minister if they could discuss his use of the family car. His father took the young man into his study and said, "Son, you bring your grades up, study your Bible a little each day and get your hair cut and we'll talk about it."

After about a month, the boy came back again and asked his father if they could discuss his use of the car. They again went into the father's study where the father said, "Son, I'm very proud of you. You've brought your grades up, you've been diligent in studying the Bible, but you didn't get your hair cut."

The young man waited for a moment and then replied, "I've been thinking about that Dad. You know Samson had long hair, Moses had long hair, and even Jesus had long hair."

The minister then said, "You're right **son, but they walked** everywhere they went."

· ·

(11) <u>Robbing the Amish</u>...

Two fellers were in desperate need of cash, but were a bit cowardly. So one suggested they break into an Amish store. The logic being that the Amish were non-resistant people and no harm would befall them.

So, they did; however, just as they were breaking into the cash register, the Amish owner turned on the lights and pointed a shotgun directly at them. "Boys," he said, "I would never do thee any harm, yet you are standing where I am about to shoot."

· ·

(12) A local priest and a pastor were fishing on the side of the road. They made a sign saying, "*The End Is Near, turn around now before it's too late!*"

They held it up to each passing car. One passer-by rolled down his window and shouted, "*Mind your own business, you religious nuts!*"

In a few seconds they heard a big splash and the priest said to the pastor, "Do you think maybe we should have just said **the bridge is out?**"

(13) Up we go...   (Prov. 13:3)

A young couple moves into a new neighborhood. The next morning while they are eating breakfast, the young woman sees her neighbor hanging the wash outside.

"That laundry is not very clean," she said. "She doesn't know how to wash correctly. Perhaps she needs better laundry soap."

Her husband looked on, but remained silent.

Every time her neighbor would hang her wash to dry, the young woman would make the same comments.

About one month later, the woman was surprised to see a nice clean wash on the line and said to her husband, "Look, she has learned how to wash correctly; I wonder who taught her that."

The husband said, "I got up early this morning and cleaned our windows."

And so it is with life. What we see when watching others depends on the purity of the window through which we look!

• •

(14) Attending a wedding for the first time, a little girl whispered to her mother, "Why is the bride dressed in white?"

The mother replied, "Because white is the color of happiness; and today is the happiest day of her life."

The child thought about this for a moment then said, "So **why is the groom wearing black?**"

• •

(15) Only a few remember who was on their side thru all the bad times...

There was a blind girl, who hated herself because she was blind. She hated everyone, except her loving boyfriend. He was always there for her. She told her boyfriend, "If I only had my sight, I would marry you."

One day, someone donated a pair of eyes to her. When the bandages come off, she was able to see everything, including her boyfriend.

He now asked her, "Will you marry me now?" The girl looked at her boyfriend and saw that he was blind. She hadn't expected that. The thought of looking at his blind eyes the rest of her life caused her to refuse to marry him.

Her boyfriend left in tears and days later wrote a note to her saying, "**Take good care of your eyes**, my dear, for before they were yours, they were mine."

Yes, sad, but only a few remember what life was like before, and who was always by their side in the most painful situations!

· ·

(16) A little girl, dressed in her Sunday best, was running as fast as she could, trying not to be late for Bible class.

As she ran she prayed, "Dear Lord, please don't let me be late! Dear Lord, please don't let me be late!"

While she was running and praying, she tripped on a curb and fell, getting her clothes dirty and tearing her dress.

She got up, brushed herself off, and started running again! As she ran she once again began to pray, "Dear Lord, please don't let me be late...But please **don't shove me either**!"

· ·

(17) A Sunday School teacher asked her class why Joseph and Mary took Jesus with them to Jerusalem.

A small child replied, "**They couldn't get a baby-sitter**."

· ·

(18) A Sunday school teacher was discussing the Ten Commandments with her five and six year olds. After explaining

the commandment to honor thy father and thy mother, she asked, "Is there a commandment that teaches us how to treat our brothers and sisters?"

Without missing a beat, one little boy answered, "**Thou shall not kill.**"

. . . .

(19) Three boys are in the school yard bragging about their fathers.

The first boy says, "My Dad scribbles a few words on a piece of paper, he calls it a poem, they give him $50."

The second boy sa ys, "That's nothing. My Dad scribbles a few words on piece of paper and he calls it a song; they give him $100."

The third boy says, "I got you both beat. My Dad scribbles a few words on a piece of paper and he calls it a sermon, and it takes **eight people to collect all the money**!"

. . . .

(20) At Sunday school they were teaching how God created everything, including human beings. Little Johnny seemed especially intent when they told him how Eve was created out of one of Adam's ribs.

Later in the week his mother noticed him lying down as though he were ill, and she said, "Johnny, what is the matter?"

Little Johnny responded, "I have pain in my side. I think I'm **going to have a wife**."

. . . .

(21) A little girl became restless as the preacher's sermon dragged on and on. Finally, she leaned over to her mother and whispered, "Mommy, **if we give him the money now**, will he let us go?"

(22) A mother was preparing pancakes for her two sons age 5 and 3. The boys began to argue over who would get the first pancake. Their mother saw the opportunity for a moral lesson. She said, "If Jesus were sitting here, He would say, 'Let my brother have the first pancake; I can wait.'"

The older brother turned to the younger and said, "Little **Brother, you be Jesus!**"

· ·

(23) A father was at the beach with his children when his four-year-old son ran up to him and said, *"Daddy, **there's a dead seagull** on the beach. What happened to him?"*

The dad said, "The seagull died and went to heaven."

A moment later the son said, "Daddy, did God throw him back down?"

· ·

(24) After the church service a little boy told the pastor, "When I grow up, I'm gonna give you lots of money." The pastor said, "Why, thank you young man, but why are you going to do that?"

The little boy said, "Because daddy says you're **one of the poorest preachers** we've ever had!"

· ·

(25) UNANSWERED PRAYER

The preacher's 5 year-old daughter noticed that her father always paused and bowed his head for a moment before starting his sermon. One day, she asked him why. "Well, Honey," he began, proud that his daughter was so observant of his messages. "I'm asking the Lord to **help me preach a good sermon.**"

"How come He doesn't answer it?" she asked.

(26) A 3-year-old boy had just put his shoes on by himself. His mother noticed that the left shoe was on the right foot. She said, *"Son, your shoes are on the wrong feet."*

The little boy looked up to her and said, *"Mommy, don't kid me;* **they're the only feet I got!***"*

. . . .

(27) On the first day of school, about mid-morning, the kindergarten teacher said, *"If anyone has to go to the bathroom,* **hold up two fingers***."* A little voice from the back asked, *"How will that help?"*

. . . .

(28) A man was driving home from work one day and stopped to watch a local Little League baseball game in the park. He sat down and asked one of the Little League Players what the score was.

"We're behind 14 to nothing," the little guy answered with a smile. "Well," the man said, "You certainly don't look very discouraged."

"Discouraged," the boy said, "why should I be discouraged? **We haven't been up to bat yet!**"

No, it's not the time to be discouraged. The devil's time is almost over and the Church is getting ready to step up to the batter's box and what a day that will be!

. . . .

(29) A little boy wanted to meet God. He knew it was a long trip to where God lived so he packed his backpack with *Twinkies* and a couple of root beer drinks and started out.

When he had gone a few blocks, he met an old man. He was sitting in the park just staring at some pigeons. The boy sat down next to him and opened his backpack. He was about to take a drink of his root beer when he noticed that the old man looked hungry so he offered him a *'Twinkie'*. The old man took it and smiled at the little boy. His smile was so pleasant that the boy wanted to see it again so he offered him a root beer.

Again he smiled and the boy was delighted. They sat there all afternoon eating and smiling, but they never talked much. As it started to grow dark, the boy realized he was quite tired and got up to leave. He had only gone a few steps when he turned around, ran back to the old man and gave him a hug. The old man gave him his biggest smile ever.

When the boy got back home his mother was surprised by the look of joy on his face. She said, "What did you do today that made you so happy?"

The little boy said, "**I had lunch with God**, and you know what? He's got the most beautiful smile I've ever seen."

Meanwhile, the old man, also radiant with joy also returned to his home. His son was stunned to see such a look of peace on his face and so he asked, "Dad, what did you do today that made you so happy?"

The old man said, "I ate *Twinkies* in the park with God; and you know what, He's much younger than I expected."

. . . .

(30) <u>Like talking to a wall!</u>

A journalist had an apartment in Jerusalem overlooking the Western Wall. Every day he watches an old bearded Jewish man come to pray. He decides to do an interview with the old man so goes down to the old man at the Wall and asks him, *"Sir, I see you praying here every day and I would like to ask you how long you have been doing this and what is it that you are praying for?"*

The old man answers, *"I have come here to pray for 25 years. In the morning I pray for world peace, and in the evening I pray for peace between the Israelis and the Palestinians."*

The journalist is impressed and says, *"How does all this praying make you feel?"* The old man says, "It is **like I'm talking to a wall.**

• •

(31) One Irishman was explaining to the other how the Lord often compensates for a person's natural deficiencies. "You see," he said, "if someone is a bit blind he might have a very good sense of hearing; or, if his sense of taste is gone, he may have a keen sense of smell."

His buddy is listening to all of this and says, "I've always believed that and have myself noticed that if someone has one short leg, **the other is just a little bit longer.**"

• •

(32) *The Preacher and the Music Director...*

There was a church where the preacher and the Music Director did not get along very well. After awhile it began to affect the worship services. One week the preacher preached on commitment and how we all should dedicate ourselves to the service of God. The closing hymn selected was…. **I Shall Not Be Moved**.

The next week the sermon was on tithing and the closing hymn was, **Jesus Paid It All**.

When the sermon was on gossiping, they sang, **I Love To Tell The Story**. In time the preacher could take it no more and announced he was going to resign. They sang, **Oh Why Not Tonight**.

The last week he announced that Jesus led him there and Jesus was now telling him it was time to leave. The Music Director had everybody stand and sing, **What A Friend We Have In Jesus**.

(33) <u>Being a Christian</u>... is like being a pumpkin. God lifts you up takes you in and washes off all the dirt off you.

He opens you up, touches you deep inside and scoops out all the yucky stuff. He removes the seeds of doubt, hate, and greed.

Then He carves you a new smiling face and puts His light inside you to shine for the entire world to see!

. . . .

(34) Moses and the people were in the desert, but what was he going to do with them? They had to be fed, and feeding 2 or 3 million people requires a lot of food. According to the Quartermaster General in the Army, it is reported that Moses would have to have had 1500 tons of food each day. Do you know that to bring that much food each day, two freight trains each at least a mile long, would be required.

Besides this, they were out in the desert, so they would have to have firewood to use in cooking the food. This would take 4000 tons of wood and a few more freight trains each a mile long, just for one day.

And the water, if they only had enough to drink and wash a few dishes, it would take 11,000,000 gallons each day and a freight train with tank cars, 1800 miles long, just to bring water.

And another thing, they had to get across the Red Sea at night. Now, if they went on a narrow path, double file, the line would be 800 miles long and would require 35 days and nights getting through. So there had to be a space in the Red Sea, 3 miles wide so that they could walk 5000 abreast to get over in one night.

And then, there is another problem...each time they camped at the end of the day, a campground two-thirds the size of the state of Rhode Island was required, or a total of 750 square miles long...think of that!

(35) **Do you think Moses figured all this out** before he left Egypt? I think not! You see, Moses believed in God and God took care of all these things for him!

Now, do you think God has any problem taking care of your needs?

. . . .

(36) A Jew and a Christian were arguing about the relative merits of their religions. The Jewish man insisted, *"You Christians have been taking things from us for thousands of years; the Ten Commandments, for instance."*

The Christian replied, "Well, it's true that we took the Ten Commandments from you, but **you can't actually say that we've ever kept them.**

. . . .

(37) Thoughts to consider...
- Good health is merely the slowest possible rate at which one can die.
- Give a person a fish and you feed them for a day. Teach a person to use the Internet and they won't bother you for weeks, months, maybe years.
- Health nuts are going to feel stupid someday, lying in the hospitals, dying of nothing.
- All of us could take a lesson from the weather. It pays no attention to criticism.

And The Number 1 Thought
"**Don't worry about old age** - it doesn't last that long."

(38) **A carrot, an egg, and a cup of coffee...**

You will never look at a cup of coffee the same way again, whether you drink coffee or not.

A young woman went to her mother and told her about her life and how things were so hard for her. She did not know how she was going to make it and wanted to give up. She was tired of fighting and struggling. It seemed as one problem was solved, a new one arose.

Her mother took her to the kitchen. She filled three pots with water and placed each on a high fire. Soon the pots came to boil. In the first she placed carrots. In the second she placed eggs and, in the last she placed ground coffee beans without saying a word. She let them sit and boil.

In about twenty minutes she turned off the burners. She fished the carrots out and placed them in a bowl. She pulled the eggs out and placed them in a bowl.

Then she ladled the coffee out and placed it in a bowl. Turning to her daughter, she asked, "Tell me what you see."

"Carrots, eggs, and coffee," she replied.

Her mother brought her closer and asked her to feel the carrots. She did and noted that they were soft. The mother then asked the daughter to take an egg and break it. After pulling off the shell, she observed the hard-boiled egg.

Finally, the mother asked the daughter to sip the coffee. The daughter smiled as she tasted its rich aroma the daughter then asked, "What does it mean, Mother?"

Her mother explained that each of these objects had faced the same adversity: boiling water. Each reacted differently.

The carrot went in strong, hard, and unrelenting. However, after being subjected to the boiling water, it softened and became weak. The egg had been fragile. Its thin outer shell had protected its liquid interior, but after sitting through the boiling water, its insides became hardened. The ground coffee beans were unique however. After they were in the boiling water, they had changed the water.

"Which are you?" she asked her daughter. "When adversity knocks on your door, how do you respond? Are you a carrot, an egg or a coffee bean?"

Think of this: Which am I? Am I the carrot that seems strong, but with pain and adversity do I wilt and become soft and lose my strength or am I the egg that starts with a malleable heart, but changes with the heat? Did I have a fluid spirit, but after a death, a breakup, a financial hardship or some other trial, have I become hardened and stiff? Does my shell look the same, but on the inside am I bitter and tough with a stiff spirit and hardened heart?

Or am I like the coffee bean? The bean actually changes the hot water, the very circumstance that brings the pain. When the water gets hot, it releases the fragrance and flavor. If you are like the bean, when things are at their worst, you get better and change the situation around you. When the hour is the darkest and trials are their greatest, do you elevate yourself to another level? How do you handle adversity? Are you a carrot, an egg or a coffee bean?

May you have enough happiness to make you sweet, enough trials to make you strong, enough sorrow to keep you human and enough hope to make you happy.

The happiest of people don't necessarily have the best of everything; they just make the most of everything that comes along their way. The brightest future will always be based on a forgotten past; you can't go forward in life until you let go of your past failures and heartaches.

(39) **When you were born**, you were crying and everyone around you was smiling. Live your life so at the end, you're the one who is smiling and everyone around you is crying.

. . . .

(40) Back in 1830 George Wilson was convicted of robbing the U.S. Mail and was sentenced to be hanged. President Andrew Jackson issued a pardon for Wilson, but he refused to accept it.

The matter went to the Chief Justice who concluded that Wilson would have to be executed. He wrote, "A pardon is a slip of paper, the value of which is determined by the acceptance of the person to be pardoned. **If it is refused, it is no pardon**."

. . . .

(41) The preacher was carefully explaining to a group of 8 year old students the story of Elijah the Prophet and the false prophets of Baal. He explained how Elijah built the altar, put wood on it, cut the steer in pieces and laid it on the altar.

And then Elijah commanded the people of God to fill four barrels of water and pour it over the altar. The preacher continued, *"Elijah had them do this four times!* Now, can anyone tell me why the Lord would have Elijah pour so much water over the steer and the altar?"

One little girl in the back of the room raised her hand and enthusiastly said, ***To make the gravy!***

. . . .

(42) Most Important Lesson...

"During my second month of nursing school, our professor gave us a pop quiz. I was a conscientious student and had breezed through the questions, until I read the last one; *"What is the first name of* **the woman who cleans the school**?"

"Surely this was some kind of a joke I thought." I had seen the cleaning woman almost every day. I remembered she was tall, she had dark hair, and she was probably in her 50's but how was I to know her name?

I handed in my paper, leaving the last question blank. Just before the class ended, one student asked if the last question would count toward our grade.

The professor said, *"Absolutely."* Then she added, *"In your profession, you will meet many people and all are significant. They deserve your attention and care, even if all you do is smile and say hello. I've never forgotten that lesson, and I since learned that her name was Dorothy."*

. . . .

(43) The preacher was wired for sound with a lapel mike.

And as he preached, he moved briskly about the platform jerking the mike cord. Then he moved to one side, getting wound up in the cord and nearly tripping before jerking it again.

After several circles and jerks, a little girl in the third pew leaned toward her mother and said, **"Mommy, if he gets loose,** will he hurt us?"

. . . .

(44) I read a quote…
- Lot's wife was a pillar of salt by day and a ball of fire at night.
- The first commandment was when Eve told Adam to eat the apple.

(45) **All I really need to know** I learned from Noah's ark...

Plan ahead – It wasn't raining when Noah built the ark.

Stay fit – When you're 600 years old someone may ask you to do something REALLY big!

Put action to your faith – Noah could have believed God, yet still drowned if he hadn't built the ark.

Don't forget that we are all in the same boat!

Remember that the Ark was built by amateurs and the Titanic was built by professionals.

If God is with you, no matter how bleak it looks, there's always a rainbow at the end!

. . . .

(46) At the funeral of a friend, the minister referred to the dates on her tombstone. He noted that first came her date of birth, and spoke lovingly of that event. Then he spoke with tears as he referred to the date of her death. BUT, he said what mattered the most was the dash between those two years; 1940-1998.

"For that dash," he said, *"represents all the time that she spent alive on earth. And now only those who love her know what that little line is worth."*

He went on to admonish the congregation that it matters not how much we own, the cars, the houses, the land or the cash. What matters most he said was how we live and love and how we spend that dash.

So, how we need to think long and hard about the dash you are making in your own life. Are there things you know you need to change?

If we could just slow down enough to consider what's true and real and always try to understand the way other people feel. Then we would be better equipped to love the people in our lives like we ought, like God commands. May we endeavor to wear a smile and perhaps that dash might be a little longer. May we live in such a way that the story told about our dash will be told by some proud people because they knew you! *Be careful how you treat* **that dash that belongs to you***!*

. . . .

(47) A visiting soloist at a church function bragged to his audience in a booming obnoxious voice, *"Two years ago I insured my voice with Lloyds of London for a million dollars."*

There was a hushed and awkward silence in the room until an elderly woman asked him, "***so what did you do with the money****?"*

. . . .

(48) <u>BEST POEM IN THE WORLD</u>

I was shocked, confused, bewildered as I entered Heaven's door,
Not by the beauty of it all, nor the lights or its decor.
But it was the folks in Heaven who made me sputter and gasp--
The thieves, the liars, the sinners, the alcoholics and the trash.
There stood the kid from seventh grade who swiped my lunch money twice.
Next to him was my old neighbor who never said anything nice.
Herb, who I always thought was rotting away in hell,
Was sitting pretty on cloud nine, looking incredibly well.
I nudged Jesus, "What's the deal? I would love to hear Your take.
How'd all these sinners get up here? God must've made a mistake.
And why's everyone so quiet, so somber - give me a clue."
"Hush, child," He said, "they're all in shock,
No one thought they'd be seeing you.

(49) <u>Palm Sunday</u>...

It was Palm Sunday and, because of a sore throat, five-year-old Johnny stayed home from Church with a baby-sitter. When the family returned home, they were carrying several palm branches. The boy asked what they were for and he was told *"people held them over Jesus' head as He walked by.*

"Wouldn't you know it," the boy fumed, **"<u>the one Sunday I don't go, and He shows up</u>.***"*

. . . .

(50) <u>Children's table grace</u>...

Last week I took my children to a restaurant. My six year old son asked if he could say grace. We all bowed our heads as he prayed, *"God is great. God is good. Thank You for the food, and I would even thank You more if mom gets us ice-cream for desert, with liberty and justice for all...Amen."*

Along with the laughter from the other customers nearby I heard a woman say, *"That's what's wrong with this country. Kids today don't even know how to pray.* **<u>Asking God for ice-cream</u>***! How ridiculous!"*

Hearing this, my son burst into tears and asked, *"Did I do it wrong? Is God mad at me?*

I held him close and assured him that he had done a terrific job and God certainly was not mad at him.

An elderly gentleman come over to our table and winked at me as he said, *"I happen to know that God thought that was a great prayer. It's just too bad that she never asks God for ice cream because a little ice cream is good for the soul".*

Naturally, I bought the kids some ice-cream at the end of the meal. My son then did something I will never forget. He picked up his ice cream and walked over to he woman and with a big smile set it in front of her and said, *"Here, this is good for you. It is good for your soul, and my soul is already good."*

(51) To my dear friend, Pastor Phil Blowhorn

I sure hope attendance at your church was better'n my church. Mercy, pastorin' ain't always easy, now is it? We had us a bunch a sick folk, and them added to all the shut-ins made for a whole lot uh pew cushions to look at from the pulpit.

I got to admit I was feelin' somewhat put out, but I went ahead and preached anyhows. Only thing was, with all them people missin' the echo in the church gave me a hoot of a headache. My wife said I needed to git out and ride a bit 'cause the fresh air would make me feel better. Well, she took to drivin' and I took to ridin' and sure nuff, she was right. Not only did my head clear up, but what I saw renewed my faith in the Good Lord. I tell you brother preacher, I seen miracle after miracle!

My S.S. Superintendant, Hank W. had called me to tell me that he wus so deathly sick, he wouldn't make it to church. But, there he wus, drivin' down the road with his favorite fishin' pole stickin' out the window! I tell you, only a miracle could-a snatched him out-a the jaws of death that way!

Then there wus my head deacon, Wilbur S. He had done and left me a message on my answerin' machine that his back wus so jerked outa line that he thought he might have to have surgery. But, I want you to know that when we drove past the golf course, there he wus, a-hittin' golf balls on the drivin' range! Hallelujah, our prayers sure work!

All told, we saw about 20 of our sick folks had taken a turn for the better and were up and about! Not only that, I just couldn't help from rejoicin' over all our shut-ins that got themselves healed too! There wus Sam B. who don't attend church much causin' of him being allergic to crowds, and he wus in line to buy tickets at the ball park...

And then there wus Horace D. who ain't been in church for six months cause-a his bum knee; he wus playing basketball down at he park and... Seein' all these mighty miracles and healings got me so worked up, I started singin' the Doxology!

Yes sir, Brother Pastor Blowhorn, I'm excited! I just know we'll be havin' us a packed house next Sunday, what with all the sick and shut-ins revived by such a touch from heaven. I look forward to givin' you a right nice report next week....Your good Brother Pastor...William (Billy-Bob) Robert from Devil's Town, Georgia.

· ·

(52) <u>DID NOAH FISH</u>?

A Sunday school teacher asked, "Johnny, do you think Noah did a lot of fishing when he was on the Ark ?"

"No," replied Johnny. "How could he, with just two worms."

· ·

(53) <u>Septic Tank Workers</u>...

As a young minister, I was asked by a funeral director to hold a graveside service for a friendless derelict man who had died while travelling through the area. The funeral was held way back in the country.

As I was not familiar with the backwoods area, I became lost. I arrived about an hour late and saw a crew of workers and a backhoe. However, even though the hearse was no where in sight, I apologized to the workers. They looked a bit puzzled as I said, "This won't take long."

I stepped to the side of the grave and saw the vault lid already in place. The workers never stopped eating their lunch as I preached like I'd never preached before. It ended up being a much longer service than I intended but the workers hung right in there with me. Finally, I closed in prayer and left for my car.

As I was opening my car door and taking off my coat, I overheard one of the workers saying to the other, *"Well, I've been putting in septic tanks for 20 years and I ain't never seen anything like this before!"*

(54) Cleaning Poem...
> I asked the Lord to tell me, why my house is such a mess.
> He asked if I'd been computing, and I had to answer 'Yes'.
> He told me to get off my fanny, and tidy up the house,
> So, I started cleaning up, the smudges off my mouse.
> I wiped and shined the top-side, that really did the trick,
> I was just admiring my work, I didn't mean to click.
> But click I did, and oops, I found, a real absorbing site,
> And I got so way into it, I was into it all night.
> So, nothing's changed except my mouse, it's very, very shinny.
> I guess my house will stay a mess, while I sit here on my hiney!

· ·

(55) The Hospital Bill...

A man suffered a serious heart attack while shopping at the Mall. Someone called 911. The paramedics came and rushed the man to the nearest hospital where he had emergency open heart surgery.

He awakened from the surgery to find himself in the care of nuns at a Catholic Hospital. A nun was seated next to his bed holding a clip-board and some forms. She asked him how was he was going to pay his medical bill.

"*Do you have health insurance?*" she asked.

He replied in a raspy voice, "*No health insurance.*"

The nun continued, "*Do you have money in the bank?*"

He replied, "*No money in the bank.*"

She continued..."*Do you have a relative who could help you with your bill?*"

The irritated gentleman said, "*I only have a spinster sister, and she is a nun.*"

Now, the nun becomes greatly irritated and announces in a loud voice, "*My good man, nuns are not spinsters! Nuns are married to God.*"

The man said, *"That's perfect, then **send the bill to my Brother-in law.***

. . . .

(56) Church Dinner

A group of friends from the Cottonwood Falls Baptist Church wanted to get together on a regular basis, socialize, and play games. The lady of the house was to prepare the meal.

When it came time for Al and Janet to be the hosts, Janet wanted to outdo all the others. She decided to have mushroom-smothered steak. But mushrooms are expensive. She then told her husband, "No mushrooms. They are too high."

He said, "Why don't you go down in the pasture and pick some of those mushrooms? There are plenty in the creek bed."

She said, "No, some wild mushrooms are poison."

He said, "Well, I see varmints eating them and they're OK." So Janet decided to give it a try. She picked a bunch, washed, sliced, and diced them for her smothered steak.

Then she went out on the back porch and gave Ol' Spot (the yard dog) a double handful. Ol' Spot ate every bite. All morning long, Janet watched Ol' Spot and the wild mushrooms didn't seem to affect him. So she decided to use them.

The meal was a great success. And Janet even hired a helper lady from town to help her serve. After everyone had finished, they relaxed, socialized, and played '42' and Dominoes. About then, the helper lady came in and whispered in Janet's ear.

She said, "Mrs. Williams, Ol' Spot is dead." Janet went into hysterics. After she finally calmed down, she called the doctor and told him what had happened.

The doctor said, "That's bad, but I think we can take care of it. I will call for an ambulance and I will be there as quickly as possible. We'll give everyone enemas and we will pump out everyone's stomach. Everything will be fine. Just keep them calm."

Soon they could hear the siren as the ambulance was coming down the road. The EMTs and the doctor had their suitcases, syringes, and a stomach pump. One by one, they took each person into the bathroom, gave them an enema, and pumped out their stomach. After the last one was finished, the doctor came out and said, "I think everything will be fine now," and he left. They were all looking pretty weak sitting around the living room and about this time the helper lady came in and whispered to Janet, "You know that **fellow that run over Ol' Spot** never even stopped.

· ·

(57) The *Orlando Sentinel* reported, "*Through a combination of good health, good luck and an innovative workplace benefit, Gary Hellender received a brand new Chrysler minivan Tuesday free of charge from his employer... He's also a father of three – his wife is expecting No. 4... (He has) an old minivan in dire need of replacement.*

"*(He) was praying for what must have seemed at the time as a miracle that he didn't have to pay for. That's exactly what he drove home in Tuesday: a Chrysler Town & Country Touring edition, a $30,000 minivan paid for by PSS, taxes included... just three days after **his prayer for a new minivan**...*"

· ·

(58) Short summary of every Jewish holiday: They tried to kill us. We won. Let's eat.

A father was reading Bible stories to his young son. He read, "A man named Lot was warned to take his wife and flea out of the city, but his wife looked back and was turned into a pillar of salt." All was well until the son answered, "Daddy, **what happened to the flea?**"

(59) <u>Worker Dead at desk for five days</u>...

New York Times: "Bosses of publishing firm are trying to find out why no one noticed that one of their employees had been sitting dead at his desk for five days and why no one even asked if he was feeling OK...He quietly passed away Monday, but nobody noticed until Saturday morning when the office asked why he was working during the weekend...

"A post-mortem examination revealed that he had been dead for five days after having a coronary. He was proofreading manuscripts on medical textbooks when he died. So...you may want to give your coworker a nudge every now and again. And...the moral of this story is don't work too hard. Nobody notices anyway!"

. . . .

(60)*The cannibal chief wrote to the head of the Missionary Society in London: **"Please send more messengers** *from the Lord. The last two were delicious!"*

   *   A man called his mother in Florida, "Mom, how are you?"

"Not too good," said the mother, "I've been very weak."

The son said, "Why are you so weak?"

She said, "Because I haven't eaten in 38 days."

The son said, "That's terrible. Why haven't you eaten in 38 days?"

The mother answered, "Because, I didn't want my mouth to be full in case you should call."

. . . .

(61) <u>THE BAPTIST WHITE LIE CAKE</u>

   Have you ever told a little white lie?

   Alice Grayson was to bake a cake for the Baptist Church Ladies' Group in Tuscaloosa, AL. She forgot until the last minute. Remembering the morning of the bake sale, Alice rummaged through cabinets, found an old angel food cake mix and quickly made it while drying her hair, dressing, and helping her son pack for scout camp.

When she took the cake from the oven, the center had dropped flat and the cake was horribly disfigured. She exclaimed, "Oh dear, there is not time to bake another cake!" So, being inventive, she looked around the house for something to build up the center of the cake. She found it in the bathroom - a roll of toilet Paper.

She plunked it into the center of the cake and then covered it with icing. Not only did the finished product look beautiful, it looked perfect! Before she left the house to drop the cake by the church and head for work, Alice woke her daughter, Amanda. She gave her some money and specific instructions: "Be at the bake sale the moment it opened at 9:30 am and buy the cake and bring it home to trash."

When the daughter arrived at the sale, she found the attractive, perfect cake had already been sold. Amanda grabbed her cell phone and called her mom. Alice was horrified -- she was beside herself! Everyone would know! What would they think? She would be ostracized, talked about, ridiculed!

All night long, Alice lay awake in bed thinking about people pointing fingers at her and talking about her behind her back. She was exhausted. The next day, Alice promised herself she would try not to think about the cake and would attend the fancy luncheon/bridal shower at the home of a fellow church member and try to have a good time.

She did not really want to attend because the hostess was a snob who more than once had looked down her nose at the fact that Alice was a single parent and not from the founding families of Tuscaloosa. But having already RSVP'd, she couldn't think of a believable excuse to stay home.

The meal was elegant, the company was definitely upper-crust Old South; but to Alice's horror, the cake in question was presented for dessert! Alice felt the blood drain from her body when she saw the cake! She started out of her chair to tell the hostess all about it, but before she could get to her feet, the Mayor's wife exclaimed, "What a beautiful cake!"

Alice, still stunned, slowly sat back in her chair when she heard the hostess who was a prominent church member say, "Why thank you, I baked it myself!"

Alice smiled and thought to herself, "God is good."

. . . .

(62) Baptist Dog…

Ever mindful of the congregation, the Baptist preacher and his wife decided to get a new dog and knew that the dog also had to be Baptist. They visited kennel after kennel and explained their needs. Finally, they found a kennel whose owner assured them he had just the dog they wanted. The owner brought the dog to meet the pastor and his wife.

"Fetch the Bible," he commanded. The dog bounded to the bookshelf, scrutinized the books, located the Bible and brought it to the owner.

"Now find Psalm 23," he commanded. The dog dropped the Bible to the floor, and showed marvelous dexterity with his paws. He leafed through, finding the correct passage, pointed to it with his paw.

The pastor and his wife were very impressed and purchased the dog. That evening, a group of church members came to visit. The pastor and his wife began to show off the dog, having him locate several Bible verses. The visitors were very impressed.

One man asked, "Can your dog do regular dog tricks too?" The pastor said, "I haven't tried yet, let's see." So, he pointed to the dog and said "Heel." The dog immediately jumped on a chair, placed his paw on the pastor's forehead and began to howl.

The pastor looked at his wife in shock and said…
"Good Lord, he's Pentecostal!"

. . . .

(63) <u>Gospel Snakes</u>

Up in the hills of old Kentuck, the meanest place that 'ere was struck; there lived a man named Jacob Job, the meanest man on this old globe. He feared not God nor cared for man, except his wild and wicked clan.

He had six boys, both mean and bad, who followed right behind their dad; they drank tat wild-cat whisky down, and painted red that country town.

And there were six gals, big buxom gals, who pranced and frolicked with their pals, they danced and capered on the hills. Sometimes they tippled at the stills.

One day an awful rattle-snake bit the oldest boy, big wicked Jake. And through his veins the venom flew, they cried, "He's bound to die, what shall we do?"

Someone said, "Run to town. Let's get the preacher and bring him down." He was a Dutchman from John Wesley's band, as good as any in the land.

The preacher prayed a strange and curious prayer. He had a faith both rich and rare. We don't know if his prayer got to heaven or not, but on earth it really hit the spot.

He prayed, "Oh God, we thank thee for this snake that Thou hast sent to bite old Jake; to fetch him down from his high hoss, and lead him to the Savior's cross! Oh God, he never would repent, until this blessed snake was sent. He would not mend his wicked ways, until this blessing came today!

"And now Oh God, the Great I Am, please send another to bite old Sam. And Mike and John, those reprobates, please dear God send more rattle-snakes! Then, dear God, send chicken snakes to bite the gals, and all their drinkin' sinful pals.

"And Mama Job, she needs one too, perhaps a copper-head would do. And dear God sent the biggest snake on the globe, to bite their daddy, old Jacob Job! And now, Oh God, before it's too late, please hurry up these Gospel Snakes. And save this old mountain state, I ask it all for Jesus' sake. AMEN!"

· ·

(64) One balmy day in the South Pacific, a navy ship noticed smoke coming from one of the three huts on an unchartered island. Upon arriving at the shore they were met by a shipwrecked survivor. He said, "I'm sure glad to see you guys. I've e been alone on this island for about five years now."

The captain replied, "If you're all alone on the island why do I see three huts?" The survivor said, "O well, I live in one, and I go to church in the other."

"Well what about the third hut?" said the captain, to which the survivor replied, "That's **where I used to go to church**."

· ·

(65) **The Rabbi and the Priest…**

A rabbi and a priest get into a car accident and it's a bad one. Both cars are totally demolished, but, amazingly, neither of the clerics is hurt. After they crawl out of their cars, the rabbi sees the priest's collar and says, "So you're a priest? I'm a rabbi. Just look at our cars. There's nothing left, but we are unhurt. This must be a sign from God. God must have meant that we should meet and be friends and live together in peace the rest of our days."

The rabbi continues, "And look at this, he said. "Here's another miracle. My car is completely demolished but this bottle of wine didn't even break! Wow! Surely God wants us to drink this wine and celebrate our good fortune." Then he hands the bottle to the priest. The priest agrees and takes a big swig and hands the bottle back to the rabbi. The rabbi takes the bottle and immediately puts the cap on it and hands it back to the priest. The priest asks, "Aren't you going to take a drink?"

The rabbi replies, "No, I think **I'll just wait for the police.**"

....

(66) **A cannibal is someone** who gets his first taste of religion when he captures a missionary…. and eats him.

....

(67) Senior citizens are criticized…for every conceivable deficiency in the world… BUT…**it was NOT the senior citizens who took:**

> **The melody out of music,**
> The pride out of appearance,
> The courtesy out of driving,
> The romance out of love,
> The commitment out of marriage,
> The responsibility out of parenthood,
> The togetherness out of the family,
> The learning out of education,
> The sevice out of patriotism,
> The Golden Rule from rulers,
> The nativity scene out of cities,
> The civility out of behavior,
> The refinement out of language,
> The dedication out of employment,
> The prudence out of spending,
> The ambition out of achievement or
> God out of government and school.

....

(68) <u>**Now that I'm older here's what I've discovered**</u>:
1. I started out with nothing, and I still have most of it.
2. My wild oats have turned into prunes and all-bran.
3. I finally got my head together, and now my body is falling apart.
4. Funny, I don't remember being absent-minded.
5. Funny, I don't remember being absent-minded.
6. If all is not lost, where is it?
7. It is easier to get older than it is to get wiser.
8. Some days, you're the dog; some days you're the hydrant.
9. I wish the buck stopped here; I sure could use a few.
10. Accidents in the back seat cause kids.
11. It's hard to make a comeback when you haven't been anywhere.
12. The only time the world beats a path to your door is when you're in the bathroom.
13. If God wanted me to touch my toes, he'd have put them on my knees.

CHAPTER 6

Florida Comedy

(1) Florida is home to a **higher percentage of the elderly** than anywhere in the nation. There are 2 million Floridians over the age of 70 with 157 million years of life on Earth.

Every hour, 14 of them die in Florida, taking with them the stories of their lives and a living piece of our collective past. Some are libraries of unread books. Others are the bestsellers of their generation.

Within the past 16 months, baseball great Joe DiMaggio died at home in Hollywood, Fl, actress Hedy Lamarr died in her Castleberry home, book editor Clifton Fadiman died on Sanibel Island and actor Durward Kirby died in a nursing home in Fort Myers. And Thomas W. Ferebee, the man who dropped the bomb on Hiroshima, died at home in Windemere. And, only God knows who will be next?

(2) A preacher made the statement to his congregation that **every church member is going to die**. He was startled to see a guy near the front of the congregation begin to laugh. So, the preacher thought he had been misunderstood, so he repeated, "Every church member here is going to die."

 Again he saw the man laugh so the preacher asked him why he was laughing and he said, "Because I'm not a church member."

. . . .

(3) Hurricane Season is like Christmas…

- * Decorating the house is like boarding up windows.
- * Last minute shopping in crowded stores.
- * Regular TV shows pre-empted for 'specials.'
- * Family and friends from out-of-state calling.
- * Days-off from work.
- * Candles in-place.

And the #1 reason Hurricanes are like Christmas…
At some point you know you're going to have a tree in your house!

. . . .

(4) Snow… I just got off the phone with a friend living in North Dakota, near the Canadian border. He said that since early this morning the snow has been nearly waist-high and is still falling. The temperature is dropping way below zero and the north wind is increasing to near gale force.

 His wife has done nothing but look through the kitchen window and just stare. He says that if it gets much worse, **he may have to let her in.**

(5) <u>Florida Hurricanes</u>...

<u>Twas the night before Hurricane</u> Francis when all through the state,
Not a gas pump was pumping, not a store opened late.
All the plywood was hung on the windows with care,
Knowing that the hurricane soon would be there.
The children were ready with flashlights in hand,
While rain-bands from the hurricane covered the land.
While out on the lawn there rose such a clatter,
I jumped out of the closet to see what was the matter.
The trees were on the fence and the neighbor's roof was torn,
Gave the fear of us dying in this terrible storm.
With a little wind gust, so lively and quick,
I just remembered our walls weren't brick.
More quickly than eagles, her courses they came,
As she whistled and wobbled and surged like insane.
Off shingles, off siding, off roof-tops and power,
Down trees, down fences, down trailers and towers.
In the center of Florida, she continued to maul.
Screaming 'blow-away, blow-away, blow-away all!
As the wind ripped and the debris flew high,
I peeked out the shutters to see cars floating by.
So off to the Safe-Room my family did go,
With a portable radio and batteries too.
And then in a twinkling, I heard on the set,
The end was not coming for a few hours yet
As I calmed down the kids and was turning around,
Through the window it came, a loud crashing sound.
A big old tree all covered in soot,
Just came through the roof and landed on my foot.
A big pile of branches now lay in a stack,
It looked like my living room had been under attack.
When the winds died down, I looked out for a peek.
I noticed the tool shed was missing its sheath.

I grabbed my last tarp and was nailing it down,
While the kids piled in the car and we headed for town.
The traffic was awful. The stores had no ice,;
My five gallon cooler would have to suffice.
Generators were scarce, not one left in town.
There were trees on the road and power lines down.
We got out of town by a zigzag routine,
And then I heard another was coming called hurricane Jean.
I sped up the car and heard the engine whistle.
Then away we all went like a Tomahawk missile.
You could hear us exclaim as we drove out of sight,
"Let's get out of this place; 'Ohio' seems just right!"

. . . .

(6) <u>The Stranger!</u>

A few years after I was born, my dad met a stranger who was new to our small town. From the beginning dad was fascinated with this enchanting newcomer and soon invited him to live with our family. The stranger was quickly accepted and was around from then on. In my young mind, he had a special niche.

My parents were complementary instructors: mom taught me good from evil, and dad taught me to obey. But the stranger... he was our storyteller. He would keep us spellbound for hours on end with adventures, mysteries and comedies. If I wanted to know anything about politics, history or science, he always knew the answers about the past, understood the present and even seemed able to predict the future! He made me laugh, and he made me cry. The stranger never stopped talking, but dad didn't seem to mind. Sometimes mom would get up quietly while the rest of us were shushing each other to listen to what he had to say, and she would go to the kitchen for peace and quiet. Dad ruled our household with certain moral convictions, but the stranger never felt obligated to honor them. Profanity, for example, was not allowed in our home - not from us, our friends or any visitors. Our long time visitor, however, got away with four-letter words that burned my ears and made my dad squirm and my mother blush. His comments were sometimes blatant, sometimes suggestive, and generally embarrassing. I now know that my early concepts about relationships were influenced strongly by the stranger. Time after time, he opposed the values of my parents, yet he was seldom rebuked ... And NEVER asked to leave. More than fifty years have passed since the stranger moved in with our family. He has blended right in and is not nearly as fascinating as he was at first. Still, if you could walk into my parents' den today, you would still find him sitting over in his corner, waiting for someone to listen to him talk and watch him draw his pictures.

His name?....**We just call him 'TV**.' He has a wife now.... we call her 'Computer.' Their first child is "Cell Phone". Second child "I Pod "

And JUST BORN LAST YEAR WAS a Grandchild: IPAD

Chapter 7

Good ole days Comedy

(1) They cooked in the kitchen in a big pot that always hung over the fire. Every day they lit the fire and added things to the pot. They mostly ate vegetables and didn't get much meat. They would eat the stew for dinner leaving leftovers in the pot to get cold overnight and then start over the next day.

Sometimes the stew had food in it that had been in there for a couple of weeks or longer. Hence the rhythm, "peas porridge hot, peas porridge cold, **peas porridge in the pot nine days old**!"

. . . .

(2) Most people got married in June because they took their **yearly bath in May** and still smelled pretty good by June. However, they were starting to smell so brides carried bouquets of pretty smelling flowers for obvious reasons.

(3) Baths equaled a big tub filled with hot water. The man of the house had the privilege of the nice clean water, then all the other sons and men, then the women and finally the children, last of all the babies.

By then the water was so dirty you could actually lose someone in it. Hence the saying, "**Don't throw the baby out** with the bathwater!"

. . . .

(4) Houses had thatched roofs. Thick straw, piled high, with no wood underneath was the only place for animals to get warm. So, all the pets, the dogs, cats, and other small animals slept up there. When it rained, it became slippery and sometimes the animals would slip and fall from the roof. Hence the saying, "**It's raining cats and dogs**."

. . . .

(5) The floor was dirt. Only the wealthy had something other than dirt, hence the saying "dirt poor." The wealthy had slate floors which would get slippery in the winter when wet.

So they spread thresh on the floor to help keep their footing. As the winter wore on they kept adding more thresh until when you opened the door it would all start slipping outside. Thus a piece of wood was placed at the entry and **called a "thresh-hold."**

. . . .

(6) Sometimes they could obtain pork and would feel really special when that happened. When company came over they would bring out some bacon and hang it to show it off. It was a sign of wealth and that the man could really "bring home the bacon." They would then cut off a little to share with guests and would sit around and "**chew the fat**."

From 'SPAM' to BALONEY

(7) Bread was divided according to status. Workers got the burnt bottom of the loaf, the family got the middle, and the guests got the top or "***the upper crust.***"

. . . .

(8) Lead cups were used to drink ale or whiskey. The combination would sometimes knock them out for a couple of days. Someone walking along the road would take them for dead and prepare them for burial. They were laid out in the kitchen table for a couple of days and the family would gather around and eat and drink and wait to see if they would wake up; hence, the custom of <u>holding</u> "*a wake!*"

. . . .

(9) England is old and small, and they started running out of places to bury the people. So they would dig up coffins and would take their bones to a house and reuse the grave. In re-opening these coffins, one out of 25 coffins were found to have scratch marks on the inside and they realized they had been burying people alive.

So they thought they would tie a string on their wrist and lead it through the coffin and up through the ground and tie it to a bell hence, "the graveyard-shift." They would know that someone was "saved by the bell" or he **<u>was "a dead ringer."</u>**

. . . .

(10) <u>Our God is Awesome!</u> ... For example...
  * Every watermelon has an even number of stripes on the rind...
  * Every orange has an even number of segments...
  * Every ear of corn has an even number of rows...
  * Every stalk of wheat has an even number of grains...

* Every bunch of bananas grows with an even number of bananas on the bottom row and each row up, decreases by one!

AND…again our Awesome God reminds us of His orderly design…

* In that all the waves of the sea come to the shore, 26 waves every minute, no variations in calm or stormy weather!

....

THE BIBLE

Did you know that… When you carry the Bible, Satan has a headache. When you open it, he collapses. When he sees you reading it, he faints. Let's read the Bible every day so he keeps on fainting. Maybe one day he'll have a stroke and never wake up.

. . . .

(11) <u>Our God is Awesome!</u> … For example… did you know…
* That **God has caused the flowers** to each blossom at specific times during the day?

Linnaeus, the great botanist, once said that if he had a conservatory containing the right kind of soil, moisture and temperature, he could tell the time of day or night by the flowers that were open and those that were closed!

* When we let our lives be ordered by Him, He will make all things work for us in ways we never dreamed of! *"He doeth all things well."*

(12) <u>Favorite Animal</u>

Our teacher asked what my favorite animal was, and I said, "Fried chicken." She said I wasn't funny, but she couldn't have been right, because everyone else laughed.

My parents told me to always tell the truth. I did. Fried chicken is my favorite animal.

I told my dad what happened, and he said my teacher was probably a member of PETA. He said they love animals very much. I do, too. Especially chicken and beef.

Anyway, my teacher sent me to the principal's office. I told him what happened, and he laughed, too. Then he told me not to do it again.

The next day in class my teacher asked me what my favorite <u>live</u> animal was. I told her it was chicken. She asked me why, so I told her it was because you could make them into fried chicken. She sent me back to the principal's office. He laughed, and told me not to do it again. I don't understand. My parents taught me to be honest, but my teacher doesn't like it when I am. Today, my teacher asked me to tell her what famous person I admired most.

I told her, "Colonel Sanders." Guess where I am now ...

CHAPTER 8

Jewish Comedy

(1) Mama's Hanukkah Letter

Dear Darling Son and that person you married,

Happy Hanukkah to you and please don't worry. I'm just fine considering I can't breathe or eat. The important thing is that you have a nice holiday, thousands of miles away from your ailing mother. I've sent along my last ten dollars in this card which I hope you'll spend on my grandchildren. God knows their mother never buys them anything nice. They look so thin in their pictures, poor babies.

Well, son, it's time for me to crawl off to bed now. I lost my cane fending off muggers last week but don't you worry about me. I'm also getting used to the cold since they turned off my heat and I'm grateful because the frost on my bed numbs the constant pain. Now don't you even think about sending any more money because I know you need it for those expensive family vacations you take every year.

Give my love to my darling grandbabies and my regards to whatever-her-name-is… the one with the black roots who stole you screaming from my bosom.

Happy Hanukkah, Love Mom

· ·

(2) Q. What did the Jewish mother ask her daughter when the daughter told her she had an affair?   A. Who catered for it?
Q. What did the waiter ask the table of *Jewish* mothers?
A. '<u>**Is anything alright?**</u>'

· ·

(3) Sadie's husband, Jake, had been slipping in and out of a coma for several months, yet his faithful wife stayed by his bedside day and night. One night, Jake comes to and motions for her to come closer. He said, "Sadie, you have been with me through all the bad times. When I got fired, you were there to support me. When my business failed, you were there. When I got shot, you were there by my side. When we lost the house, you gave me support. When my health started failing, you were there still by my side.

You know what I think, Sadie?"

"What dear?" she asked gently.

The dying man said, "<u>**I think you're bad luck.**</u>"

· ·

(4) Mike wandered into the local tavern and saw his friend Pat sitting down at the end of the bar. He puts his hand over his heart and shouts out, "Oh my dear Pat, I'm so sorry to hear about your shop burning down." Pat quickly spins around and says, "<u>**Hush up you. It's tomorrow.**</u>"

(5) *The High Holidays have nothing to do with marijuana.
   * Israel is the land of milk and honey; Florida is the land of milk of magnesia.
   * Why Jewish women like Chinese food so much; "wonton" spelled backwards is "not-now".
   * When the doctor called Mrs. Goldberg to tell her that her check came back she said, "**And so did my arthritis!**"

. . . .

(6) A Jewish boy comes home from school and tells his mother he's been given a part in the school play. "That's wonderful," says his mother, "what's the part?"
   The boy says, "I play the part of a Jewish husband."
   The mother scowls and says, "Go back and tell the teacher **you want a speaking part!**"

. . . .

(7) A young gay man called home suddenly and told his Jewish mother that he had met a wonderful girl and that they were going to be married. He told his mother that he assumed she would be happier now because she'd been very disturbed about his homosexuality.
   His mother responded that she was indeed delighted and asked, "I suppose it would be too much to hope that she would be a good Jewish girl?" He told his mother that not only is his fiancée a Jewish girl but also was from a wealthy Beverly Hills family. The mother admitted that she was overwhelmed by the news, and asked, "What's her name?"
   He replied, "Her name is Monica Lewinsky."
   There was a pause and then his mother asked, "What happened to **that nice black boy** you were dating last year?"

(8) Two nuns were discussing their travel plans and couldn't decide where to go for vacation.

"Go to Israel," said the first nun to which her friend answered, "No, there are too many Jews there."

"Well, then let's go to New York" and back came the remark, "No, there are too many Jews there."

"Well, how about Miami" was the next suggestion, but back came the same reply. "No, there are too many Jews there too."

There was a Jewish lady listening to all of this and she retorted, "Well, why don't you go to hell, **there are no Jews there**."

· ·

(9) A Jewish man went to eat at a Chinese restaurant and wondered whether there were any Chinese Jews. When the waiter came over to take his order he asked, "Pardon me sir, but I would like to know if there are any Chinese Jews?"

The waiter looked directly at him and said, "I not know. I go into kitchen and ask manager." When he came back his remark was, "No, no Chinese Jews. We have orange Jews, tomato Jews, grape Jews but **no Chinese Jews**."

· ·

(10) An IRS official came to a rural synagogue for an inspection. During the visit, the Rabbi accompanied him around the premises. The IRS man said, "So, Rabbi, tell me, please, after you have distributed all your unleavened bread, what do you do with the crumbs?"

The Rabbi replied, "Why, we gather them carefully and send them to the city where they make bread with the crumbs and send it to us." "Ah," said the IRS man, "so what about all these candles? What do you do with all these wax drippings?"

The Rabbi said, "Why, we send them to the city as well, and they make new candles from them and send them to us."

From 'SPAM' to BALONEY

Again, the IRS official asked another question, "And what about all these circumcisions? What do you do with all the leftover pieces?" The Rabbi wearily replies, "Why, we send them to the city as well." "To the city?" the puzzled IRS man asked. "And what do they send you?"

"Well," said the Rabbi, "**Today they have sent us you**."

· ·

(11) The newlyweds were walking out of the church. The groom's new brother-in-law whispered in his ear, "When they start throwing the rice, open your mouth - **it's the last good meal** you're going to get!"

· ·

(12) An elderly Rabbi retired from his duties with the congregation and he decided to fulfill his lifelong fantasy --- to taste pork. He went to a hotel in the Catskills in the off-season and chose a table in the back corner. The waiter arrived and the Rabbi ordered a roast suckling pig. As the Rabbi waited, struggling with his conscience, a family from his congregation walked in. They immediately saw the Rabbi and joined him at the table. The Rabbi began to sweat and finally the waiter arrived with a huge dome platter. He lifted the lid and saw a whole roast suckling pig, complete with an apple in its mouth.

"This place is amazing," cried the Rabbi, "**You order a baked apple** and look what you get!"

Chapter 9

Married Comedy

(1) A dog is truly man's best friend, did you know that?
   If you don't believe it, just try this experiment.
   Put your dog and **you wife in the trunk** of your car for an hour. When you open the trunk…see who is really happy to see you.

· ·

(2) A Doctor, examining a woman who had been rushed to the Emergency Room, took the husband aside and said, "I don't like the looks of your wife at all."
   The husband said, "Me neither Doc, but she's a great cook and **really good with the kids**."

· ·

(3) A couple celebrated their 50th wedding anniversary at a church reception. The minister asked Brother Ralph to share some insights on how he managed to live with the same woman all these years.

The husband replied to the audience, "Well, I treated her with respect, spent money on her, but mostly took her travelling on special occasions."

The minister inquired, "Trips to where?"

"Well," the husband said, "For our 25th anniversary, I took her to Beijing, China."

"Wow!" said the minister, "What a terrific example you are to all husbands. Ralph, please tell us what you're going to do for your wife on your 50th anniversary?"

Brother Ralph said, <u>"I'm going back to get her!"</u>

. . . .

(4) <u>Top 5 reasons why God created Eve…</u>
- God knew if the world was to be populated, men would never be able to handle the pain and discomfort of childbearing.
- As the keeper of the Garden, Adam would never remember where he left his tools.
- Apparently, Adam needed someone to blame his absence on when God caught him hiding in the garden.
- As the Bible says, "It is not good for man to be alone."

<u>And the #1 reason why God created Eve…</u>

- When God finished the creation of Adam, He stepped back, scratched His head and said, "I can do better than that!"

. . . .

(5) <u>Bad timing…</u>

A married couple was driving along a highway doing about 60 mph with the wife behind the wheel. Her husband suddenly looks over at her and says, "Honey, I know we've been married for 30 years, but I want a divorce."

The wife says nothing but slowly increases the speed to 70 mph. Then the husband says, "I don't want you to try and talk me out of it because I've been seeing your friend Erma. She and I have a lot more in common than we do."

Again the wife remains quiet but slowly speeds up to 80 mph. And the husband says, "I want the house and the car." By now they're going 90 mph. The wife starts veering towards a bridge overpass piling. This makes him a bit nervous and says, "Isn't there anything you want?"

"No!" she yells, "I've got everything I need!"

"Oh really!" he says, "So what have you got?"

And right before they are about to slam into the concrete pier at 100 mph she smiles back and says, "<u>I GOT THE AIRBAG</u>!"

· ·

(6) After the christening of his baby brother in church, little Johnny sobbed all the way home in the back seat of the car. His father asked him three times what was wrong. Finally, the boy replied, "The priest said he wanted us brought up in a Christian home and <u>**I want to stay with you guys**</u>."

· ·

(7) Terri asked her Sunday school class to draw pictures of their favorite Bible stories. She was puzzled by one little guy whose picture showed four people on an airplane. She asked him which story it represented.

The little guy said, "The flight to Egypt."

The teacher said, "I see. That must be Mary and Joseph and Baby Jesus but who is the fourth person?"

"Oh," said the student, "<u>**that's Pontius, the pilot.**</u>"

(8) <u>How to start a fight</u>...
   My wife's not here tonight but I do want to report that we're still on speaking terms. It was only this morning that she said to me, "What ya doin today?"
   I said, "Nothing."
   She said, "Well, I thought **you did that yesterday**!"
   To that I replied, "Yes, I did but I didn't finish." And that's how the fight started!

· ·

(9) A couple were married for 25 years and both turned 60 that year. During the celebration, a fairy appeared and said she would grant them one wish each. The wife said she would like to travel around the world, and poof...she had the tickets in her hand.
   The husband said shyly, "I'd like to have a woman that was 30 years younger than me." The fairy picked up her wand and **poof...the husband was 90**!

· ·

(10) Two guys were discussing popular family trends on sex, marriage and values. One guy said, "I didn't sleep with my wife before we got married. Did you?"
   The other guy said, "I'm not sure; **what was her maiden name**?"

· ·

(11) An old man goes to the witchdoctor to ask him if he can remove a curse he has been living under for the last 40 years. The witchdoctor says, "Maybe, but you'll have to tell me the exact words that were used to put the curse on you."
   The old man says, without hesitation, "**I now pronounce you** man and wife."

(12) Mr. Smith goes to the doctor's office to collect his wife's test results. The lab technician tells him, "I'm sorry sir, but there's been a bit of a mix-up and we have a problem. When we sent the samples from your wife to the laboratory, the samples from another Mrs. Smith were sent as well. We are not certain which one belongs to <u>your</u> wife. Regardless, the results are either bad or terrible!"

At that Mr. Smith asked, "What do you mean?"

"Well," said the technician, "one Mrs. Smith has tested positive for Alzheimer's and the other tested positive for Aids. We can't tell which one applies to your wife."

Mr. Smith says, "That's terrible, can we do the test over?"

To which the technician replies, "Normally yes, but you have an insurance plan that won't pay for this expensive test twice. I did call the insurance company and here's what they suggested. Drop your wife off in the middle of downtown and **if she finds her way home**, don't sleep with her!

. . . .

(13) <u>Signs in kitchens…</u>
- No husband has ever been shot while doing the dishes.
- A husband is one who takes the trash out and gives the impression he just cleaned the whole house.
- If we are what we eat, then I'm easy, fast and cheap!
- A balanced diet is a cookie in each hand.
- Thou shalt not weigh more than thy refrigerator.
- A clean house is a sign of a mis-spent life.
- Countless numbers of people have eaten in this kitchen and go on to lead normal lives.

(14) <u>Marriage - man's perspective</u>...
- I haven't spoken to my wife in 18 months; I don't like to interrupt.
- Marriage is a 3-ring circus; Engagement ring, wedding ring, suffering.
- In the beginning God created the earth and rested. Then God created man and rested. Then God created woman.
- A beggar walked up to a well-dressed woman in the Mall and said, "I haven't eaten anything in four days."
- She looked at him and said, "I wish I had your will power."
- The punishment for bigamy is two mother-in-laws.
- A young man said, "Is it true, dad, that in some countries a man doesn't know his wife until he marries her?"
- The dad replied, "Son, that's true in every country."
- Just think, if it weren't for marriage, men would go through life thinking they had no faults at all!

. . . .

(15) <u>Listen</u>...

Married life is very frustrating. In the first year of marriage, the man speaks and the woman listens. In the second year of marriage, the woman speaks and the man listens. In the third year, they both speak **and the neighbors listen**.

. . . .

(16) A few days ago, I saw a man in the shopping mall that was really in a panic. I said to him, "Why on earth are you in such a pickle?"

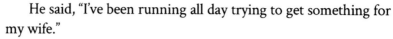

He said, "I've been running all day trying to get something for my wife."

I said to him, "Don't sweat it, **I'll make you an offer!**"

· ·

(17) <u>Oh! If I Could Have One Wish</u>...

A man was walking along a Florida beach and stumbled across an old lamp. He picked it up, rubbed it and a genie popped out. The genie said, "OK, OK, you get one wish; what will it be?"

The man thought for awhile and said, "I've always wanted to go to Hawaii but I'm afraid to fly and I get very seasick. Could you build me a bridge to Hawaii so I can visit?"

The genie laughed and said, "That's impossible! How would you ever get supports to the bottom of the ocean, and think of all the concrete and steel! No way…make another wish."

The man said "OK, I've been married and divorced four times. My wives always said that I didn't care enough and that I'm insensitive. So I wish that I could understand women, know how they feel, what they're thinking, why they cry and know how to make them truly happy."

The genie rubbed his head, wrinkled his brow and stood back with an amazed look in his eyes. Then he said…

"Would you want that bridge **a two-lane or a four-lane?**"

· ·

(18) <u>A little boy was attending his first wedding</u>…

After the service his cousin asked the little boy, "How many women can a man marry?"

The little guy answered, "Sixteen."

The cousin was surprised that he answered so quickly so he asked, "How'd you know that?"

"Easy," said the little guy, "the preacher said, 4 better, 4 worse, **4 richer and 4 poorer**."

....

(19) A little boy was watching his father, a preacher, writes a sermon. After awhile he asked, "Dad, how do you know what to say?"

His dad responded, "Well son, God tells me what to write."

"Well," said the boy, "How come you **keep erasing things out**?"

....

(20) A mother was trying hard to get her little boy to sit still in church during the sermon. She finally got through to him when she said, "If you don't sit still and be quiet, the pastor is going to lose his place and **have to start all over again**." - **It worked!**

....

(21) **Climb the walls…**

"Oh, I'm so happy to see you," the little boy said to his grandmother, "Now maybe daddy will do the trick he has been promising us."

The grandmother was curious, "what trick is that?" she asked.

The little boy said, "Daddy told mommy if you came to visit, he would climb the walls and now we will be able to see him do it."

....

(22) **The mood ring…**

The wife told some friends about the mood ring the husband had bought for her. She said, "When I'm in a good mood, it turns green.

When I'm in a bad mood, it leaves a red mark on his forehead."

(23) <u>Monkeys in a coconut tree...</u> –
    Three monkeys sat in a coconut tree,
    Discussing things as are said to be.
    Said one to the other, "Now listen you two,
    There's a certain rumor that can't be true:
    That humans descended from our noble race,
    That idea is a shocking disgrace."
    "Never did a monkey desert his wife,
    Starve her babies and ruin her life
    And pass them on one to another,
    'Til they scarcely know who is their mother.
    And another thing you'll never see,
    Is a monk build a fence 'round a coconut tree.
    And let all the coconuts go to waste,
    Forbidding all other monks to have a taste."
    "If I put a fence 'round a coconut tree,
    Starvation would cause you to steal from me.
    And here's another thing a monk won't do,
    Go out at night and get in a stew.
    Making whoopee and disgracing his life,
    Then stagger home and beat up his wife."
    "They call this all pleasure and make a big fuss,
    They've descended from something," said the monkey,
    "But certainly not from us!"

· ·

(24) A man and his wife had some problems at home and gave each other the silent treatment. The next week the man realized he would need his wife to wake him at 5 a.m. for an early flight. Not wanting to be the first to break the silent treatment, he finally wrote on a piece of paper, <u>please wake me at 5 a.m.</u>.
    The next morning the man woke up only to discover it was 9 a.m. and that he had missed his flight. He was furious and

was about to go see why his wife hadn't awakened him when he noticed a piece of paper by the bed. It said... **it's 5 a.m. wake up!**

. . . .

(25) <u>I Miss The Old Clothesline</u>

    A clothesline was a news report to neighbors passing by.
There were no secrets you could keep when clothes were hung to dry.
It also was a friendly link, for neighbors always knew,
If company had stopped on by to spend a night or two.
For then you'd see the *fancy sheets* and towels upon the line.
And you'd see the company table cloths, with intricate design.
The clothesline announced a baby's birth from folks who lived inside,
As brand new infant clothes were hung so carefully with pride.
The ages of the children could so readily be known.
By watching how the sizes changed, you'd know how much they changed.
It also told when illness struck as extra sheets were hung,
The night clothes and bathrobes too, haphazardly were strung.
It also said "Gone on vacation now" when the clothes lines were bare.
And they said "We're back!" when lines were full with not an inch to spare.
New folks in town were scorned upon if the wash was dingy and gray.
When neighbors raised their eye-brows and looked the other way.
But, clotheslines are of the past, for dryers make work much less.
Now what goes on inside a home is anybody's guess!

From 'SPAM' to BALONEY

(26) NEED HELP ?

A police officer pulls over a speeding car. The officer says, "I clocked you at 80 miles per hour, sir."

The driver says, "Gee, officer, I had it on cruise control at 60; perhaps your radar gun needs calibrating."

Not looking up from her knitting the wife says: "Now don't be silly, dear -- you know that this car doesn't have cruise control."

As the officer writes out the ticket, the driver looks over at his wife and growls, "Can't you please keep your mouth shut for once?"

The wife smiles demurely and says, "Well dear you should be thankful your radar detector went off when it did or your speed would have been higher."

As the officer makes out the second ticket for the 'illegal' radar detector unit, the man glowers at his wife and says through clenched teeth, "Woman, can't you keep your mouth shut?"

The officer frowns and says, "And I notice that you're not wearing your seat belt, sir; that's an automatic $75 fine."

The driver says, "Yeah, well, you see, officer, I had it on, but I took it off when you pulled me over so that I could get my license out of my back pocket."

The wife says, "Now, dear, you know very well that you didn't have your seat belt on. You never wear your seat belt when you're driving."

And as the police officer is writing out the third ticket, the driver turns to his wife and barks, "WILL YOU PLEASE SHUT UP?"

The officer looks over at the woman and asks, "Does your husband always talk to you this way, Ma'am?" (I love this part)

"**Only when he's been drinking**," she says!

(27) *The best way for a man to remember his wife's birthday is to forget it just once.

* The husband describes his wife by saying, "She's an angel - always up in the air and harping on things!"

* Ad in British newspaper: "Joining nudist colony – must sell washer & dryer"

* Another ad: "<u>**Wedding dress for sale**</u>...worn once by mistake...Call Stephanie."

* Ad: For Sale By owner- "Complete 45 volume set of encyclopedias. Excellent condition. No longer needed. Just got married, wife knows everything"

. . . .

(28) <u>Letter to my darling husband...</u>

(I have here a picture of an SUV Ford sitting on top of a nice sleek red convertible. The SUV has obviously done some serious damage to the little red car as they are both wedged inside a two-car garage attached to this lovely residential home. Got the picture?) Here is the note that was sent via mail...

To my darling husband...

Before you return from your overseas trip, I just want to let you know about the small accident I had with my SUV this morning when I turned into our driveway. Fortunately, it was not too bad and I really didn't get hurt, so please do not worry too much about me.

I was coming home from Wal-Mart and when I turned into the driveway, I accidentally pushed down on the accelerator instead of the brake pedal. The garage door is slightly bent but the SUV fortunately came to a halt when it bumped into your little red convertible.

I am really sorry but I know with your kindhearted personality you will forgive me. You know how much I love you and care for you my sweetheart. I am enclosing a picture for you. I cannot wait to hold you in my arms again.

Signed: Your loving wife.
P.S. <u>**Your girlfriend called**</u>!

. . . .

(29) <u>Shirts for women</u> (who don't take no lip)...
- I'm busy. You're ugly. Have a nice day!
- Warning! I have an attitude and I know how to use it!
- Remember my name; you'll be screaming it later!
- Of course I don't look busy; I did it right the first time!
- I'm multi-talented; I can talk and tick you off at the same time!
- You have the right to remain silent; so SHUT UP!
- Don't tick me off; I'm running out of places to hide the bodies!

. . . .

(30) Here are the Five Rules for Men to follow for a Happy Life that Russell J. Larsen had inscribed on his headstone in Logan, Utah. He died not knowing that he would win the "Coolest Headstone" contest.

FIVE RULES FOR MEN TO FOLLOW FOR A HAPPY LIFE:
1. It's important to have a woman who helps at home, cooks from time to time, cleans up and has a job.
2. It's important to have a woman who can make you laugh.
3. It's important to have a woman who you can trust and doesn't lie to you.

4. It's important to have a woman who is good in bed and likes to be with you.
5. It's very, very important that these four women do not know each other or you could end up dead like me.

. . . .

(31) The Curtain Rods...

The wife spent the first day packing her belongings into boxes, crates and suitcases. On the second day, she had the movers come and collect her things. On the third day, she sat down for the last time at their beautiful dining room table by candlelight, put on some soft background music and feasted in a pound of shrimp, a jar of caviar and a bottle of wine. When finished, she went into every room and stuffed half-eaten shrimp shells dipped in caviar into the hollow of all the curtain rods. She then cleaned up the kitchen and left.

When the husband returned with his new girlfriend, all was bliss for the first few days. Then, slowly, the house began to smell. They tried everything; cleaning, moping, and airing the place out. Vents were checked for dead rodents, carpets were steam cleaned and air fresheners were hung everywhere. Eventually, exterminators were brought in to set off gas canisters while everyone moved out for a few days. In the end, they even paid to replace the expensive wool carpeting but nothing worked. People stopped coming to visit, repairmen refused to work in the house and the maid quit. Finally, they could not take the stench any longer and decided to move.

A month later, even though they had cut their price in half, they could not find a buyer for their stinky house. Word spread fast and eventually, even the local realtors refused to return their calls. Finally, they had to borrow a huge sum of money to purchase a new place. The ex-wife called the man and asked how things were going. He told her his sad story about the rotting house. She listened politely and said that she missed her old home terribly and would he be willing to reduce her divorce settlement in exchange for getting the house back.

Knowing his ex-wife had no idea how bad the smell was, he agreed on a price that was about 1/10 of what the house had been worth, but only if she were to sign the papers that very day. She agreed and within an hour, his lawyer delivered the paperwork.

A week later, the man and his girlfriend stood smiling as they watched the moving company pack everything to take to their new home, including the curtain rods!

Don't you just love a happy ending?

. . . .

(32) Blue Silk P.J.'s...

A man calls home to his wife and says...

"Honey, I have been asked to go fishing at a big lake up in Canada with my boss and several of his friends. We'll be gone for a week. This is a good opportunity for me to get that promotion I've been wanting. So would you please pack me enough clothes for a week and set out my rod and tackle box. We're leaving from the office and I will stop by the house to pick my things... Oh, and by the way, please pack my new blue silk pajamas."

The wife thinks this sounds a little fishy but being a good wife she does exactly what her husband asks. The following weekend he comes home a little tired but otherwise looking good. The wife welcomes him home and asks if he caught many fish.

He says, "Oh Yes! We caught lots of Walleye, some Bluegill, and a few Pike. But," he asks, "Why didn't you pack my new blue silk pajamas like I asked you to?"

The wife replies, "I did. They were in your tackle box."

(33) <u>Happy Valentine's Day</u>

    I go to work and pay the bills and mow the grass and such,
    But when it comes to loving, I'll admit I'm not that much.
    I usually buy you flowers on your very special days.
    I thought that it would make up for the words I didn't say.

    I told you that I'd love you, until the end of time,
    And that I would let you know, if I ever changed my mind.
    But that's not what you want to hear, you need more than that,
    You want burning passion, and at that I'm a little flat.

    Life goes on and the days go by, and months turn into years.
    Some are filled with laughter, and some are filled with tears.
    But one thing that will never change and that's my love for you.
    Although I don't express it, it's honest and it's true.
    Lots of things that matter, some I can't recall.
    But having you beside me is what matters most of all.
    <u>I Love You…Happy Valentine's Day</u>!

• •

(34) <u>Husband Problem</u>

    A nice, calm and respectable lady went into the pharmacy, right up to the pharmacist, looked straight into his eyes, and said, "I would like to buy some cyanide."

    The pharmacist asked, "Why in the world do you need cyanide?" The lady replied, "I need to poison my husband."

    The pharmacist's eyes got big and he exclaimed, "Lord have mercy! I can't give you cyanide to kill your husband! That's against the law. They'll throw both of us in jail! All kinds of bad things will happen. Absolutely not! I will certainly not sell you cyanide!"

    The lady reached in her purse and pulled out a picture of her husband in bed with the pharmacist's wife.

The pharmacist looked at the picture, thought for a minute and said, "Well now, that's different. You didn't tell me **you had a prescription!**

· ·

(35) New Brain

A man went to see the doctor for his test results. The doctor said, "Well, I've got some good news and some bad news. The bad news is that you have an inoperable brain tumor. The good news is that our hospital has just been certified to do brain transplants and there has just been a donation of a young man's brain and a young woman's brain and you can have whichever one you want."

The doctor went on to say, "The man's brain is $100,000 and the woman's brain is $25,000."

The patient could not help but ask, "Why such a difference in the price between the man's brain and the woman's brain?"

The doctor replied, "**The woman's brain is used!**"

· ·

(36)*I just got back from a pleasure trip. I took my mother-in-law to the airport.

   * I've been in love with the same woman for 49 years. If my wife finds out, she'll kill me!

   * Someone stole all my credit cards, but I won't be reporting it. The thief spends less than my wife did.

   * We always hold hands. If I let go, she shops.

   * The Doctor gave a man six months to live. The man couldn't pay his bill, so the doctor gave him another six months.

* Q. Did you hear about the bum who walked up to a Jewish mother on the street and said, "**Lady I haven't eaten in three days?**"

A. "Force yourself," she replied.

. . . .

(37) Three men were hiking through the woods, and they come to a raging river. The water was so deep and so fast that it seemed impossible to cross. The first man offers a prayer, "Please Lord, give me the strength to cross this river." The Lord decides that this is a reasonable request and a cloud settles over the man. When the cloud lifts, he is taller, his legs are like tree trunks and with his massive arms he makes it across the raging river.

The second man offers a prayer, "Please Lord, give me the strength and the ability to cross this river." Once more a cloud descends and when it lifts, the man is made into a massive creature and there is a rowboat next to him. After 3 or 4 hours of hard rowing he makes it safely to the other side.

The third man prays, "Please Lord, give me the strength and ability and wisdom to cross this river." Again the cloud descends but when it lifts this time he is made into a woman. She looks at the map, walks 100 yards **downstream, and crosses on the bridge**! Be particular when you pray!

. . . .

(38) First you forget names, and then you forget faces. Then you forget to pull up your zipper. But, it's worse when you forget to pull it down.

Long ago when men cursed and beat the ground with sticks, it was called **witchcraft; today, it's called golf**.

(39) <u>Why Men are seldom depressed...</u> (written by a woman!)

Men are just happier people! What do you expect from such simple people? Your last name stays the same, the garage is all yours. Wedding plans take care of themselves, and chocolate is just another snack!

You can be President, you can never get pregnant, you can wear a white t-shirt to a water-park, you can wear NO t-shirt to a water park, and car mechanics tell you the truth!

You never have to drive to another gas station because this one is just too icky, you don't have to stop and think which way to turn a nut on a bolt, you do the same work but get more pay, phone calls are over in 30 seconds, a five-day vacation requires only one small suitcase, and you get extra credit for the slightest act of thoughtfulness!

If someone else forgets to invite you, he or she can still be your friend. Your underwear is $8.95 for a three-pack, three pairs of shoes are more than enough, you almost never have strap problems in public, and you are unable to see wrinkles in your clothes!

Everything on your face stays the original color, the same hairstyle lasts for years, maybe decades, and you only have to shave your face and neck!

You can play with toys all your life, your belly usually hides your big hips, one wallet and one pair of shoes, one color for all seasons, and you can wear shorts no matter how your legs look.

You can 'do' your nails with a pocket knife and you have the freedom of choice about growing a moustache. You can do Christmas shopping for 25 relatives on Dec. 24 and do it all in 25 minutes!

No wonder men are happier! Now tell me, what's fair about that?

<u>Aren't We Fortunate To Be Seniors?</u>

(40) A friend of mine was sitting on a lawn chair, sunning and reading, when he was startled by a fairly late model car crashing through a hedge and coming to rest on his lawn.

He helped the elderly driver out and sat her on a lawn chair.

"My goodness" he exclaimed, "you are quite old to be driving!"

"Yes" she replied, "I am old enough that I don't need a license. The last time I went to my doctor, he examined me and asked if I had a driver's license. I told him 'yes' and handed it to him. He took scissors out of a drawer, cut the license into pieces and threw them in the wastebasket."

He told me I **won't be needing this anymore**.

"I' was *so thankful* for his help. No need to worry about remembering to renew the thing," she said sweetly as she piled back into her car and careened on down the street.

. . . .

(41) The Jewish Elbow

A Jewish grandmother is giving directions to her grown grandson who is coming to visit with his wife.

"You come to the front door of the apartments. I am in apartment 301. There is a big panel at the front door. With your elbow, push button 301. I will buzz you in. Come inside and the elevator is on the right.

Get in, and with your elbow, push 3rd floor. When you get out, I'm on the left. With your elbow, hit my doorbell. OK?"

"Grandma, that sounds easy, but, why am I hitting all these buttons with my elbow?""

What?! You're coming empty handed?"

CHAPTER 10

Military (Memories)

(1) He was getting old and paunchy, and his hair was falling fast.
And he sat around the Legion, telling stories of the past.
Of a war that he had fought in, and the deeds that he had done,
In his exploits with his buddies, they were heroes every one.
And 'tho sometimes to his neighbors, his tales became a joke,
All his Legion buddies listened, for they knew whereof he spoke.
But we'll hear his tales no longer, for old <u>BILL</u> has passed away,
And the world's a little poorer, for a soldier died today!
He will not be mourned by many, just his children and his wife,
For he lived an ordinary and uneventful life.
Held a job and raised a family, quietly going his own way,
And the world won't note his passing, tho a soldier died today!
When politicians leave this earth, their bodies lie in state.
Thousands note their passing and proclaim they were great.
It is not the politicians, with their compromise and ploys,
Who won for us the freedom that our country now enjoys.
He was just a common soldier, and his ranks are growing thin,
But his presence should remind us, we may need his like again.

For when countries are in conflict, then we find the soldier's part
Is to clean up all the troubles that the politicians start.
If we cannot do him honor while he's here to hear the praise,
Then at least let's give him homage at the ending of his days,
Perhaps just a simple headline in a paper that would say…
Our country is in mourning, for **a soldier died today**!

· ·

(2) <u>Dear Grandma and Grandpa,</u>

  I am well. Hope you are. Tell brother Walt and brother Elmer the Marine Corp sure beats working on the farm. Tell them to join up quick before all the places are filled. I was restless at first, because we get to stay in bed till nearly 6 AM but I am getting so I like to sleep late.

  Tell Walt and Elmer all you do before breakfast is smooth your cot and shine some things. No hogs to slop, feed to pitch, mash to mix, wood to split or fire to start, practically nothing!

  Men got to shave but it's not so bad; there's warm water. Breakfast is strong on trimmings like fruit, juice, cereal, eggs and bacon, though not much regular food like steak or fried eggplant. The food holds you though until noon when you get food again.

  It's no wonder these city boys can't walk much. We go on route marches which the platoon sergeant says are long walks to harden us. Shoot, if he thinks so, it's not my place to tell him different. A route march is about as far as to our mailbox back home.

  Then the city guys get sore feet and we all ride back in trucks. The sergeant nags a lot, sort of like our old school teacher. I think he really likes us a bunch though.

  Oh, here's something that will kill Walt and Elmer with laughing. I keep getting medals for shooting. I don't why. The bull's-eye is nearly as big as a chipmunk's head and know don't move. All you got to do is lie down and get all comfortable and hit it! You don't even have to load your own cartridges. They come in boxes.

Then there's what they call hand-to-hand combat training; you get to wrestle with them city boys. I have to be real careful though; they break real easy. It ain't like fightin' with that old bull at home! I'm about the best they got in that category.

My best competition comes from a guy from the other side of the county who joined up about the same time I did. I beat him only once but I'm only 5'6" and weigh 130 pounds and he is 6'8" and weighs nearly 300 pounds.

Got to go but be sure to tell Walt and Elmer to hurry and sign up before too many other fellers come stampedin' in... Signed...YOUR LOVING DAUGHTER – ALICE!

· ·

(3) Three Marines were walking through the forest when they came upon a set of tracks. The first Marine said, "Those are deer tracks."

The second Marine said, "No, those are elk tracks."

The third Marine said, "You are both wrong. They are moose tracks."...They were still arguing **when the train hit them**.

· ·

(4) The Jock Strap...

Twenty-eight years ago, Herman James, a West Virginian mountain man, was drafted into the army. On his first day in boot camp, the Army issued him a comb. That afternoon an Army barber shaved his head.

On the second day, the Army issued him a tooth brush. That afternoon an Army dentist yanked out several of his teeth.

On the third day, he was issued a jock strap and the Army is still looking for him!

(5) An RCMP (Royal Canadian Mounted Police) stopped to help a stranded rider beside a stalled motorcycle high up on a mountain road. It was extremely cold and the rider was heavily dressed in a helmet, snow goggles and a snowmobile suit.

In a muffled voice, the rider told the Mountie that the carburetor was frozen. The Mountie, being a motorcyclist himself, remembered an old trick for just such an occasion. He said to the rider, "Try peeing on it. That should unfreeze it."

"I can't." replied the rider.

So, the helpful **Mountie took out his own equipment**, liberally hosed down the carburetor and the bike soon fired up.

A few days later, the local department received a thank you note from a father, grateful for the roadside assistance his young daughter had received from the RCMP.

· ·

(6) <u>Air Flight</u>

I sat in my seat of the Boeing 767 waiting for everyone to hurry and stow their carry-ons and grab a seat so we could start our long flight home. The slow-moving people never seemed to pay much attention to the long lines forming behind them. I just shook my head and expected a long boring flight. I guess I was focused on my interests and knew I could do nothing but wait.

Finally everyone got seated and we just sat there with the door open; no one seemed in any hurry to get us in the air. But, before long we heard the attendant on the speaker telling us we would be delayed a bit longer. She said, "We are holding the plane for some very special people and they should be here in another 5 minutes or so."

We waited for what seemed to be a half hour and I wondered who could be that special. I thought surely it must be some celebrity or famous sports person so why all this commotion over them anyway? Then, the attendant came back on the speaker and excitedly said, "They are here! We have some Marines who are just **returning home from Iraq**!"

When they walked on board, the entire plane load of people erupted into applause. The Marines were surprised and overjoyed as they searched for their seats. As they came down the aisle, I saw one elderly woman kiss the hand of a Marine as he passed by. After handshakes and thank-yous they eventually settled in.

I don't think I was the only civilian that day to question my impatience about getting home to relax in my easy chair with my remote control in my hand. Sure, I took for granted of the everyday freedoms I enjoy and all the conveniences of the American way of life. I tried to get my selfish outlook back under control before we landed. I was not disgruntled in the least when the attendant announced that we remain in our seats until the Marines gathered their gear and dis-bark the plane first. The cheers again erupted from the passengers and continued until the last Marine left.

I felt proud and honored to be able to say a big "Thank-You for a job well-done!" May we all do the same whenever we have the opportunity to be in the presence of any servicemen and women. And may we be quick to say a prayer for their safe return home!

. . . .

(7) Abraham Lincoln was elected to Congress in 1846.
John F. Kennedy was elected to Congress in 1946.
Abraham Lincoln was elected President in 1860.
John F. Kennedy was elected President in 1960.
The names *Lincoln* and *Kennedy* each have seven letters.
Both were particularly concerned with civil rights.
Both wives lost their children while living in the White House.
Both Presidents were shot on a Friday.
Both Presidents were shot in the head.
Lincoln's secretary was named *Kennedy* and

Kennedy's secretary was named *Lincoln*.
Both were succeeded by Southerners named *Johnson*.
Andrew *Johnson*, who succeeded Lincoln, was born in 1808, Lyndon *Johnson*, who succeeded Kennedy, was born in 1908.
John Wilkes Booth, who assassinated Lincoln, was born in 1839, Lee Harvey Oswald, who assassinated Kennedy, was born in 1939.
Both assassins were known by their three names.
Both names are composed of fifteen letters.
Lincoln was shot at a theater named *Ford*.
Kennedy was shot in a car called *Lincoln*.
Booth ran from the theater and was caught in a warehouse.
Oswald ran from a warehouse and was caught in a theater.
Booth and Oswald were assassinated before their trials.
And here's the kicker...A week before Lincoln was shot, he was in Monroe, Maryland and a week before Kennedy was shot, **he was with Marilyn Monroe!**

....

(8) <u>My Kind Of Teacher</u> - Semper Fidelis

This is dedicated to all my friends who ever taught school, parented children or served their country. There should be one like this in every school! - My kind of teacher (I'm still laughing!)

A former Sergeant, having served his time with the Marine Corps, took a new job as a school teacher. But just before the school year started, he injured his back. He was required to wear a plaster cast around the upper part of his body.

Fortunately, the cast fit under his shirt and wasn't noticeable.

On the first day of class, he found himself assigned to the toughest students in the school. The punks, having already heard the new teacher was a former Marine, were leery of him and decided to see how tough he really was before trying any pranks.

Walking confidently into the rowdy classroom, the new teacher opened the window wide and sat down at his desk.

When a strong breeze made his tie flap, he picked up a stapler and promptly stapled the tie to his chest.

There was dead silence. He had no trouble with discipline that year.

HAVE A GREAT DAY! IN GOD WE TRUST

When everything's coming your way, you're in the wrong lane!

. . . .

(9) Can't wiggle out of this one...

To make it possible for everyone to attend church next Sunday, we are going to have a special 'NO EXCUSE SUNDAY.'

There will be cots placed in the foyer for those who say "Sunday is my only day to sleep in."

Eye drops will be available for those with tired eyes from watching too much TV late Saturday night.

We will have steel helmets for those who say, "The roof would fall in if I ever went to church."

Blankets will be furnished for those who think the church will be too cold, and fans for those who think it will be too hot.

We will have hearing aids for those who say, "The preacher speaks too softly" and cotton for those who say "he preaches too loud."

Also, score cards will be available for those who wish to list the hypocrites present.

Some relatives will be present for those who like to go visiting on Sunday.

There will be TV dinners for those who can't go to church and cook dinner also.

One section will be devoted to trees and grass for those who like to see God through nature.

And finally, the sanctuary will be decorated with both Christmas poinsettias and Easter lilies for those who have never seen the church without them!

. . . .

(10) A Navy destroyer stops four **Mexicans in a row boat** rowing towards California. The Captain gets on the loud-hailer and shouts, "Ahoy, small craft. Where are you headed?"

One of the Mexicans puts down his oar, stands up, and shouts, "We are invading the United States of America!"

The entire crew of the destroyer doubled over in laughter. When the Captain is finally able to catch his breath, he gets back on the loud-hailer and asks, "Just the four of you?"

The same Mexican stands up again and shouts, "No, we're the last four. The rest are already there!"

. . . .

(11) A REDNECK LOVE POEM

>Susie Lee done fell in love,
>She planned to marry Joe.
>She was so happy 'bout it all,
>She told her Pappy so.
>
>Pappy told her Susie Gal,
>You'll have to find another.
>I'd just as soon yo' Ma don't know,
>But Joe is yo' half brother.

From 'SPAM' to BALONEY

So susie put aside her Joe,
And planned to marry Will.
But after telling Pappy this,
He said, "there's trouble still".

You can't marry Will, my Gal,
And please don't tell yo' Mother.
But Will and Joe, and several mo'
I know is yo' half brother.

But Mama knew and said, "my child"
Just do what makes yo' happy.
Marry Will *or* marry Joe,
You ain't no kin to Pappy!

Chapter 11

One-liner Comedy

(1) **Will Rogers**, who died in a 1935 plane crash, was one of the greatest political sages this country has ever known.

Some of his sayings:
- Never slap a man who's chewing tobacco.
- There are two theories to arguing with a woman. Neither works.
- Never miss a good chance to shut up.
- Always drink upstream from the herd.
- If you find yourself in a hole, stop digging.
- The quickest way to double your money is to fold it and put it back into your pocket.
- If you're riding' ahead of the herd, take a look back every now and then to make sure it's still there.
- Lettin' the cat outta the bag is a whole lot easier'n puttin' it back.

- After eating an entire bull, a mountain lion felt so good he started roaring. He kept it up until a hunter came along and shot him.
- The moral: When you're full of bull, keep your mouth shut.

• •

(2) <u>ABOUT GROWING OLDER...</u>
- Eventually you will reach a point when you stop lying about your age and start bragging about it.
- The older we get, the fewer things seem worth waiting in line for.
- You know you are getting old when everything either dries up or leaks.
- I don't know how I got over the hill without getting to the top.

• •

(3) <u>For Educated Minds</u>
- She was only a whiskey maker **but he loved her still**.
- A dog gave birth to puppies near the road and was cited for littering.
- Atheism is a non-prophet organization.
- Two hats were hanging on a hat rack in the hallway. One hat said to the other, "You stay here; I'll go on a head."
- I wondered why the baseball kept getting bigger. Then it hit me.
- A sign on the lawn at a drug rehab center said: 'Keep off the Grass.'
- When cannibals ate a missionary, they got a taste of religion.

- Two fish swim into a concrete wall. One turns to the other and says 'Dam!'

(4) <u>Being Thankful</u>

A Rabbi said to a precocious six-year-old boy, "So your mother says your prayers for you each night? That's very commendable. What does she say?"

The little boy replied, "**Thank God he's in bed!**"

. . . .

(5)*<u>**Don't take candy from strangers**</u> unless they offer you a ride. OK?
- He used to hit me but now I miss him.
- My latest song title, "My cell-mate thinks I'm sexy."
- Drive carefully: It's not only cars that can be recalled by their Maker.
- If you can't be kind, at least have the decency to be vague.
- If you lend someone $20 and never see that person again, it was probably worth it.
- Since it's the early worm that gets eaten by the early bird, sleep late. (Remember it's the second mouse that gets the cheese).
- A truly happy person is the one who can enjoy the scenery on a detour!
- Your fences need to be horse-high, pig-tight, and bull-strong!
- Life is simpler when you plow around the stumps!
- A bumble-bee is considerably faster than a John Deere tractor!
- Meanness doesn't just happen overnight!
- Forgive your enemies, it messes up their heads!
- It doesn't take a very big person to carry a grudge.
- You cannot un-say a cruel word.

* Remember, that silence is sometimes the best answer.

* Live a good and honorable life, and then when you get older and think back, you'll enjoy it a second time.

* Live simply, love generously, care deeply, speak kindly, and leave the rest to God!

. . . .

(6) <u>Coincidence is when God chooses to remain anonymous!</u>
- Don't wait for six strong men to take you to church.
- Exercise daily; walk with the Lord!
- Forbidden fruits create many jams.
- God doesn't call the qualified, He qualifies the called!
- God doesn't want shares in your life, He wants controlling interest.
- God grades on the cross, not on the curve.
- Watch your step carefully, everyone else does!
- We're too blessed to be depressed.
- You can tell how big a person is by what it takes to discourage him.
- Birthdays are good for you; the more you have the longer you live!
- Ever notice that the people who are late are often much jollier than the people who have to wait for them?
- You may be only one person in the world, but you may also be the world to one person.
- Don't cry because it's over; smile because it happened.
- Once over the hill you pick up speed.
- I love cooking with wine; sometimes I even put it in the food.
- Whatever hits the fan will not be evenly distributed.

- We cannot change the direction of the wind, but we can adjust our sails.

A health Expert said: "If you have a lot of tension and you get a headache, do what it says on the aspirin bottle, "Take two aspirins and keep away from children"

. . . .

(7) <u>DID YOU KNOW?</u>
- Most lipstick contains fish scales?
- The first product to have a bar-code was Wrigley's gum?
- No piece of square dry paper can be folded more than 7 times in half?
- There are more than 10,000 bricks in the Empire State Building?
- A crocodile always grows new teeth to replace the old teeth?
- The sun is 330,330 times larger than the earth?
- A *'jiffy'* is an actual unit of time for 1/100th of a second?
- The sentence <u>*The quick brown fox jumps over a lazy dog*</u> uses every letter of the alphabet?
- The average life span of a major league baseball is 5-7 pitches?
- The longest recorded flight of a chicken is 13 seconds?
- Cat urine glows under a black light?
- A rubber band pistol was confiscated from algebra class, because it was a weapon of math disruption.

(8) <u>Breaking News</u>... "Six toilets were stolen from the police station. The police have **nothing to go on!**"

....

(9) <u>Did I read that sign right?</u>

* Toilet out of order. PLEASE USE FLOOR BELOW.

* At laundromat: Automatic Washing Machines Please remove all your clothes when the light goes out.

....

(10) <u>On Philosophy</u>...

Philosopher, Rene Descartes, says, "I think, therefore I am."
A comedian says, "I stink, therefore I am."
Carlin says, "I think I am, **therefore I am, I think**."

....

(11) <u>On Being Thankful</u>...

- If you have food in the refrigerator, clothes on your back, a roof overhead and a place to sleep... *You are richer than 75% of this world's population.*

- If you have money in the bank, some in your wallet and spare change in a dish... *You are among the top 8% of the worlds wealthy.*

- If you woke up this morning with more health than illness... *You are more blessed than the million who will not survive this week.*

- If you can attend a church meeting without fear of harassment, arrest, torture or death... *You are more blessed than half the people of the world.*

(12) <u>Modern Proverbs...</u>
- He who laughs last, thinks the slowest.
- Change is inevitable, except from a vending machine.
- Indian Chief says... "When chips are down...buffalo is empty!"
- Honk if you love peace and quietness.
- Nothing is foolproof to a sufficiently talented fool.
- It is hard to understand how a cemetery raised its burial costs and blamed it on the cost of living.
- Latest survey showed that 3 out of 4 people make up 75% of the world's population.

. . . .

(13) A person needs only two tools - - WD-40 and duct tape!
　　If it doesn't move and it should, use WD-40;
　　If it moves and it shouldn't, use duct tape!

. . . .

(14) <u>Bumper Stickers...</u>
- Women who seek to be equal with men... lack ambition!
- Where there is a will...I want to be in it!
- I don't suffer from insanity...I enjoy every minute of it!
- A bartender is just a pharmacist with a limited inventory!
- Always remember, you're unique...just like everybody else!
- Be nice to your kids...they'll choose your nursing home someday!
- There are three kinds of people in the world...those who can count and those who can't!

(15) When you make a mistake, make amends immediately; It's easier to **eat crow while it's still warm**!

....

(16) **If you woke up breathing**, congratulations! You have another chance.

....

(17) Be nice to your friends because you never know when you're going to **need them to empty your bedpan** and hold your hand.

....

(18) Being happy doesn't mean everything's perfect; it just means you've decided **to see beyond the imperfections**.

....

(19) **Thoughts to live by...**

- Accept the fact that **some days you're the pigeon** and some days you're the statue!
- Be wary of strong drink. It can make you shoot at tax collectors, and miss!
- Drive carefully. It's not only cars that can be recalled by their maker!
- Eat a live toad early in the morning and nothing worse will happen to you for the rest of the day!
- If you can't be kind, at least have the decency to be vague!
- If you lend somebody $20 and never see them again, it was probably worth it!
- Never try to teach a pig to sing. It wastes your time and it annoys the pig!

- Be nice to nerds and geeks. One day you'll probably be working for them!

. . . .

(20) <u>From a High School Principal</u> - given at a school speech.
- Life is not fair, get used to it!
- The world doesn't care about your self-esteem; get that on your own!
- If you think your teacher is tough, wait till you get a boss. He doesn't have to deal with your parents!
- Flipping burgers is not beneath your dignity. Your parents called that 'opportunity'!
- In school there may not be winners and losers. You may get as many times as you want to get the right answer. That doesn't bear the slightest resemblance to <u>anything</u> in real life!
- Life is not divided into semesters. You don't get the summers off and very few employers are interested in helping you find yourself. Do that on your own time!

. . . .

(21) <u>Quotes from Ronald Reagan...</u>
- Socialism only works in two places;
- Heaven, where they don't need it, and Hell where they already have it!
- Here's my strategy on the Cold War; we win, they lose!
- The most terrifying words in the English language are; I'm from the Government and I'm here to help!
- Government is like a baby; A canal with a big appetite at one end and no sense of responsibility at the other.

- It has been said that politics is the second oldest profession. I have learned that it bears a striking resemblance to the first.
- If we ever forget that we're One Nation Under God; then we will be One Nation Gone Under!

· ·

(22) <u>I want to go back to the time when...</u>
- Decisions were made by going 'Eeny-meeny-miney-mo'.
- Mistakes were corrected by simply exclaiming, 'do over.'
- 'Race Issues' meant arguing about who ran the fastest.
- Catching fireflies could happily occupy an entire evening.
- It wasn't odd to have two or three 'best friends.'
- Being old referred to anyone over 30.
- When it was unbelievable to think that dodge ball wasn't an Olympic event.
- Having a weapon in school meant being caught with a slingshot.

· ·

(23) <u>Rules of Life...</u>
- Money cannot buy happiness, but it's more comfortable to cry in a Cadillac than on a bicycle.
- Forgive your enemy but remember his name.
- If you help someone when they are in trouble, they will remember you when they're in trouble again.
- Many people are alive only because it's illegal to shoot them.

- Alcohol does not solve any problems, but then neither does milk.
- I hear that in (any town) they go to the dentist to have their wisdom teeth put in.
- The conscience does not stop you from doing anything, it just keeps you from enjoying it.

The original point and click interface was a Smith & Wesson.

....

(24) More Rules of Life...
- Regular naps prevent old age... especially if you take them while driving.
- Having one child makes you a parent; having two makes you a referee.
- Marriage is a relationship in which one person is always right and the other is the husband!
- Don't feel bad. A lot of people have no talent.
- True friends stab you in the front.
- Forgiveness is giving up my right to hate you for hurting me.
- My wife and I always compromise. I admit I'm wrong and she agrees with me.
- They call our language the mother tongue because the father seldom gets to speak.

....

(25) Thoughts For Today...
- Birds of a feather flock together and poop on your car.

- There's always a lot to be thankful for if you take time to look for it. For example, I am sitting here thinking how nice it is that wrinkles don't hurt.
- When I'm feeling down, I like to whistle. It makes the neighbor's dog run to the end of his chain and gag himself.
- If you can't be kind, at least have the decency to be vague.
- Don't assume malice for what stupidity can explain.
- A penny saved is a government oversight.
- The real art of conversation is not only to say the right thing at the right time, but also to leave unsaid the wrong thing at the tempting moment.
- The easiest way to find something lost around the house is to buy a replacement.
- He who hesitates is probably right.
- If you think there is good in everybody, you haven't met everybody.
- If you can smile when things go wrong, you have someone in mind to blame.
- Saving is the best thing; especially when your parents have done it for you.
- Wise men talk because they have something to say; fools talk because they have to say something.
- There are two theories to arguing with a woman. Neither works.
- Never miss a good chance to shut up.
- Always drink upstream from the herd.
- If you find yourself in a hole, stop digging.

From 'SPAM' to BALONEY

(26) Women should **not have children after 35**, because 35 is certainly enough!

* I live in my own little world, but it's OK, they all know me here!
* Nobody is perfect 'til you fall in love with them!
* If God had intended for man to use the metric system, Jesus would have had only 10 disciples!
* I see your IQ tests were negative!
* When I was born, I was so surprised I could not talk for a year or so!
* A Shopping tip: you can get shoes for 85 cents at the bowling alley!
* I married my wife for her looks, but not the ones she's been giving me lately!
* I gave my son a hint. I put a sign on his bedroom door, "Check-out time eighteen!"
* Ever notice that people who spend their money on beer, cigarettes and lottery tickets, are always complaining about being broke and not feeling well?
* The next time you feel like complaining, remember; your garbage disposal probably eats better than 30% of the people in the world!
* The Irishman/Redneck took his necktie back to the store because it was too tight!

THE MOST WASTED DAY OF ALL IS ONE IN WHICH WE HAVE NOT LAUGHED!

- Change is inevitable; except from a vending machine.
- Love may be blind but marriage is a real eye-opener.
- If at first you don't succeed, then skydiving isn't for you.

(27) Remember: **you're unique. Just like everyone else**.
- Never test the depth of the water with both feet.
- If you think nobody cares if you're alive, try missing a couple of car payments.
- If at first you don't succeed, skydiving is not for you.
- A closed mouth gathers no foot.
- Generally speaking, you aren't learning much when your lips are moving.
- Experience is something you don't get until just after you need it.
- Never miss a good chance to shut up.
- Everyone seems normal until you get to know them.

· ·

(28) Some people **say that I'm superficial**, but that's just on the surface.
* The person who invented thumb twiddling didn't do it singlehandedly.

* Where I come from, the valleys are so narrow; dogs have to wag their tail up and down.

* Cleaning with kids in the house is like brushing your teeth while eating Oreos.

* "Good Eye Might" is impossible to say that without sounding like a friendly Australian.

* There is only one difference between a long life and a good dinner: in the dinner, the sweets come last.

* Borrow money from a pessimist, they don't expect it back.

* No one is listening till you make a mistake.

* A clear conscience is usually a sign of a bad memory.

(29) Anyone who thinks **old age is golden** must not have had a very exciting youth.
- How come it takes so little time for a child who is afraid of the dark to become a teen-ager who wants to stay out all night?
- No one has more driving ambition than the boy who wants to buy a car.
- How come we choose from just two people for president and 50 for Miss America?
- Money will buy a fine dog, but only kindness will make him wag his tail.
- Learn from the mistakes of others. You won't live long enough to make them all yourself.
- A backyard barbecue draws two things....flies and relatives.
- The nicest thing about the future is that it always starts tomorrow.
- You know you're old when you reach down to get the wrinkles out of your hose and realize you aren't wearing any.

· ·

(30) For those who take life too seriously
- **Save the whales**; collect the whole set.
- On the other hand; you have more fingers.

Chapter 12

Patriotic (Memories)

(1) A Dutchman was explaining the red, white, and blue Netherlands flag to an American. He said. "Our flag is symbolic of our taxes. We get red when we talk about them, white when we get our tax bills, and blue after we pay them."

    The American nodded and said, "It's the same in the U.S. **only we see stars too**!"

. . . .

(2) A woman applying for a job in a Florida lemon grove seemed to be far too qualified for the job. The foreman frowned and said,

    "I have to ask you this; have you had any actual **experience in picking lemons?**

    She answered, "Well, as a matter of fact I have! I've been divorced three times, I owned two Chryslers, and I voted for Obama!"

(3) <u>Slow Response…</u>

While hiking down along the border this morning, I saw a Muslim extremist fall into the Rio Grande River. He was struggling to stay afloat because of all the guns and bombs he was carrying.

Along with him was a Mexican who was also struggling to stay afloat because of the large backpack of drugs that was strapped to his back. If they didn't get help, they'd surely drown.

Being a responsible Texan and abiding by the law to help those in distress, I informed the El Paso County Sheriff's Office and Homeland Security.

It is now 4 PM, both have drowned, and neither authority has responded. I'm starting **to think I wasted two stamps.**

· ·

(4) You might be a Redneck if…
- It never occurred to you to be offended by the phrase, "One Nation Under God."
- You never protested about seeing the 10 commandments posted in public places.
- You still say, "Merry Christmas" instead of "winter festival" or "happy holidays."
- You bow your head and remove your hat when someone prays.
- You stand and place you hand over your heart when they play the National Anthem.
- You treat our armed forces veterans with great respect, and always have.
- You know what you believe and you aren't afraid to say so, no matter who is listening.

(5) Origin of Left & Right...

I have often wondered why it is that Conservatives are called the 'right' and Liberals are called the 'left.' Then I discovered this in the Bible Book of Ecclesiastes 10:2 (NIV)...

"The heart of the wise inclines to the right but the heart of the fool to the left."

The answer can't get any simpler than that!

. . . .

(6) A Spelling Lesson...
- The last **four letters in American**... I Can...
- The last four letters in Republican...I Can...
- The last four letters in Democrats...Rats

There will be a test in Nov. 2012... Remember that November is set aside as 'National Rodent Removal' month...

. . . .

(7) Military Medals...
- The Bronze Star – for acts of valor.
- The Silver Star – for more and greater acts of valor.
- The Congressional Medal of Honor is known as 'The Gold Star'.

However, God gives out the greatest medal of all.

The Morning Star' – The Star that continues to shine in the morning twilight hours, after all the other stars have lost their luster.

(8) <u>Wal-Mart vs. The Morons</u>
- Americans spend $36,000,000 at Wal-Mart every hour of every day.
- *This works out to $20,928 profit every minute!
- *Wal-Mart will sell more from January 1 to St. Patrick's Day (March 17th) than Target sells all year.
- *Wal-Mart is bigger than Home Depot + Kroger + Target +Sears + Costco + K-Mart combined.
- *Wal-Mart employs 1.6 million people, is the world's largest private employer, and most speak English.
- *Wal-Mart is the largest company in the history of the world.
- *Wal-Mart now sells more food than Kroger and Safeway combined, and keep in mind they did this in only fifteen years.
- *During this same period, 31 big supermarket chains sought bankruptcy.
- *Wal-Mart now sells more food than any other store in the world.
- *Wal-Mart has approx 3,900 stores in the USA of which 1,906 are Super Centers; this is 1,000 more than it had five years ago.
- *90% of all Americans live within fifteen miles of a Wal-Mart.

You may think that I am complaining, but I am really laying the ground work for suggesting that MAYBE we should hire the guys who run Wal-Mart to fix the economy.

(9) <u>To President Obama and all 535 voting members</u> of the <u>Legislature</u>

It is now official that the majority of you are corrupt morons:

1. The U.S. Postal Service was established in 1775. You have had 234 years to get it right and it is broke.

2. Social Security was established in 1935. You have had 74 years to get it right and it is broke.

3. Fannie Mae was established in 1938. You have had 71 years to get it right and it is broke.

4. War on Poverty started in 1964. You have had 45 years to get it right; $1 trillion of our money is confiscated each year and transferred to "the poor" and they only want more.

5. Medicare and Medicaid were established in 1965. You have had 44 years to get it right and they are broke.

6. Freddie Mac was established in 1970. You have had 39 years to get it right and it is broke.

7. The Department of Energy was created in 1977 to lessen our dependence on foreign oil. It has ballooned to 16,000 employees with a budget of $24 billion a year and we import more oil than ever before. You had 32 years to get it right and it is an abysmal failure.

You have FAILED in every "government service" you have shoved down our throats while overspending our tax dollars.

AND YOU WANT AMERICANS TO BELIEVE YOU CAN BE TRUSTED WITH A GOVERNMENT-RUN HEALTH CARE SYSTEM??

(10) West Virginia FARM KID in Marines

Dear Ma and Pa,

   I am well. Hope you are. Tell Brother Walt and Brother Elmer the Marine Corps beats working for old man Minch by a mile. Tell them to join up quick before all of the places are filled.

   I was restless because they make you get to stay in bed till nearly 6 a.m. But I am getting so I like to sleep late. Tell Walt and Elmer all you do before breakfast is smooth your cot, and shine some things. No hogs to slop, feed to pitch, mash to mix, or wood to split. Practically nothing.

   Men got to shave but it is not so bad, there's warm water.

   Breakfast is strong on trimmings like fruit juice, cereal, eggs, bacon, etc., but kind of weak on chops, potatoes, ham, steak, fried eggplant, pie and other regular food, but tell Walt and Elmer you can always sit by the two city boys that live on coffee. Their food, plus yours, holds you until noon when you get fed again. It's no wonder these city boys can't walk much.

   We go on 'route marches,' which the platoon sergeant says are long walks to harden us. If he thinks so, it's not my place to tell him different. A 'route march' is about as far as to our mailbox at home. Then the city guys get sore feet and we all ride back in trucks.

   This next will kill Walt and Elmer with laughing. I keep getting medals for shooting. I don't know why. The bulls-eye is near as big as a chipmunk head and don't move, and it ain't shooting at you like the Higgett boys at home. All you got to do is lie there all comfortable and hit it. You don't even load your own cartridges. They come in boxes.

   Then we have what they call hand-to-hand combat training. You get to wrestle with them city boys. I have to be real careful though, they break real easy. It ain't like fighting with that ole bull at home. I'm about the best they got in this except for that Tug Jordan from over in Silver Lake. I only beat him once. He joined up the same time as me, but I'm only 5'6' and 130 pounds and he's 6'8' and near 300 pounds dry.

Be sure to tell Walt and Elmer to hurry and join before other fellers get onto this setup and come stampeding in.

Your loving daughter, Alice

. . . .

(11) <u>I Am Your Flag</u>

Some people call me 'Old Glory', others call me the Star Spangled Banner, but whatever they call me, I am your flag – the Flag of the United States of America.

Something has been bothering me, so I thought I might talk it over with you, because you see, it is about you and me.

I remember some time ago people lined up on both sides of the street to watch the parade and naturally, I was leading every parade, proudly waving in the breeze. When your daddy saw me coming, he immediately removed his hat and placed it against his left shoulder so that his hand was directly over his heart, remember?

What happened? I'm still the same old flag. Oh I have a few more stars since you were a boy and a lot more blood has been shed since those parades of long ago.

But now I don't feel as proud as I used to. When I come down your street and you just stand there with your hands in your pockets, I may get a small glance and you look away. Then I see children running around and shouting – they don't seem to know who I am…

I saw a man take his hat off, then look around. He didn't see anybody with theirs off, so he quickly put it back on; and what about that night at the ball game? When they played 'The Star Spangled Banner' and I waved so proudly in the breeze and nobody bothered to sing?

Is it a sin to be patriotic? Have you forgotten what I stand for or where I have been? Remember Germany, France, Japan, Holland Belgium, Korea, Vietnam, Persian Gulf, Afghanistan, and Iraq? Take a look at the memorial honor rolls sometime and read the names of those who never came back. They gave their lives to keep this republic free and rightfully labeled, 'One Nation Under God!' When you salute me, you are saluting them!

I may not be coming down your street for a long time, as it seems that patriotic parades are becoming a thing of the past. But, if I do, will you do me a big favor…?

…Stand up straight, place your hand over your heart, and if they play the 'Star Spangled Banner' sing out loud and clear. I will salute you by waving back! Show me you remember; <u>I AM YOUR FLAG!</u>

· ·

(12) <u>A great political idea</u>… Limit all politicians to <u>two</u> terms, one term in office and one term in prison. (<u>**I guess Illinois already does this!**</u>)

· ·

(13) Subject: <u>My Son</u>

Two men were having coffee, when one of them said:

"Last night, my son just walked into the living room and said, '**<u>Dad, cancel my allowance</u>** immediately, rent my room out, throw all my clothes out the window, take my TV, stereo, i-Phone, iPad, and my laptop.

"Please give my jewelry to the Salvation Army or Goodwill. Then sell my car. Take my front door key away from me and throw me out of the house. Then disown me and never talk to me again. And don't forget to write me out of your will and leave my share to my brother.'"

From 'SPAM' to BALONEY

The other man said: "Wow, he really said that?"

"Well, he didn't put it quite that way. He actually said, 'Dad, I've decided to work for Obama's re-election campaign.'"

. . . .

(14) Subject: $1000 Check every month...

Without any paperwork, Grandpa started getting a $1000 check every month. So Grandpa and Grandma started cashing them. It turns out an insurance company made a mistake with the address. The checks were intended for another person with the same name.

Grandpa then received a notice that he had to pay back $10,000 and became very upset. He called up his grandson, an accountant, and explained the situation.

The Grandson asked, *"Grandpa, didn't you wonder why you were receiving the checks for doing absolutely nothing?"*

Grandpa answered, *"No, I didn't. I just figured the Democrats were back in power."*

. . . .

(15) Things got you down? Well then, consider these...

In a hospital's Intensive Care Unit, patients always died in the same bed, on Sunday morning, at about 11:00 am, regardless of their medical condition. This puzzled the doctors and some even thought it had something to do with the supernatural.

No one could solve the mystery as to why the deaths occurred around 11:00 AM Sunday, so a worldwide team of experts was assembled to investigate the cause of the incidents. The next Sunday morning, a few minutes before 11:00 AM all of the doctors and nurses nervously waited outside the ward to see for themselves what the terrible phenomenon was all about. Some were holding wooden crosses, prayer books, and other holy objects to ward off the evil spirits. Just when the clock struck

147

11:00, Fernando Rodriguez, the part-time Sunday sweeper, entered the ward and **unplugged the life support** system so he could use the vacuum cleaner.

. . . .

(16) Still Having a Bad Day?

The average cost of rehabilitating a seal after the Exxon Valdez Oil spill in Alaska was $80,000.00 At a special ceremony, two of the most expensively saved animals were being released back into the wild amid cheers and applause from onlookers... A minute later, in full view, **a killer whale ate them both**.

Signs:...In an office:
AFTER TEA BREAK, STAFF SHOULD EMPTY THE TEAPOT AND STAND UPSIDE DOWN ON THE DRAINING BOARD.

Outside a secondhand shop:
WE EXCHANGE ANYTHING -- BICYCLES, WASHING MACHINES, ETC. WHY NOT BRING YOUR WIFE ALONG AND GET A WONDERFUL BARGAIN?

Spotted in a safari park:
ELEPHANTS PLEASE STAY IN YOUR CAR

Chapter 13

Redneck Comedy

(1) <u>Mule For Sale</u>... In Starkville Miss. someone ran an ad in the newspaper, 'Mule For Sale.' A couple of locals, Curtis and Leroy bought the mule for $100 The mule was supposed to be delivered the next day.

The next day a farmer drove up and said to Curtis and Leroy, "Sorry fellas, I have some bad news. The mule died last night." They said, "That's OK just give us our money back."

"Well," the farmer said, "I'd like to but I can't because I already went and spent it."

They said, "OK, just bring us the dead mule." The farmer asked what on earth they wanted the dead mule for. Curtis said, "We are going to raffle him off."

The farmer said, "You can't get away with raffling off a dead mule." "Sure enough we can," said Leroy, "we don't have to tell anybody he's dead."

A couple of weeks later, the farmer ran into Curtis and Leroy in town and asked, "What'd you fellers ever do with that dead mule?"

They said, "We raffled him off, jes like we said we'd do, and we made a couple hundred dollars."

The farmer said, "Didn't anybody complain?"

Curtis said, "Well, the feller that won did so we gave him his two dollars back."

P.S. Curtis and Leroy now work for the government; they're overseeing the Bailout Stimulus Program!

. . . .

(2) Pat: "Mike, you haven't said much today. Is something wrong?"
Mike: "Well, sorta, I had to **shoot my old coon dog** last night."
Pat: "Well, Mike, was he mad?"
Mike: "No, not really, but I don't think he liked it very much."

. . . .

(3) <u>You know you're a true Red-Neck when...</u>
- You've been married three times and still have the same in-laws.
- Someone in your family died right after saying, "Hey guys, watch this!"
- You wonder how service stations keep their restrooms so clean.

. . . .

(4) <u>You Just Can't Fix Stupid</u>... I was driving when I saw the flash of a traffic camera. I figured that my picture had been taken for exceeding the speed limit, even though I knew that I was not speeding.

Just to be sure, I went around the block again and passed the same spot driving even more slowly, but again the camera flashed.

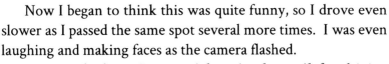

Now I began to think this was quite funny, so I drove even slower as I passed the same spot several more times. I was even laughing and making faces as the camera flashed.

Two weeks later, **I got 5 tickets in the mail** for driving without my seat belt fastened! <u>You just can't fix stupid!</u>

. . . .

(5) <u>Mississippi</u>... A young man from Mississippi came running into the store and said to his buddy, "Bubba, **somebody just stole your pick-up** truck from the parking lot."

Bubba said, "Did you see who it was?"

"No," his friend answered, "I couldn't tell who it was, but I did get his tag number."

. . . .

(6) <u>In Texas</u>... The Sheriff pulled up next to a guy dumping garbage into the ditch. The Sheriff asked, "Why are you dumping garbage in the ditch? Don't you see that sign right over your head?"

"Yep," the man said, "that's why I'm dumping it here, 'cause it says, '**Fine for dumping garbage**.'"

. . . .

(7) <u>In Alabama</u>... A group of Alabama friends went deer hunting and paired off in twos for the day. That night, one of the hunters returned alone, staggering under the weight of an 8-point buck.

"Where's Henry?" the others asked. "Well," the man replied, "the bad news is that Henry had a stroke a couple of miles back up the trail, and just wanted to lie there for awhile."

"Don't tell me you just left Henry out there in the woods and you carried this deer back?"

"Well," the hunter said, "it was a tough call" but I figured **nobody is gonna steal ole Henry**."

(8) A man walked into a Louisiana Circle-K, put a $20 bill on the counter, and asked for change. When the clerk opened the cash drawer, the man pulled a gun and asked for all the cash in the register, which the clerk promptly provided. The man took the cash from the clerk and fled, leaving the $20 bill on the counter. The total amount of cash he got from the drawer was $15. (The question to consider is…if someone points **a gun at you and gives you money,** is it really a crime?)

. . . .

(9) <u>Southern Advice…</u>
- If you run your car into a ditch, don't panic. Four men in a 4-wheel drive pick-up truck with a tow chain will be along shortly. Don't try to help them; just stay out of their way. That is what they live for!
- Don't be surprised to find movie rentals and bait in the same store. Just don't buy food there.
- Be advised that 'He needed a killin' is a valid defense in the southern court of law.
- If you hear a Southerner exclaim, *"Hey, y'all, watch this"* try to get it on video and stay out of the way because these are likely to be his last words.

. . . .

(10) <u>In need of a push…</u>

    One night a man and his wife were in bed when they hear a knock on the door. He gets up and answers it only to find a very drunk guy asking if he could get a push.

    "What?" exclaims the husband in an angry voice, and promptly slams the door in the drunken man's face. He goes back to bed and when his wife asks what that was all about, he says, *"O, it was just some drunk wanting a push."*

The wife said to him, *"Well, why didn't you help him?"* The husband says, *"Because its 3 o'clock in the morning and it's raining like crazy."*

The wife is by now getting quite angry and says, *"Remember when your car broke down and someone in the middle of the night was kind enough to come to our rescue? I think you ought to get up and go help the man."*

Well, what choice does this poor husband have? So, he gets up, gets dressed, finds a raincoat, and goes outside with a flashlight and yells out, *"Where are you? Do you still need a push?"*

He hears a muffled voice reply, *"I'm over here."*

He makes his way in the pouring rain in the direction of the voice and yells out again, *"Where are you?"* And then he hears the drunken man yell back, *"Over here on the swing set!"*

· ·

(11) <u>Darwin Awards...</u>

When his 38 caliber revolver failed to fire at his intended victim during a hold-up in Long Beach, California, the would-be robber, James Elliot, did something that can only inspire wonder. He peered down the barrel and tried the trigger again. This time it worked!

· ·

(12) <u>A Fish and Game Warden</u> caught a man shooting loons. He arrested him on the spot and took him right to town and brought him up before the judge. The judge said, *"This is terrible. These birds are endangered and I've got a good mind to throw the book at you."*

The guilty defendant said, *"You're right, Your Honor, I have no excuse. It's just that they taste so good, I couldn't help myself."*

"Well," the judge said, "That's certainly no excuse. I would think you'd have better sense than to break the law and risk going to jail just because loons taste good. So, tell me just what do they taste like?"

"Well," your honor," he said, "the taste is about half-way between a blue heron and a bald eagle!"

. . . .

(13) <u>Dying of Thirst...</u>

A traveler was stumbling through the desert, desperately searching for water, when he saw something in the far distance. Hoping to find water, he walked toward the image only to find an old peddler sitting at a card table with a bunch of ties for sale.

The parched wanderer asked, *"Please, I'm dying of thirst, can I have some water?"* The man replied, *"I don't have any water, but why don't you buy a tie?*

The desperate man shouted curses at the old peddler, called him a lot of vulgar names and said he didn't need a tie, he needed some water.

The old peddler said, *"OK, don't buy a tie. But to show you how nice a guy I am, I'll tell you that over that hill there, about 5 miles is a nice restaurant. Just keep walking and eventually you will get all the water you want."*

The man took off in a huff walking and eventually disappeared out of sight. About 3 hours later he returned. The old peddler asked him, *"What happened? Didn't you find the restaurant?"*

"I found it all right", said the traveler, **"but they wouldn't let me in without a tie!"**

. . . .

(14) <u>The Tiny Cabin...</u>

A social worker from a big city in Massachusetts recently transferred to the Mountains of West Virginia and was on her first tour in her new territory, when she came upon the tiniest cabin she had ever seen in her life. Intrigued, she went up and knocked on the door.

"*Anybody home?*" she asked. "*Yep,*" came a kid's voice through the door.

"*Is your father there?*" asked the social worker.

"*Pa? Nope, he left before Ma came in.*" said the kid.

"*Well, is your mother there?*" persisted the social worker.

"*Ma? Nope, she left just before I got here,*" said the kid.

"*But*" protested the social worker, "*Are you never together as a family?*"

"*Sure*" said the kid through the door, "*But not here, this is the outhouse.*"

Government workers are so very smart. Aren't you happy that they'll soon be handling all our financial, educational, and medical dilemmas?

• •

(15) <u>West Virginia Drivers Application</u>...

Last name_____

First name (Check appropriate box)

_____ Billy-Bob   Age ___ (If unsure, guess)

_____ Billy-Joe   Sex ___M ___F ___Not Sure

_____ Billy-Ray   Shoe Size ___Left ___Right

_____ Billy-Sue

_____ Bobby-Jo   Occupation

_____ Bobby-Ann   ___ Farmer   ___ Mechanic

_____ Bobby-Lee   ___ Hair Dresser ___ Waitress

_____ Bobby-Ellen   ___ Unemployed   ___ Dirty Politician

_____ Bobby Beth-Ann Sue

Leonard O'Donnell

Relationship with Spouse (Check all that apply)
___ Sister ___ Brother ___ Mother ___ Father ___ Cousin
___ Aunt ___ Uncle ___ Son ___ Daughter ___ Pet

Number of children living in household ___
Number of children living in shed ___
Number of children that are yours ___

Mother's name ___ (if not sure leave blank)
Father's name ___ (if not sure leave blank)
Education: 1 2 3 4 (circle highest grade completed)

Do you ___ own ___ rent your mobile home?

Vehicles you own & where you keep them:
___ Total vehicles you own.
___ Number of vehicles in front yard.
___ Number of vehicles that still crank.
___ Number of vehicles on cement blocks.
___ Number of vehicles in back yard.

Firearms you own & where you keep them
_____ Truck _____ Kitchen _____ Bedroom
_____ Bathroom _____ Shed

Do You Have A Gun Rack?
___ Yes ___ No
If 'No' explain _____

Newspapers/Magazines you subscribe to
___ The National Enquirer ___ The Globe ___ T.V. Guide
___ Soap Opera Digest ___ Rifle & Shotgun

___ Number of times you've seen a UFO

From 'SPAM' to BALONEY

___ Number of times you've seen Elvis
___ Number of times you've been on Jerry Springer

How often do you bathe?
___ Weekly
___ Monthly
___ Not Applicable
___ No. of teeth you have?

Color of teeth:
___ Yellow
___ Brownish Yellow
___ Brown
___ Black

Brand of chewing tobacco you prefer:
___ Red Man ___ Copenhagen

How far is your home from a paved road?
___ 2 miles ___ 3 miles ___ don't know

. . . .

(16) <u>I hope its blood</u>

An old drunk was cautiously walking across an icy street and he had a pint of whiskey in his back pocket. He slipped and fell on his rear. Putting his hands down to help himself up, he felt something wet. He thought for a moment and then said, *"I hope its blood."*

. . . .

(17) <u>Jaundice...</u>

The Doctor was treating his patient for "Jaundice" until he realized his patient was "Chinese".

. . . .

(18) A Redneck friend was trying to convince Bubba that he ought not to be staying in his shack in the woods with the cold winter coming on. He only wanted to help him endure the winter, so

he said... "Bubba, you're out here in the woods all alone. Aren't you afraid of the dark?"

Bubba said, *"No I'm not afraid of the dark."*

Then his redneck friend said, *"Well, what about the bears?"*

Bubba thought for a moment and then said, *"**I don't know if they are afraid of the dark or not**."*

• •

(19) <u>Blessed are the cracked, for they let in the light!</u>
   1. My husband and I divorced over religious differences. He thought he was God and I didn't.
   2. I don't suffer from insanity; I enjoy every minute of it.
   3. Some people are alive only because it's illegal to kill them.
   4. I used to have a handle on life, but it broke.

• •

(20) A man in North Carolina had a flat tire. He pulled off on the side of the road, and proceeded to put a bouquet of roses in front of the car and one behind it. Then he got back in the car to wait.

A passerby studied the scene as he drove by and was so curious he turned around and went back. He asked the fellow what the problem was.

The man replied, "I got a flat tahr." The passerby asked, "But what's with the flowers?"

The man responded, "When you break down they tell you to **put flares in the front and flares in the back**. I never did understand it neither."

• •

(21) A Tennessee State trooper pulled over a pickup on I-65. The trooper asked, "**<u>Got any ID?</u>**" The driver replied, "Bout whut?"

(22) Y'all kin say whut y'all want 'about the South, but y'all never heard **o' nobody retirin' an' movin' up North**.

. . . .

(23) <u>Redneck Birthday Present</u>...

    A redneck is on the phone… "Hello, is this the FBI?"

    "Yes," came the response, "what do you want?"

    "Well, I'm calling to report about my neighbor Billy Bob Smith. He is hiding marijuana inside his firewood."

    "Thank you very much for the call sir."

    The next day the FBI descended on Billy Bob's property. They searched the woodshed. Using axes, they bust open every piece of wood but found no marijuana. They warned Billy Bob and left. Then the phone rings at Billy Bob's house. **"Hey, Billy Bob! Did the FBI come?**

    "Yeah" he said. "Did they split your firewood?"

    "Yup, they sure did. Happy Birthday buddy."

. . . .

(24) An Irishman, a Mexican and a Blonde Guy were doing construction work on scaffolding on the 20th floor of a building. They were eating lunch and the Irishman said, *"Corned beef and cabbage. If I get corned beef and cabbage one more time for lunch I'm gonna jump off this building!"*

    The Mexican opened his lunch box and exclaimed, *"Burritos again? If I get burritos one more time I'm jumping too!"*

    The blonde guy opened his lunch and said, *"Bologna again? If I get a bologna sandwich one more time I'm jumping too!"*

    The next day the Irishman opened his lunch box, saw the corned beef and cabbage, and jumped to his death. Then the Mexican opened his lunch box, saw a burrito, and jumped too. The blonde guy opened his lunch, saw the bologna and jumped to his death as well.

At the funeral, the Irishman's wife was weeping. She said, *"If I had known how really tired he was of corned beef and cabbage, I never would have given it to him again!"*

The Mexican's wife also wept and said, *"I could have given him tacos or enchiladas! I didn't realize he hated burritos so much."*

Everyone turned and stared at the blonde's wife. The blonde's wife said, *"Don't look at me.* **He makes his own lunch***!"*

· ·

(25) <u>The Little House Behind The House</u>

One of my fondest memories, as I recall the days of yore,
Was the little house behind the house, with the crescent o'er the door.
'Twas a place to sit and ponder, with your head all bowed down low,
Knowing that you wouldn't be there, if you didn't have to go.
Ours was a multi-holer, with a size for everyone,
You left there feelin' better, after your job was done.
You had to make those frequent trips in snow, rain, sleet or fog,
To that little house where you usually found the Sears-Robuck catalogue.
Oft times in dead of winter, that seat was spread with snow,
'Twas then wit much reluctance, to that little house you'd go.
With a swish you'd clear that wooden seat, bend low with dreadful fear,
You'd shut your eyes and grit your teeth, as you settled on your rear.
I recall the day Old Grandpa, who stayed with us one summer,
Made a trip to that little house, which proved to be a bummer.
'Twas the same day that my dad had finished painting the kitchen green,
He'd just cleaned up the mess he'd made, with rags and gasoline.
He tossed the rags down the hole, went on his usual way,
Not knowing that by doing so, he'd eventually ruin the day.
For Grandpa had an urgent call, I never will forget,

This trip he made to the little house stays in my memory yet!
He sat down on the wooden seat, with both feet on the floor,
He filled his pipe and tapped it down and struck a match on the outhouse door.
He lit the pipe and sure enough, it soon began to glow,
He slowly raised his rear a bit, and tossed the flaming match below.
The blast that followed, I am told, was heard for miles around,
And there was poor old Grandpa, sprawled out there on the ground.
The smoldering pipe still in his mouth, his eyes were shut real tight,
The celebrated three-holer, was blown clear out of sight.
We asked him what had happened, what he'd said I'll ne'er forget,
He said he thought it must have been, the pinto beans he'd et!
The next day we had a new one, dad put it up with ease,
But this one had a door-sign, 'No Smoking, please!'
Now that's the story's end, my friend, of memories long ago,
When we went to the house behind the house, because we had to go!

. . . .

(26) ATTORNEY: What was the first thing your husband said to you that morning?
WITNESS: He said, 'Where am I, Cathy?'
ATTORNEY: **And why did that upset you?**
WITNESS: My name is Susan!
ATTORNEY: What is your date of birth?
WITNESS: July 18th.
ATTORNEY: What year?
WITNESS: Every year.

(27)*If walking is good for your health, the postman would be immortal.

* *A whale swims all day, only eats fish, drinks water, and is fat. A rabbit runs and hops and only lives 15 years.

* *A tortoise doesn't run and does nothing, yet it lives for 450 years. And you tell me to exercise?? I don't think so.

I'm retired. Go around me.

....

(28) <u>From Hawaii Pastor</u> ... (It pays to serve God faithfully)

Some of the greatest men ever used came from Godly families. John and Charles Wesley, Billy Graham and James Dobson, to name a few.

Jonathan Edwards was brought up in a Christian home and 400 of his descendants were traced, just to see how his kids and grand-kids turned out. Out of the 400, there were...

- 14 college presidents and over 100 college professors;
- Over 100 ministers and missionaries,
- Over 100 judges and about 60 doctors.
- And the rest were authors, editors or journalists. Then, living about the same time was the 'Jukes' family who had no use for God and over 1000 of their descendants were traced, and this is what was found...
- Over 400 were homeless street people, hooked by addictions,
- There were 310 professional beggars and 130 convicted criminals,
- 60 habitual thieves and 7 murderers. The best account is that 20 of them learned a good trade while serving time in prison!

Chapter 14

School Comedy

(1) <u>Mother:</u> "Doctor, little Johnnie swallowed a 22 shell, what should I do?"

<u>Doctor:</u> "Give him a double dose of **<u>Castor Oil and point him towards the woods.</u>**

· ·

(2) A little girl had just finished her first week of school and was complaining that she was just wasting her time. She told her mother…

"I can't read, I can't write, and they won't let me talk."

"One day the teacher **<u>told me 2 plus 2 is 4 and now</u>** she says 3 plus 1 is four…I'm not going back till she makes up her mind!"

· ·

(3) <u>Little Johnny</u>'s father said, "**<u>Let me see your report card</u>**."

Johnny replied, "I don't have it."

"Why not?" asked his father.

Little Johnny replied, "My friend wanted to borrow it; he wants to scare his parents!"

. . . .

(4) <u>The Mirror:</u>

According to a radio report, a middle school in Oregon was faced with a unique problem. A number of girls were beginning to use lipstick and would put it on in the bathroom. That was fine, but after they put on their lipstick, they would press their lips to the mirror leaving dozens of little lip prints.

Finally the principal decided that something had to be done. She called all the girls to the bathroom and met them there with the maintenance man. She explained that all these little lip prints were causing a major problem for the custodian who had to clean the mirrors every night. To demonstrate how difficult it was to clean the mirrors, she asked the maintenance man to clean one of the mirrors.

He took out a long handle squeeze, dipped it in the toilet and then proceeded to clean the mirror.

Since then, there have been no lip prints on the mirror.

. . . .

(5) <u>A Student's Letter to Dad</u>

Dear Father,

$chool i$ really great. I am making lot$ of friend$ and $tudying very hard. With all my $tuff, I $imply Can't think of anything I need, $o if you would like, you can ju$t $end me a card, a$ I would love to hear from you.

Love, Your $on.

After receiving his son's letter, the father immediately replies by sending a letter back.

Dear Son,

    I kNOw that astroNOmy, ecoNOmics, and oceaNOgraphy are eNOugh to keep even an hoNOr student busy. Do NOt forget that the pursuit of kNOwledge is a NOble task, and you can never study eNOugh.

Love, Dad

. . . .

(6) <u>Goldfish</u>...

    Little Mary was in the garden filling in a hole when her neighbor peered over the fence. Interested in what the cute little cheeky-faced youngster was up to, he politely asked, "What are you up to there Mary?"

    "My goldfish died," Mary said tearfully, "and I've just buried him."

    "Well," said the neighbor, "that's an awfully big hole for a goldfish, isn't it?"

    Mary patted down the last heap of earth and then replied, "That's **<u>because he's inside your cat</u>**."

. . . .

(7) <u>School Daze:</u>

    It was the end of the school year, and a kindergarten teacher was receiving gifts from her pupils. The florist's son handed her a gift. She shook it, held it overhead and said, "I bet I know what it is, some flowers!"

    "That's right," said the boy, "but how did you know?"

    "Oh, just a wild guess" said the teacher.

The next student was the candy shop owner's daughter. The teacher held her gift overhead, shook it and said, "I bet I can guess what this is; a box of candy!"

"That's right," said the little girl, "but how did you know?"

"Oh, just a wild guess," said the teacher.

The next gift came from the son of the liquor store owner. The teacher held the package overhead, and noticed it was leaking. She touched a drop of the leakage wither finger and tasted it with her tongue. "Is it wine?' she asked.

"No," the boy said with excitement.

The teacher repeated the process, taking an even larger taste and said, "Is it champagne?"

"NO" the boy again said, with even more excitement. The teacher took one more taste before declaring, "I give up, what on earth it is then?"

And with great glee, **the boy blurted out, "It's a puppy!"**

. . . .

(8) The teacher gave her fifth grade class the following assignment, "Get your parents to tell you a story with a good moral at the end of it." The next day the innocent kids began, one by one, to tell their stories.

Soon it was little Johnny's turn and he said, "My daddy told me about my Aunt Karen. She was a pilot in Desert Storm and her plane got shot down. She had to bail out over enemy territory and all she had was a flask of whiskey, a pistol and a survival knife."

"Well," my daddy said, "she drank the whiskey on the way down so it wouldn't break, and then her parachute landed right in the middle of twenty enemy troops."

Daddy said, "She shot 15 of them with her pistol before it ran out of bullets. Then she killed 4 more with her knife before the blade broke. And then, she killed that last one with her bare hands!" "Good heavens," exclaimed the horrified teacher. "What kind of a moral did your daddy tell you from this horrible story?"

"Daddy just told me," said little Johnny, "<u>to stay away from Aunt Karen when she is drinkin'!</u>"

· ·

(9) <u>Dream Job</u>... One day, while working as an aide at the local high school, my duty was to stand in the front hall and direct the parents to the proper classroom for the parent/teachers conference.

A friend came in and said to me, "Why are you standing there?"

I said, "<u>I'm supposed to tell people where to go.</u>"

"Man, that's great." He said, "I've always wanted a job like that!"

· ·

(10) An old Jewish teacher stood in front of his class and said, "The Jewish people have observed their 5800 year as a people. Consider that the Chinese, for example, have only observed their 4800th year as a people.

"Now, what does that tell you about us Jews?" asked the teacher. After a moment of silence, my grandson, David raised his hand and said, "It means that the Jews had <u>to suffer without Chinese food for over 1000 years.</u>"

· ·

(11) Two boys were walking home from Sunday school after hearing a strong preaching on the devil. One said to the other, "What do you think about <u>all this Satan stuff?</u>"

The other boy replied, "Well, you know how Santa Claus turned out. It's probably just your Dad."

(12) The Children had all been photographed and the teacher was trying to persuade each one of them to buy a copy of the group picture. "Just think," she said, "one day when you're all grown up, you will be able to look at this picture and say there's Jennifer, she's a lawyer, and there's Michael, he's a doctor and so on."

A small voice from the back of the room rang out, "and **there's our teacher, she's dead!**"

. . . .

(13) A teacher was giving a lesson on the circulation of the blood. Trying to make the matter clearer, he said, "Now boys, if I stood on my head the blood, as you know, would run into it, and I would turn red in the face." "Yes sir," the boys said, "that's why it is that when I'm standing up straight, the blood doesn't run into my feet. And that's **cause your feet ain't empty**!"

. . . .

(14) <u>College Dorm...</u>On the first day of college, the Dean addressed the students, pointing out some of the rules:

"The female dormitory will be out-of-bounds for all male students, and the male dormitory to the female students. Anyone caught breaking this rule will be fined $40 the first time, $100 the second time and the third time it will cost you $200. Are there any questions?"

At that point a male student in the crowd inquired: **"How much for a season pass?**

. . . .

(15) A mother calls 911 very worried asking the dispatcher if she needs to take her kid to the emergency room, the kid had eaten

ants. The dispatcher tells her to give the kid some Benadryl and he should be fine.

The mother says, '**I just gave him some ant killer**......'
Dispatcher: 'Rush him in to emergency right now!'

Life is tough. It's even tougher if you're stupid!!!!

....

(16) **Don't take life too seriously**; No one gets out alive.

- You're just jealous because the voices only talk to me
- I'm not a complete idiot -- Some parts are just missing.
- God must love stupid people; He made so many.
- The gene pool could use a little chlorine.
- Consciousness: That annoying time between naps.
- Ever stop to think, and forget to start again?
- Being 'over the hill' is much better than being under it!
- Wrinkled Was Not One of the Things I Wanted to Be When I Grew up.

....

(17) Dear Dad…

Let me hear from you more often**, even if it's only a five or ten**

Chapter 15

Senior Comedy

(1) _The Importance of Walking_

    Walking can add minutes to your life. This enables you at 85 years old to spend an additional 5 months in a nursing home at $7000 per month.

    My grandpa started walking five miles a day when he was 60. Now he's 97 years old and we don't know where he is.

    I joined a health club last year, spent about 400 bucks, I haven't lost a pound. Apparently you have to go there.

    The advantage of exercising every day is so when you die, they'll say, "Well, she looks good, doesn't she."

· ·

(2) A doctor examining a woman, who had been rushed to the Emergency Room, took the husband aside & said, "I don't like the looks of your wife at all."

    "Me neither doc," said the husband.

    "But she's **a great cook & really good with the kids**."

(3) An elderly woman died last month. Having never married, she requested no male Pallbearers.

In her handwritten instructions for her memorial service, she wrote: "They wouldn't take me out while I was alive, I don't want them to <u>take me out when I'm dead.</u>"

. . . .

(4) <u>Pat</u>: "Hey Mike, I got a really good report from my Doctor today; he said I could go any day now."

<u>Mike</u>: "Hey, Pat, that doesn't sound like a good report to me."

<u>Pat</u>: "Well, Mike, it does to me. I haven't been **able to go for three weeks.**"

. . . .

(5) <u>The $2.99 Special</u>

We went to breakfast at a restaurant where the "seniors' special" was two eggs, bacon, hash browns and toast for $2.99.

"Sounds good," my wife said, "But I don't want the eggs."

"Then, I'll have to charge you $3.49 because you're ordering a la carte," the waitress warned her.

"You mean I'd have to pay for not taking the eggs?" my wife asked incredulously.

"YES," stated the waitress.

"I'll take the special then," my wife said.

"How do you want your eggs?" the waitress asked.

"Raw and in the shell," my wife replied.

She took the two eggs home and baked a cake.

DON'T MESS WITH SENIORS!!!

We've been around the block more than once!

(6) <u>If My body were a car!</u>

If my body were a car, this is the time I would be thinkin' about trading it in for a newer model. I've got bumps, dents and scratches in my finish and my paint job is getting a little dull.

But, that's not the worst of it. My headlights are out of focus, and it is especially hard to see things up close. My traction is not as graceful as it once was. I slip and slide and skid, and bump into things even in the best of weather. It takes me hours to reach my minimum speed. My fuel rate burns inefficiently.

But here's the worst of it -- almost every time I sneeze, cough or sputter, either my radiator leaks or my exhaust backfires!

. . . .

(7) <u>Best ever senior joke…</u>

A little silver-haired lady calls her neighbor and says, "Please come over here and help me. I have a killer jigsaw puzzle, and I can't figure out how to get started."

Her neighbor asks, "What is it supposed to be when it's finished?"

The little silver haired lady says, "According to the picture on the box, it's a rooster."

Her neighbor decides to go over and help with the puzzle. She lets him in and shows him where she has the puzzle spread all over the table.

He studies the pieces for a moment, then looks at the box, then turns to her and says, "First of all, no matter what we do, we're not going to be able to assemble these pieces into anything resembling a rooster."

He takes her hand and says, "Secondly, I want you to relax. Let's have a nice cup of tea." And as he sighs deeply, he says …

"<u>Now, let's put all the Corn Flakes back in the box.</u>

(8) <u>I've sure gotten old</u>! I've had two bypass surgeries, a hip replacement, new knees, fought prostrate cancer and diabetes. I'm half blind, can't hear anything quieter than a jet engine, take 40 different medications that make me dizzy, winded, and subject to frequent blackouts...BUT, the good news is...
   I still have my Florida Driver's License!

· ·

(9) *<u>Wrong Way!</u>*
   As a senior citizen was driving down the freeway, his car phone rang. When he answered, he heard his wife's voice urgently warning him. *"Herman,"* she said, *"I just heard on the news that there's a car going the wrong way on the freeway. Please be careful."*
   Herman answered back...
   "There's not just one; there's hundreds of them!"

· ·

(10) When Sally and I were walking home from school.
   No one believes seniors...everyone thinks they are senile. An elderly couple was celebrating their 60th anniversary. The couple had married as childhood sweethearts and had moved back to their old neighborhood after they retired.
   Holding hands, they walked back to their old school. It was not locked, so they entered and found the old desk they'd shared, where Andy had carved, "I love you, Sally."
   On their way back home, a bag of **money fell out of an armored car**, practically landing at their feet. Sally quickly picked it up, but not sure what to do with it, they took it home. There, she counted the money...$50,000.
   Andy said, "We've got to give it back."
   Sally said, "No way, finders keepers." So Sally put the money in a bag and hid it in the attic.

From 'SPAM' to BALONEY

The next day, two police officers stopped by as they were canvassing the neighborhood looking for the money. They knocked on the door and asked if either of them found a bag of money that had fallen out of a car near there yesterday.

Sally said "No!"

Andy said, "She's lying…she hid it up in the attic."

Sally said, "Don't believe him, he's getting senile."

The police officer turned to Andy and began to question him. One said, "Tell us the story from the beginning."

Andy said, "Well, when Sally and I were walking home from school yesterday…"

The police officer turned to his partner and said, "Let's get outta here."

. . . .

(11) A tough old cowboy all his life was counseling his grandson as to what he learned about living so long. He said it was always his habit to sprinkle a little gunpowder on his oatmeal every morning. The old man lived to be 99 years old and when he died, he left 14 children, 28 grandchildren and 35 great-grandchildren and…<u>a 15 foot hole **in the wall of the crematory**</u>!

. . . .

(12) My Irish friend, getting up in years, said to his best drinking buddy, "Me son, when I pass on, would ye be so kind as to slowly pour a bottle of the Pub's finest brew on me as I lay in me casket?"

"I will, I will," said his buddy as he sobbed at the thought, "but, I have one request…would ye mind if I passes it **<u>through me kidneys first?</u>**

(13) Arriving in New York, O'Malley was asked whether he flew or came by boat. O'Malley says, "I dunno, me friend, **me mother bought the ticket.**

. . . .

(14) There were these two elderly people living in a Florida Mobile Park. He was a widower and she was a widow. They had known each other for years but their memory wasn't quite what it used to be.

One evening at the community center gathering they were eating at the same table and as the meal went on, the man leaned over and said to her, *"Will you marry me?"*

She thought a few seconds and said, *"Why, yes! Yes I will!"*

The next morning he was troubled, *"Did she say yes or no"* he couldn't remember. He didn't have the faintest idea what she said so he telephoned her.

With some embarrassment he asked her whether she said *yes* or *no*. He was delighted to hear her say that she had said "yes, and I mean it with all my heart."

Then she continued, "I'm so glad that you called, because I couldn't remember who had asked me."

. . . .

(15) An old gentleman was showing off, as usual. He told his friend, "**I bought a hearing aid** yesterday. It cost me two thousand bucks, but it is state of the art, digital, invisible and I can hear *everything.*"

"What kind is it?" his friend asked.

The old man answered, "It's a quarter to twelve."

(16) While shopping for vacation clothes, the wife said as they passed a display of female bathing suits, **"Do you think I should get a bikini type or get an all-in-one?"**

The husband said, "You'd better get a bikini. You'd never get it all in one." The husband is still in intensive care!

. . . .

(17) An elderly woman and her little grandson whose face was sprinkled with bright freckles, spent the day together at the zoo. Lots of children were waiting inline to get their cheeks painted by a local artist.

"You've got so many freckles," she said to her grandson, "there's no place to paint." The little grandson became embarrassed and hung his head. His grandmother knelt down next to him and said, *"I love your freckles. When I was small I always wanted freckles,"* as she ran her fingers across his little cheeks. *"Freckles are beautiful,"* she said.

The little boy looked up and said, *"Really?"*

"Of course," said the grandmother, *"Why, just you **name me one thing that's prettier than freckles."***

The little boy thought for a minute, peered intently into his granny's face and said softly... *"Wrinkles."*

. . . .

(18) <u>In My Day</u>! – "grass" was mowed, "coke" was a cold drink and "pot" was something your mother cooked in.

"Rock music" was your grandmother's lullaby, "Aids" were helpers in the Principal's office and "chip" was a piece of wood.

"Hardware" was found in a hardware store, "software" wasn't even a word, and believe it or not, we were the last generation to actually believe that a woman needed a husband to have a baby.

No wonder people call us "old and confused," but how old do you actually think I am? - The answer may shock you…I would be only 58 years old!

. . . .

(19) <u>In The Beginning</u>…

God covered the earth with broccoli, cauliflower and spinach; lots of green, yellow and red vegetables so that man would live long, healthy lives. Then using God's bountiful gifts, Satan created Ben & Jerry's Ice Cream and Krispy-Kreme Doughnuts. Then Satan said, *"You want hot fudge with that?"*

Man said, *"Yes."*

And the woman said, *"Put sprinkles on mine too"*.

And lo, they both gained 10 pounds. Then God created beautiful yogurt that Woman might keep the figure that man found so fair. Then Satan brought forth white flour from the wheat and sugar from the cane and combined them. Woman then went from size 2 to size 18.

So God said, *"Try my fresh green garden salad."* Satan then presented crumbled bleu cheese dressing and garlic toast on the side. Man and Woman unfastened their belts following their feast.

God said, *"I have sent you heart healthy vegetables and olive oil which to cook them."* Satan then brought forth deep-fried cocoanut shrimp, butter-dipped lobster chunks and chicken-fried steaks, so big it needed its own platter….

God then gave lean beef so that man might consume fewer calories and still satisfy his appetite. Satan created McDonalds and the 99 cent double cheeseburger. Then Satan said, *"You want fries with that?"*

Man replied, *"Yes, and super-size 'em."*

Satan said, *"It is good!"*

Man and woman went into cardiac arrest. God sighed.... and created quadruple by-pass surgery. Satan chuckled... and created HMO's.

. . . .

(20) Memories, from a local newspaper – "I can **usually remember Monday through Thursday**. If you can remember Friday, Saturday and Sunday, let's put our heads together."

. . . .

(21) <u>I need a Gun - New Medicare Program</u>...

If you're a senior citizen and the government says there is no nursing home available for you, here's a plan designed for you! This plan gives anyone over 65 years old a gun and 4 bullets. You are allowed to shoot 4 politicians.

Of course, this means you will be sent to prison where you will get three chef-prepared meals a day for the rest of your life, a roof over your head, central heating and air with no power bill to pay, and all the health care you need!

If you need new teeth, no problem; need glasses? No problem. Need a new hip, knees, kidney, lungs or heart? They're all covered and you don't have to pay a dime. And, as an added bonus, your kids can come and visit you as often as they do now. And who will be paying for all of this? It's the same government that just told you that they cannot afford for you to go into a home.

Plus, because you are a prisoner, you'll never have to pay any income taxes anymore! *Is this a great country, or what?*

(22) Long-Term Commitment... Recent widow who has just buried husband number four is looking for someone to round out a six-unit plot. Dizziness, fainting, shortness of breath is not a problem.

. . . .

(23) <u>The Bathtub Test</u>...

During a visit to the mental asylum, a visitor asked the Director what criteria was used to determine whether or not a patient should be institutionalized. *"Well,"* said the Director, *"we fill up a bathtub, and then we hand out a teaspoon, a teacup, and a bucket to the patient and ask him or her to empty the bathtub."*

"Oh," I understand," said the visitor. *"A normal person would use the bucket because it's bigger than the spoon or the teacup."*

"No," said the Director... *"A normal person would pull the plug. Do you want a bed near the window?"*

. . . .

(24) <u>When I get old</u>...

There will be **no nursing home in my future**...When I get old and feeble, I am going to get on a Princess Cruise Ship. The average cost for a nursing home is $200 per day. I checked on reservations at Princess and I can get a long term discount and senior discount price of $135 per day.

That leaves $65 per day for...
- Gratuities which will be $10 per day.
- I will have as many as 10 meals a day if I can waddle to the dining room or I can have room service, which means I can have breakfast in bed every day of the week.
- Princess has as many as 3 swimming pools, a work-out room, free washers and dryers, and a show

every night.
- They have free toothpaste and combs, and free soap and shampoo.
- They will even treat you like a customer, not a patient. An extra $5 worth of tips will have the entire staff scrambling to help you.
- I will get to meet new people every 7 or 14 days.
- Clean sheets and towels every day, and you don't even have to ask for them.
- Do you want to see South America, the Panama Canal, Australia, Asia, or you name where you want to go and Princess will have a ship ready in a few days. So don't look for me in a nursing home, just call shore to ship and you'll get me!
- … And best of all…when you die, they just dump you over the side at no charge! *What, pray tell, could be better than that?*

· ·

(25) <u>Mint Condition</u>… Male, 1932, high mileage, good condition, some hair, many new parts including hip, knee, cornea and valves. Doesn't run but walks well!"

· ·

(26) <u>One more</u>. . .

A little old man shuffled slowly into an ice cream parlor and pulled himself slowly, painfully, up onto a stool… After catching his breath, he ordered a banana split.

The waitress asked kindly, "**<u>Crushed nuts</u>?**"

"No," he replied, "Arthritis."

(27) <u>Senior Moment</u>...

Several days ago, as I left a meeting at our church, I desperately gave myself a personal TSA pat down. I was looking for my car keys. They were not in my pockets. A quick search in the meeting room revealed nothing.

Suddenly I realized I must have left them in the car. Frantically, I headed for the parking lot. My wife, who shall remain nameless, has scolded me many times for leaving the keys in the ignition.

My theory is the ignition is the best place not to lose them. Her theory is that the car will get stolen. As I burst through the doors of the church, I came to a terrifying conclusion. Her theory was right. The parking lot was empty.

I immediately called the police. I gave them my location, confessed that I had left my keys in the car, and that it had been stolen.

Then I made the most difficult call of all, "Honey," I stammered (I always call her honey in times like this), Í left my keys in the car and it was stolen."

There was a period of silence. I thought my call had been cut off, but then she barked back at me, "I dropped you off at the church, remember?"

Now it was my time to be silent. Embarrassed, I said, "Well, can you come and get me?" She retorted, "I will, as soon as I convince this policeman **I haven't stolen your car**."

Life is short – forgive quickly – love deeply – laugh loudly - and you'll live longer!

. . . .

(28) Three old guys are out walking. **First one says, "Windy, isn't it?"** Second one says, "No, it's Thursday!" Third one says, "So am I. Let's go get something to drink."

(29) Great to be old

A couple in their nineties are both having problems remembering things. During a checkup, the doctor tells them that they're physically okay, but they might want to start writing things down to help them remember. Later that night, while watching TV, the old man gets up from his chair. "Want anything while I'm in the kitchen?" he asks.

She responds, "Will you get me a bowl of ice cream?"

"Sure," the husband says.

"Don't you think you should write it down so you can remember it?" she inquires. "No, I can remember it."

"Well, I'd like some strawberries on top, too. Maybe you should write it down, so as not to forget it?"

He says, "I can remember that. You want a bowl of ice cream with strawberries."

"I'd also like whipped cream. I'm certain you'll forget that, write it down?" she says.

Irritated, he says, "I don't need to write it down, I can remember it! Ice cream with strawberries and whipped cream - I got it, for goodness sake!"

Then he toddles into the kitchen. After about 20 minutes, the old man returns from the kitchen and hands his wife a plate of bacon and eggs. She stares at the plate for a moment and says, "**Where's my toast?**

· ·

(30) An elderly couple had dinner at another couple's house. And after eating, the wives left the table and went into the kitchen.

The gentlemen were talking, and one said, "Last night we went out to a new restaurant and it was really great. I would recommend it very highly."

The other man said, "**What is the name of the restaurant?**

The first man thought and thought and finally said, "What is the name of that flower you give to someone you love? You know the one that's red and has thorns."

"Do you mean a rose?"

"Yes, that's the one," replied the man. He then turned towards the kitchen and yelled, "Rose, what's the name of that restaurant we went to last night?"

. . . .

(31) <u>Senior Thoughts</u>… <u>Cremation? – Think outside the box.</u>

Retired? – I was tired yesterday and I'm tired today.

Florida? – God's waiting room.

When I was younger, all I wanted was a BMW, but now I'd settle for a BM.

I was always taught to respect my elders, now I don't have anyone to respect.

Some days I wake up grumpy, and some days I let her sleep.

The secret to staying young is to live honestly, eat slowly, and lie about your age.

He's not old, he's just chronologically gifted.

And finally, never should a senior take a sleeping pill and a laxative at the same time.

The gene pool could use a little chlorine.

Ever stop to think, and forget to start again?

<u>Being 'over the hill' is much better than being under it!</u>

. . . .

(32) A senior citizen said to his eighty-year old buddy:

"So I hear you're getting married?"

"Yep!"

"Do I know her?"

"Nope!"

"This woman, is she good looking?"
"Not really."
"Is she a good cook?"
"Naw, she can't cook too well."
"Does she have lots of money?"
"Nope! Poor as a church mouse."
"Well, then, is she good in bed?"
"I don't know."
"Why in the world do you want to marry her then?"
"Because she can still drive!"

. . . .

(33) Morris, an 82-year-old man, went to the doctor to get a physical.

A few days later, the doctor saw Morris walking down the street with a gorgeous young woman on his arm.

A couple of days later, the doctor spoke to Morris and said, "You're really doing great, aren't you?"

Morris replied, "Just doing what you said, Doc, **get a hot mama and be cheerful.**"

The doctor said, "I didn't say that. I said, You've got a heart murmur; be careful."

. . . .

(34) A WELL PLANNED LIFE?

Two women met for the first time since graduating from high school. One asked the other, "You were always so organized in school. Did you manage to live a well planned life?"

"Yes," said her friend. "My *first* marriage was to a millionaire, my *second* marriage was to an actor, my *third* marriage was to a preacher, *and now* I'm married to an undertaker."

Her friend asked, "What do those marriages have to do with a well planned life?" "One for the money, two for the show, three to get ready, and four to go."

(35) First you forget names, and then you forget faces. Then you forget **to pull up your zipper**. However, it's worse when you forget to pull it down.

. . . .

(36) <u>Aren't We Fortunate To Be Seniors</u>?

    A friend of mine was sitting on a lawn, sunning and reading, when he was startled by a fairly late model car crashing through a hedge and coming to rest on his lawn.

    He helped the elderly driver out and sat her on a lawn chair.

    "My goodness," he exclaimed, "you are quite old to be driving!"

    "Yes." she replied, "I am old enough that I don't need a license. The last time I went to my doctor, he examined me and asked if I had a driver's license. I told him *yes* and handed it to him. He took scissors out of a drawer, cut the license into pieces and threw them in the wastebasket."

    "Then **he said I wouldn't be needing this anymore**. I'm so thankful for his help. No need to worry about remembering to renew the thing," she sweetly said as she piled back into her car and careened on down the street.

Chapter 16

Sports Comedy

(1) If you are going to try **cross-country skiing**, start with a small country.

. . . .

(2) <u>The Bear Family</u>: Mama and Papa Bear were getting a divorce, and Baby bear had to decide who he was going to live with. So, the Judge wanted to talk to Baby Bear to see what he thought about living with either of his parents.

When he asked Baby Bear about living with his father, Baby Bear said, "Oh No! I can't live with Papa Bear, he beats me terribly."

"O.K." said the Judge, "Then you want to live with your mother, right?"

"Oh, no way!" said Baby Bear, "She beats me worse than Papa Bear does."

The Judge was a bit confused by this and asked if he had any relatives he would like to live with. Baby Bear said, "Yes, I have an Aunt in Chicago, I want to go live with her there."

The Judge said, "Are you sure she will treat you well and won't beat you?"

"Oh, I'm definitely sure," said Baby Bear, "**The Chicago Bears don't beat anybody!**"

· ·

(3) A guy just died and he's at the Pearly Gates, waiting to be admitted, while Saint Peter is leafing through the Big Book. St. Peter goes through the Book several times and finally says to the guy, "You know, I can't see that you ever did anything really bad in your life, but you never did anything really good either. If you can point to just one really good deed, you're in!"

The guy thinks for a moment and says, "Yeah, I was driving down the highway and saw a big group of Bikers assaulting this poor girl. I slowed down my car, and saw a couple of dozen big guys with leather jackets and chains and knives!"

"I became infuriated. I got out of my car, grabbed the tire iron out of my trunk and walked up to the leader of this gang. He was a big guy with a studded leather jacket and had a chain running from his nose to his ear."

"I grabbed that chain and ripped it off his face and smashed him over the head with my tire iron and laid him out cold. Then I turned and yelled at the rest of them, 'Leave this poor girl alone, or I'll give you all a taste of this tire iron.'"

Saint Peter was impressed, and says, "Really? When did this happen?"

To which the guy said, "Oh, **about two minutes ago!**"

· ·

(4) Two guys were roaring down the road on a motorcycle when the driver slowed up and pulled over. His leather jacket had a broken zipper, and he told his friend, "I can't drive anymore with the air hitting me in the chest like that."

"Well," his friend said, "just put the jacket on backwards."

They continued down the road but around the next bend, they lost control and wiped out. A nearby farmer came upon the accident and ran to call the police.

The police asked him if there were any signs of life. "Well," the farmer explained, "the driver was gasping for breath, **until I turned his head around the right way.**

· ·

(5) It would have been more than enough for the polarizing Denver Broncos quarterback to simply lead his underdog team to victory over the Pittsburgh Steelers on Sunday in the AFC wild-card game. And Tim Tebow did, thanks to his 80-yard touchdown pass on the first play of overtime that left the Steelers and the watching world simply stunned.

But then the facts and figures emerged, and the Internet verily exploded: **Tebow threw for exactly 316 yards** in the 29-23 upset win, presenting an eerie allusion to the Bible's John 3:16 passage — whose number Tebow famously wore in the black under his eyes when he led the Florida Gators to victory in the 2009 Collegiate National Championship Game.

What's more, that event took place exactly three years ago on the same day as his latest miracle comeback. And that wasn't it for the coincidences: Tebow set an NFL playoff record with, you guessed it, 31.6 yards per completion and the TV rating on CBS peaked between 8.00-8.15pm ET with a rating of, say it ain't so, 31.6.

· ·

(6) In a supermarket, Kurtis the stock boy was busily working when a new voice came over the speaker asking for a carry-out at cash register #4. Kurtis was almost finished, and wanted to get some fresh air anyway, so he decided to answer the call.

As he approached the cash register a smile caught his eye; the new check-out girl was beautiful. She was an older woman, maybe 26 and he was only 22, and he fell in love right then and there that day.

After their shift was over, he waited by the punch-out-clock to find out her name. She arrived to punch out and gave him another big smile, then left. He looked at her card and noticed that her name was *Brenda*.

He walked outside only to see her walking up the street. Next day, he again waited outside and offered her a ride home. He looked harmless enough so she accepted a ride home.

When he dropped her off, he asked if maybe he could see her again. She simply said it wasn't possible and he pressed her, "why not?" She explained that she had two children and she couldn't afford a baby-sitter. So he offered to pay for the baby-sitter. Reluctantly she accepted his offer for a date for the following Saturday.

That Saturday evening he arrived at her door only to have her tell him that she was unable to go with him. The baby-sitter had called and cancelled. To which Kurtis simply said, "Well, let's take the kids with us." She tried to explain that taking the kids was not an option. But again, not taking *no* for an answer, he pressed, "why not?"

Finally, Brenda brought him inside to meet the children. She had an older daughter who was just as cute as a bug Kurtis thought. And then Brenda brought out her son, who was in a wheelchair. He was born a paraplegic with Downs Syndrome. Kurtis said to Brenda, "I still don't understand why the kids can't come with us!"

Brenda was amazed. Most men would run away from a woman with two kids, especially if one had disabilities, just like her first husband, the father of these kids had done.

That evening, Kurtis and Brenda loaded up the kids and went to dinner and the movies. When her son needed anything

Kurtis would take care of him. The kids loved Kurtis. At the end of the evening, Brenda knew this was the man she was going to marry.

Within a year, they were married and Kurtis adopted both of her children. Since then they have added two more kids. So, what happened to the stock boy and the check-out girl? Well, Mr. and Mrs. Kurt Warner, now live in St. Louis, where he is employed by the **St. Louis Rams and plays quarterback!**

• •

(7) <u>Mood Swings</u>...
- Next mood swing; ten seconds.
- I hate everybody, and you're next!
- I used to be schizophrenic, but now we're OK.
- All stressed out and no one to choke!
- I'm one of those bad things that happen to good people!
- How can I miss you if you won't go away!

Chapter 17

Travel Comedy

<u>Kulula is an Airline with head office situated in Johannesburg.</u>

(1) On a Kulula flight, (there is no assigned seating, you just sit where you want) passengers were apparently having a hard time choosing, when a flight attendant announced, "People, people, we're not picking out furniture here, find a seat and get in it!"

....

(2) "There may be 50 ways to leave your lover, but there are **only 4 ways out of this airplane.**

....

(3) "Thank you for flying Kulula. We hope you enjoyed giving us the business as much as we enjoyed <u>taking you for a ride.</u>

(4) From a Kulula employee: "Welcome aboard Kulula 271 to Port Elizabeth. **To operate your seat belt**, insert the metal tab into the buckle, and pull tight. It works just like every other seat belt; and, if you don't know how to operate one, you probably shouldn't be out in public unsupervised."

. . . .

(5) "In the event of a sudden loss of cabin pressure, masks will descend from the ceiling. Stop screaming, grab the mask, and pull it over your face. If you have a small child travelling with you, secure your mask before assisting with theirs. If you are travelling with **more than one small child, pick your favorite**."

. . . .

(6) "Your seats cushions can be used for flotation. And in the event of an emergency water landing, please **paddle to shore and take your seat** with our compliments."

. . . .

(7) "As you exit the plane, make sure to gather all of your belongings. Anything left behind will be distributed evenly among the flight attendants. Please do not leave children or spouses."

Another flight attendant's comment on a less than perfect landing: "We ask you to please remain seated **as Captain Kangaroo bounces us to the terminal.**"

. . . .

(8) After a real crusher of a landing in Johannesburg, the attendant came on with, "Ladies and Gentlemen, please remain in your seats until Captain Crash and the Crew have brought the aircraft to a screeching halt against the gate. And, once the tire smoke has cleared and the warning bells are silenced, we will open the

door and **you can pick your way through the wreckage** to the terminal."

....

(9) Part of a flight attendant's arrival announcement. "We'd like to thank you folks for flying with us today. And, the next time you get the insane urge to go **blasting through the skies** in a pressurized metal tube, we hope you'll think of Kulula Airways."

....

(10) Heard on a Kulula flight: "Ladies and Gentlemen, if you wish to smoke, the smoking section on this airplane is on the wing. **If you can light 'em, you can smoke 'em.**

....

(11) <u>Rough Landing</u>

After landing hard, the pilot got on the PA system and announced, "Sorry folks for the hard landing. It wasn't my fault; blame it on the rough asphalt."

However, the airline policy was that he had to stand at the exit and apologize to each passenger getting off the plane.

As one little old lady was getting off the plane, adjusting her hearing aid, she said to the pilot, "Did we have a rough landing, or were we shot down?"

....

(12) A plane was taking off from Durban Airport. After it reached a comfortable cruising altitude, the captain made an announcement over the intercom, "Ladies and Gentlemen. This is your captain speaking. Welcome to Flight Number 293, non-stop from Durban to Cape Town. The weather ahead is good

and, therefore, we should have a smooth and uneventful flight. Now sit back and relax... OH, MY GOODNESS!"

Silence followed, and after a few minutes, the captain came back on the intercom and said, "Ladies and Gentlemen, I am so sorry if I scared you earlier. While I was talking to you, the flight attendant accidentally spilled a cup of hot coffee in my lap. You should see the front of my pants!"

A passenger then yelled, "That's nothing. **You should see the back of mine!**"

. . . .

(13) <u>Things are not always as they appear</u>... A buddy of mine was flying across the country. The plane landed along the way to pick up more passengers and the flight attendant explained that there would be a short delay. She said if the passengers wanted to get off and stretch their legs a bit the plane would re-board in about 30 minutes.

Most everybody got off the plane except my buddy and an old gentleman who was blind. My buddy had noticed the seeing-eye dog lying on the floor by the old man's seat. He could also tell the blind man had flown that flight quite frequently because the pilot came by his seat and spoke to him by name.

The pilot said, "Keith, we're making a short stop here, would you like to get off and stretch your legs?"

The blind guy replied, "No thanks, but maybe my dog would like to stretch his legs."

Picture this: All the people in the gate area came to a complete quiet standstill when they looked up and saw the pilot walk off the plane with the seeing-eye dog!

Just to add to the effect the pilot was wearing sunglasses. The people scattered. They not only tried to change planes, they were even <u>trying to change airlines</u>!

Have a great day and remember things are not always as they appear.

(14) Two Irishmen were collaborating as they were consuming a case of their favorite Irish brew, when one was explaining to the other how the Lord often compensates for a person's natural deficiencies. (An intelligent conversation, you can be sure!) "You see," said one, "if someone is a wee bit blind he might have a very good sense of hearing. Or, if his sense of taste is a wee bit gone, he may have a keen sense of smell."

His buddy responded, "I certainly agree with you, my friend." Then he continued with, "I've always noticed **that if someone has one short leg,** the other one is just a wee bit longer!" (This started a ferocious argument!)

· ·

(15) It is so rare to be offered a meal on airlines these days that I was surprised to hear the flight attendant ask the man in front of me, "Would you like dinner?"

"**What are my choices?**" the man asked.

"Yes or no" said the attendant.

· ·

(16) <u>Crafty Millionaire</u>…

Before going to Europe on business, a man drove his Rolls-Royce to a downtown NY City bank and went in to ask for an immediate loan of $5,000. The loan officer asked if he had any collateral.

"Well," said the millionaire, "I can give you the keys to my Rolls-Royce." The loan officer promptly had the car driven into the bank's underground parking for safe keeping, and gave the man a $5,000 loan.

Two weeks later, the millionaire walked back into the bank to pay off the loan to get his car back. The loan officer said, "That will be $5,000 plus $20.30 for interest." The man wrote out a check to the bank and started to walk away. "Wait, just a minute," said the loan officer, "While you were gone I found out you are a millionaire. Why in the world would you need to borrow $5,000?

The man smiled and said, "Where else in Manhattan could I park my Rolls-Royce for two weeks and pay only $20.30?"

. . . .

(17) <u>How hot is it in Missouri?</u>

<u>IT'S SO HOT AND DRY in MISSOURI</u>...
- the birds have to use potholders to pull the worms out of the ground.
- the best parking place is determined by shade instead of distance.
- hot water comes from both taps.
- you can make sun tea instantly.
- you learn that a seat belt buckle makes a pretty good branding iron.
- the temperature drops below 95 F (35 C) and you feel a little chilly.
- you discover that in July it only takes two fingers to steer your car.
- you discover that you can get sunburned through your car window.
- you actually burn your hand opening the car door.
- your biggest motorcycle wreck fear is, "What if I get knocked out and end up lying on the pavement and cook to death?"
- you realize that asphalt has a liquid stage.
- the potatoes cook underground, so all you have to do is pull one out and add butter.
- the cows are giving evaporated milk.

- farmers are feeding their chickens crushed ice to keep them from laying boiled eggs

IT'S SO DRY IN Missouri That the Baptists are starting to baptize by sprinkling;
  ...the Methodists are using wet-wipes.
  ...the Presbyterians are giving rain checks, and
  ...the Catholics are praying for the wine to turn back into water!

CHAPTER 18

Work Comedy

(1) I handed the teller at my bank a withdrawal slip for $400.00. I said, "**May I have large bills**, please?"

She looked at me and said, "I'm sorry sir. All the bills are the same size." When I got up off the floor I explained it to her.

. . . .

(2) When my husband and I arrived at an automobile dealership to pick up our car, we were told the keys had been locked in it. We went to the service department and found a mechanic working feverishly to unlock the driver side door. As I watched from the passenger side, I instinctively tried the door handle and discovered that it was unlocked. "Hey," I announced to the technician, "<u>its open</u>!"

His reply: "I know. <u>I already got that side</u>."

This was at the Ford dealership in Canton, Ohio.

(3) We had to have the garage door repaired. The Sears repairman told us that one of our problems was that we did not have a large enough motor on the opener. I thought for a minute and said that we had the largest one Sears made at that time, a 1/2 horsepower. He shook his head and said, "Lady, you need a 1/4 horsepower." **I responded that 1/2 was larger than 1/4.**

He said, "NO, it's not. Four is larger than two." We haven't used Sears repair since.

• •

(4) My daughter and I went through the McDonald's take-out window and I gave the clerk a $5 bill. Our total was $4.25, so I also handed her a quarter.

She said, "You gave me too much money."

I said, "Yes I know, but this way you can **just give me a dollar bill back.** She sighed and went to get the manager, who asked me to repeat my request.

I did so and he handed me back the quarter. He said that they were sorry but could not do that kind of thing.

The clerk then proceeded to give me back $1 and 75 cents in change. Do not confuse the clerks at McD's.

• •

(5) One day, at a local buffet, a man suddenly called out, "My son's choking! **He swallowed a quarter**! Help! Please, anyone! Help!" A man from a nearby table stood up and announced that he was quite experienced at this sort of thing. He stepped over with almost no look of concern at all, wrapped his hands around the boy's chest and squeezed. Out popped the quarter. The man then went back to his table as though nothing had happened

Thank you!" the father cried. "Are you a paramedic?"

"No," replied the man. "I work for the IRS."

From 'SPAM' to BALONEY

(6) I was in Home Depot the other day pushing my cart around when I collided with a young guy pushing his cart. I said to the young guy, "Sorry about that. I'm looking for m wife and I guess I wasn't paying attention to where I was going."

The young guy said, "That's O.K.; it's a coincidence; I'm looking for my wife too! I can't find her and I'm getting a little desperate."

I said, "Well, maybe we can help each other out. What does your wife look like?" The young guy said, "Well, she is 24 years old, tall, blonde and is wearing white skimpy shorts and a halter top. What does your wife look like?"

I said. "Oh it doesn't matter, **let's look for yours**!"

• •

(7) <u>Airport Full Body Scanner Solution</u>... All we need to do is develop a booth that you can step into that will <u>not</u> X-Ray you but <u>will</u> detonate any explosives you may have hidden on or in your body. The explosion will be contained within the sealed booth.

This would be a win-win situation for everyone. There would be none of this crap about racial profiling and the device would eliminate long and expensive trials.

This is so simple that it's brilliant! I can see it now; you're in the airport terminal and you hear a muffled explosion. In a few minutes an announcement comes over the P.A. system, "Attention standby passengers, we now have another seat available!"

• •

(8) <u>Be Nice To Your Nurse</u>... When you're hospitalized, it pays to be nice to your nurse, even when you're feeling miserable. A bossy businessman learned the hard way after ordering his nurses around as if they were his employees. BUT, the head

nurse stood up to him. One morning as she entered his room she announced, "I have to take your temperature."

After complaining for several minutes, he finally settled down, crossed his arms and opened his mouth. "No, said the nurse, "I'm sorry but for this reading, I can't use an oral thermometer."

This started another round of complaining, but eventually he rolled over and bared his bottom. After feeling the nurse insert the thermometer, he heard her announce, "I have to get something. Now you stay just like that till I get back." She left the door to his room open on her way out, and he cursed under his breath as he heard people walking past his door and laughing. After almost an hour, the man's doctor entered the room.

"What's going on here?" asked the doctor.

Angrily the man answered, "What's the matter Doc? Haven't you ever seen someone having their temperature taken?"

"Yes," said the doctor, "but never with a carnation!"

. . . .

(9) <u>Autopsy</u>:

The lawyer questioned the doctor:

"Doctor," he said, 'before you performed the autopsy, did you check for a pulse?" Doctor: "No."

Q. "Did you check for blood pressure?"

A. 'No.'

Q. "Did you check for breathing?"

A. "No."

The lawyer continued questioning, "So then it is possible that the patient was alive when you began the autopsy?" A. "No."

The lawyer continued, "How can you be so sure, Doctor?" The Doctor said, "Because his brain was sitting on my desk in a jar."

"But," the lawyer continued, "Could the patient have still been alive nevertheless?"

The frustrated doctor said, "Yes, it is possible that the patient could have been alive and practicing law somewhere!"

....

(10) A little boy got lost at the YMCA and found himself in the women's locker room. When he was spotted, the room burst into shrieks, with ladies grabbing towels and running for cover.

The little boy watched in amazement and then asked, "What's the matter? **Haven't you ever seen a little boy before?**

....

(11) A police recruit was asked during the exam, "What would you do if you had to arrest your own mother?"

He answered, **"I'd call for backup.**

....

(12) A man is recovering from surgery when the Special Nurse appears and asks him how he is feeling. The patient says, "I'm OK, but I didn't like the four-letter word the doctor used in surgery."

"And what did the Doctor say" the nurse asked. And the patient told her **the awful word he heard was "OOPS."**

....

(13) Nice Not To Know You...

In a trial in a small town, the prosecuting attorney called his first witness, an elderly woman to the stand. As he approached her, he asked, "Mrs. Jones, do you know me?"

The elderly lady answered, "Yes, Mr. Williams, I know you. I've known you since you were a young boy, and frankly you've been a big disappointment to me. You lie, you manipulate people, and talk about them behind their back. You think you're a big-shot, but you haven't the brains to realize you'll never amount to anything."

The lawyer was stunned of course. Not quite knowing what to do next he pointed across the room and asked, "Mrs. Jones, do you know the defense attorney?"

Mrs. Jones answered, "Yes I do. I've also known Mr. Bradley since he was a youngster. He's lazy and bigoted; he can't hold a job nor keep a relationship with anyone. He's a womanizer and his wife is about fed up with him too."

The judge, having keenly observed the proceedings, asked both attorneys to approach the bench. And in a very quiet voice, the judge said to them, "If either of you two idiots asks her if she knows me, I'll send you both to the electric chair!"

• •

(14) <u>The Lost Poem of Dr. Seuss</u>:

<u>I love my job</u>, I love the pay; I love it more and more each day!

I love my boss, he is the best; I love his boss and all the rest.

I love my office, and its location; I hate to have to go on vacation. I love my furniture, so drab and grey; and piles of paper that grow each day!

I love my computer, and all the software; I hug it often, though it don't care. I love each program and every file; I'd love them more if they'd work awhile.

I am happy to be here, I am, I am. I'm the happiest slave of the Firm, I am. I love my job, I'll say it again, I even love those friendly men...Those friendly men who've come today... In clean white coats to take me away!

(15) <u>Farmer Brown</u> phoned the old town veterinarian and said he had a sick cat. "The cat just lies around all day and whines," he

told the vet. The old doctor said, "That's nothing. Give him a pint of castor oil."

So the farmer did, and a few days later he met the vet in town. "How's that sick calf?" asked the doctor. "Calf?" exclaimed the farmer, "It wasn't a calf; it was my cat."

"Good Heavens," exclaimed the vet, "Did you give your cat a whole pint of castor oil?

"Yep, shore did," said the farmer.

"Well," asked the old doctor "how's the cat doing?"

Farmer Brown said, "Well, the last time I seen him he was going over the hill with 5 other cats. Two were digging holes, two were covering up the holes and one went on ahead **scoutin' out for more ground.**

· ·

(16) <u>Pregnant at Age 71</u>...

A woman went to the doctor's office where she was seen by one of the younger doctors. After about four minutes in the examination room, she burst out screaming as she ran down the hall.

The older doctor stopped her and asked what the problem was, and she told him her story. After listening, he had her sit down and relax in another room.

The older doctor marched down the hallway to where the young doctor was writing on his clipboard. "What on earth is wrong with you?" the older doctor demanded. "This woman is 71 years old, has 4 grown children and several grandchildren, and you told her she was pregnant?"

The younger doctor continued writing and without looking up said, "**Does she still have the hiccups?**

(17) <u>A Cardiologist and a Motorcycle Mechanic</u>...

    A motorcycle mechanic was removing a cylinder head from the motor of a big Harley bike when he spotted a well-known cardiologist in his shop. The doctor was there waiting for the service manager to come and take a look at his car when the mechanic shouted across the garage, "Hey, Doc, want to take a look at this?" The cardiologist, a bit surprised, walked over to where the mechanic was working on the motorcycle.

    The mechanic straightened up, wiping his hands on a rag and said, "Hey Doc, look at this engine. I opened its heart, took the valves out, repaired or replaced anything damaged, and then put everything back in and, it works just like new. So, how is it that I make $30 thousand a year and you make $1 million when you and I are doing basically the same work?"

    The doctor paused, leaned over with a grin and said to the mechanic... **"Try doing that with the engine running!**

. . . .

(18) <u>LAWYERS</u>

    A lawyer purchased a box of very rare and expensive cigars, and then insured them against, among other things, fire. Within a month, having smoked his entire stockpile of these great cigars, the lawyer filed a claim against the insurance company. In his claim, the lawyer stated the cigars were lost "***in a series of small fires***'"

    The insurance company refused to pay, citing the obvious reason, that the man had consumed the cigars in the normal fashion. The lawyer sued - and WON!

    Rather than endure lengthy and costly appeal process, the insurance company paid $15,000 to the lawyer for his loss of the cigars that perished in the "*fires.*"

    NOW FOR THE BEST PART... After the lawyer cashed the check, the insurance company had him arrested on 24 counts of ARSON!!! With his own insurance claim and testimony from the previous case being used against him, the lawyer was convicted of intentionally burning his insured property and was sentenced to 24 months in jail and a $24,000 fine. ONLY IN AMERICA!

· ·

(19) A guy walks into a post office one day and sees this middle-aged, bald-headed man methodically placing 'Love' stamps on bright pink envelopes with hearts all over them. Then he takes out a perfume bottle and sprays perfume all over them.

The guy watching all of this goes up to the man and says, "What are you doing?"

The man says, "I'm sending out **1000 Valentine cards** signed, *Guess who?*"

The observer asks, "But why?"

The man replies, "I'm a divorce lawyer."

· ·

(20) A young man was hired by a supermarket and on his first day of work. The manager greeted him and gave him a broom and said, "Your first job will be to sweep out the store."

The young man indigently replied, "But I am a college graduate."

The store manager apologized by saying, "Oh, I'm sorry. I didn't know that. Here, give me **the broom and I'll show you how**."

· ·

(21) <u>Famous Skier Picabo (Peek-a-boo) Street</u>

The famous skier Pickabo Street is not just a great athlete; she is also a registered nurse. She now works in the Intensive Care Unit of a large hospital. However, they had to restrict her from answering incoming phone calls. It was causing too much confusion when the phone would ring and she would say, **"Peek-a-boo I.C.U!**

• •

(22) ATTORNEY: She had three children, right?
WITNESS: Yes.
ATTORNEY: How many were boys?
WITNESS: None.
ATTORNEY: Were there any girls?
WITNESS: Your Honor, I think I need a different attorney. **Can I get a new attorney?**

• •

(23) A police officer pulled over a guy for speeding and says…
"May I see your driver's license?"
Driver:"I don't have one. I got it suspended when I got my 5th DUI."
Officer:"May I see the vehicle's registration?"
Driver:"It's not my car. I stole it."
Officer:"Did you say this car is stolen?
Driver:"That's right. But come to think of it, I think I did see the registration in the glove box when I was putting my gun in there."
Officer:"Is there a gun in the glove box?"
Driver:"Yes sir. That's where I put it after I shot and killed the woman who owns this car; before I stuffed her body in the trunk."
Officer:"Did you say **there's a body in the trunk**?"
Driver:"Yes sir, that's what I just said."

After hearing this, the officer immediately called his Captain for back-up. The Captain quickly arrived and cautiously approached

From 'SPAM' to BALONEY

the driver and said..."Sir, can I see your license?" The driver handed over his license.

Captain: "Looks OK to me. Whose car is this?"
Driver: "It's mine sir. Here is the registration."
Captain: "Looks OK to me. Would you slowly open the glove box so I can see if there is a gun in it?"
Driver: "Yes sir, but there is no gun in there."
Captain: "Would you mind opening the trunk? I was told there was a dead body in there." <u>The trunk was opened but no dead body in there!</u>
Captain: "Sir, I'm sorry to bother you like this but the officer who stopped you told me you didn't have a license, that you stole the car, that you had a gun in the glove box and had a dead body in the trunk."
Driver: "Yeah and I bet he also told you I was speeding."
Captain: "Sorry for inconveniencing you sir. Have a good day!"

• •

(24) <u>The Teacher</u>...

The teacher was helping one of her kindergarten students put on his boots. The little guy asked for help and the teacher pulled and pushed but **the boots still didn't want to go on**. After a lot of sweat and tears, she finally got his boots on, only to hear the little guy whimper, "Teacher, they're on the wrong feet."

She looked and sure enough they were. Well, it wasn't any easier getting them off, but she finally did. She managed to keep her cool as together they worked to get the boots back on the right feet.

Then the little guy announced, "These aren't my boots." The teacher bit her tongue rather than to scream like she wanted, "Why didn't you say so?"

Once again they struggled to get the boots off, and then he said, "These are my brother's boots; my mother made me wear them!"

At this point the teacher didn't know whether to laugh or cry. But, she mustered up whatever grace and courage she had left to wrestle the boots back on his feet again.

Finally she said, "Now, where are the mittens?"

The little guy said, "I stuffed them in the toe of my boots." The teacher's trial starts next week!

● ●

(25) Two heavily intoxicated men stood looking at the Newspaper headlines which read, "Man wanted for armed robbery in Brooklyn." One man looked at the other and said, "**If that job was in Manhattan, I'd take it!**"

● ●

(26) **Dear I.R.S (Internal Revenue Service)**...

Enclosed you will find this years tax return showing that I owe $3400 in taxes. Please note the attached article from our newspaper wherein you will see where the Dept. of Defense is paying $171 for hammers and NASA has paid $600 for toilet seats.

I am enclosing 4 toilet seats, valued at $2400 and 6 hammers valued at $1026 bringing my total to $3426. Please apply the overpayment of $26 to the (Obama) Presidential Election Fund as noted on my return.

It has been a pleasure to pay my tax bill this year and I look forward to paying it again next year.

Signed: Sincerely, A Satisfied Taxpayer.

(27) <u>The Police</u>…in one city were interrogating a suspect by placing a metal colander on his head and connecting it with wires to a photocopy machine. The words "He's lying" were place in the copier and the police pressed the copy button each time they thought the suspect wasn't telling the truth.

Believing the so-called lie detector was working, the suspect confessed.

• •

(28) <u>Not a Morning Person</u>…

John had this problem of getting up late in the morning and was always late for work. His boss was mad at him and threatened to fire him if he didn't do something about it.

So, John went to his doctor who gave him a pill and told him to take it before he went to bed.

John slept well and in fact beat the alarm in the morning. He had a leisurely breakfast and drove cheerfully to work. "Boss," he said, "The pill actually worked!"

"That's all fine," said the boss, "**But where were you yesterday?**"

• •

(29) <u>Baskin in the Sun</u>… Two robins were sitting in a tree when one said to the other, "I'm really hungry, let's fly down and find some lunch."

They flew to the ground and found a nice plowed field full of worms. They ate and ate and ate 'till they could eat no more. One robin then said to the other, "I'm so full I don't think I can fly back up to the tree."

"Me neither," said the other robin, "let's just lay here and bask in the warm sun." "O.K." said the other. So they plopped down basking in the sun.

No sooner had they fallen asleep when a big fat tomcat snuck up and gobbled them up. As the old cat washed his face after such a delicious meal, he chirped, "I love baskin robins!"

. . . .

(30) <u>How to Use Your IRS Rebate Check</u>...

Yes, our Government wants us to use our IRS Rebate check to stimulate the economy.

If we spend the money at Wal-Mart, all the money will go to China.

If we spend it on gasoline, it will go to the Arabs.

If we purchase a computer, it will go to India,

If we purchase fruit and vegetables, our money will go to Mexico, Honduras, or Guatemala,

If we buy a good car, it will go to Japan,

If we purchase useless crap our money will go to Taiwan,

AND NONE OF IT WILL HELP THE AMERICAN ECONOMY!

It has been suggested that in order to keep the money here in America, we ought to spend it at Yard Sales and Flea Markets since these are the only businesses still in our country!

. . . .

(31) <u>Dust If You Must</u>...

Dust if you must, but wouldn't it be better to paint a picture or write a letter, bake a cake or plant a seed, or help someone who has a need?

Dust if you must, but there is not much time, with rivers to swim and mountains to climb;

There's music to play and books to read, friends to laugh with and souls to feed.

Dust if you must, but the world's out there, with sun in your eyes and wind in your hair; a flutter of snow, a shower of rain, this day will not come 'round again.

Dust if you must, but bear in mind, old age will come and it's not kind. And when you go, and go you must, you, yourself, will make more dust.

....

(32) Quality of Life... An American businessman was at the pier of a small coastal Mexican village when a small boat with just one fisherman docked. In the small boat were several large yellow-fin tuna. The American complimented the Mexican on the quality of his fish and asked how long it took to catch them.

The Mexican replied, "Only a little while, Senor."

The American then asked, "Why didn't you stay out longer and catch more fish?" The Mexican said he had enough to support his family's immediate needs.

The American then asked, "But, what do you do with the rest of your time?"

The Mexican fisherman said, "I sleep late, fish a little, play with my children, take siestas with my wife. Then in the evening we stroll into the village where we sip a little wine and I play the guitar with my amigos. I have a full and busy life, Senor."

The American scoffed, "Listen amigo, I am a Harvard Business Major and I can help you. You should spend more time fishing and with the proceeds you could buy a bigger boat; then you could buy several boats. Eventually you could own a fleet of boats."

"Then," said the Harvard businessman, "instead of selling your catch to a middleman, you could sell directly to the processor, and eventually open your own cannery. You could control the whole processing and distribution process."

"Of course," the professor continued, "You would need to leave this small costal fishing village and move to the big city where you could expand your market to several big cities."

The Mexican scratched his head and said, "But Senor, how long would this take?" To which the American replied, "Maybe 15 or 20 years."

"But what then, Senor," asked the fisherman. The American businessman laughed and said, "This is the best part. When the time is right you could sell your company stock to the public and become very rich, you would make millions."

"Millions, Senor? Then what?

"Well," laughed the American, "Then you would retire, move to a small coastal fishing village where you could sleep late, fish a little, play with your grandkids, take siestas with your wife, stroll onto the village in the evenings where you could sip wine and **play your guitar with your amigos!**

. . . .

(33) <u>Tators</u>: Some people are very bossy and like to tell others what to do, but don't want to soil their own hands. They are called '**<u>Dick Tators.</u>**' Some people never seem motivated, but are content to watch while others do the work. They are called 'Speck Tators'.

Some people never do anything to help, but are gifted at finding fault with the way others work. They are called 'Comment Tators.' Some people are always looking to cause problems by asking others to agree with them that it is too hot, too cold, too sour or too sweet.

These are… 'Agie Tators.' There are those who say they will help, but somehow never get around to actually doing the promised help. These are called 'Hezzie Tators.' Some people put up a front and continually pretend to be someone they are not, often to the point where they actually believe it. They are called 'Emma Tators'.

Then there are those few who love and do what they say they will. They are always prepared to stop what they are doing and lend a helping hand. They bring sunshine into the lives of others. These are the 'Sweet Tators.'

....

(34) <u>All Potatoes Have Eyes</u>:

Well, Mr. and Mrs. Potato had eyes for each other, and finally they got married and had a little 'sweet potato,' which they called 'Yam.'

Of course, they wanted the best for Yam. When it was time, they told her about the facts of life. They warned her about going out and getting half-baked, so she wouldn't get accidently mashed and make a bad name for herself, like 'Hot-Potato' and end up with a bunch of 'Tater-Tots.'

Yam said not to worry; no 'Spud' would get her into the sack and make a 'Rotten-Potato" out of her! But, on the other hand, she wouldn't stay home and become a 'Couch-Potato' either. She said she would get plenty of exercise so as not to be skinny like her 'Shoestring' cousins.

When she went off to Europe, Mr. and Mrs. Potato told Yam to watch out for the 'Hard-Boiled' guys from Ireland and the greasy guys from France called 'French-Fries.' And when she went out west, to watch out for the Indians so she wouldn't get 'Scalloped.'

Yam said she would stay on the straight and narrow and wouldn't associate with those high class 'Yukon Golds,' or the ones from the other sides of the tracks who advertise their trade on all the trucks that say, 'Frito-Lay.'

Mr. and Mrs. Potato sent Yam to Idaho P.U. (that's Potato University) so that when she graduated she'd really be in the 'Chips.' But, in spite of all they did for her, one day Yam came home and announced she was going to marry Tom Brokaw.

"Tom Brokaw!" Mr. and Mrs. Potato exclaimed, "You cannot marry Tom Brokaw because he's just....well, a COMMON-TATOR!"

(35) The waiter said, "**Would you like your coffee black?**"
And the customer said, "What other color do you have?"

. . . .

(36) <u>Cutting Down The Forest</u>...

A large, well-established, Canadian lumber camp advertised that they were looking for a good lumberjack. The very next day, a skinny little man showed up at the camp with his axe, and knocked on the head lumberjack's door.

The head lumberjack took one look at the little man and told him to leave. "Just give me a chance to show you what I can do," said the skinny little man.

"OK, see that big oak over there?" said the boss-man, "Take your axe and go cut it down."

The skinny little man headed for the tree, and in a few minutes he was back knocking on the lumberjack's door. "I cut the tree down," said the man.

The lumberjack couldn't believe his eyes and said, "Where did you get the skill to chop down trees like that?"

"In the Sahara Forest," the little man replied.

"Sahara Forest? Do you mean the Sahara Desert?" said the lumberjack.

The little man laughed and answered back, "Oh sure, that's what they call it now!"

. . . .

(37) <u>Dumb and Dumber</u>...

    Q. Can you describe the individual?
    A. Yes, he was about medium height and had a beard.
    Q. Was this a male or a female?
    Q. All your responses must be oral, OK? So, what school did you go to?
    A. Oral

Q. Do you recall the time that you examined the body?
A. Yes, the autopsy began around 8:30 p.m.
Q. And the patient was indeed dead at the time?
A. No, he was sitting on the table wondering why I was doing an autopsy.
Q. Are you qualified to take a urine test?
A. Probably not, the last one I took I failed.

....

(38) <u>Noah in the Year 2010</u>

In the year 2010, the Lord came unto Noah, who was now living in Malibu, California. The Lord said, "Noah, once again, the earth has become so wicked and over-populated we need to build another Ark. Again, we need to save two of every living thing along with a few good people.

God gave Noah the blueprint and said, "You have six months to build the Ark before I will start the unending rain for forty days and forty nights.

Six months later, the Lord looked down and saw Noah weeping in his yard...but no Ark. "Noah!" God roared, "I'm about to start the rain! Where is the Ark?"

"Forgive me Lord," begged Noah, "but things have changed. I needed a building permit. I've been arguing with the inspector about the need for a sprinkler system. My neighbors claim that I've violated the neighborhood zoning laws by building the Ark in my yard and exceeding the height limitations. We had to go to the Development Appeal Board for a decision.

Getting the wood was another problem. There's a ban on cutting local trees in order to save the spotted owl. I tried to convince the environmentalist that I needed the wood to save the owls...but they would hear nothing of that. The Animal Rights Group insisted that I was confining wild animals against their will. They argued the accommodations were too restrictive, and it was cruel and inhumane to put so many animals in a confined space.

I'm still trying to resolve a complaint with the Human Rights Commission on how many minorities I'm supposed to hire for my building crew. Immigration and Naturalization is checking the green-card status of most of the people who want to work. The Trade Union says I can't use my sons. I have to hire only Union Workers with Ark-Building experience.

To make matters worse, the IRS seized all my assets, claiming I'm trying to leave the country illegally with endangered species. So, forgive me Lord, but I am trying."

Suddenly the sky cleared, the sun began to shine, and a rainbow stretched across the sky. Noah looked up in wonder and asked, "Lord, does this mean you're not going to destroy the world?"

"NO," said the Lord, "the Government has already done it!"

· ·

(39) Assassin Wanted...

The CIA had an opening for an assassin. After all of the background checks, interviews and testing were done, there were three finalists, two men and a woman.

For the final test, the CIA agents took one of the men to a large metal door and handed him a gun. "We must know that you will follow your instructions, no matter what the circumstances. Inside this room, you will find your wife sitting in a chair. Kill her!"

The man said, "You can't be serious. I could never shoot my wife!"

The agent said, "Then you're not the man for the job."

The second man was given the same instructions. He took the gun, and went into the room. All was quiet for about five minutes. Then the man came out with tears in his eyes and said, "I tried, but there is no way I can kill my wife."

The agent said, "You don't have what it takes for the job. Take your wife and go home." <u>Finally</u>, it was the woman's turn. She was given the same instructions; to kill her husband. She took the gun and went into the room.

Shots were heard, one shot after another. They heard screaming, crashing, banging on the walls. After a few minutes, all was quiet. The door opened slowly and there stood the woman. She wiped the sweat from her brow and said, "This gun is loaded with blanks! **<u>I had to beat him to death with a chair!</u>**

• •

(40) <u>Our God is Awesome</u>! ... For example...
- Because of the tremendous weight of the elephant, it is the only 4 legged creatures in which all 4 legs that bend forward to facilitate its movement!
- Because the horse rises from the ground on its two front legs first, and the cow rises from the ground with its two hind legs first...it's awfully hard to believe in evolution!
- Yes, our God is awesomely efficient and orderly, and when you and I were created, He looked at us and said, "*That's very good.*"

(41) DOES GOD EXIST?

A man went to a barbershop to have his hair cut and his beard trimmed. As the barber began to work, they began to have a good conversation.

They talked about so many things and various subjects. When they eventually touched on the subject of God, the barber said, "I don't believe that God exists."

"Why do you say that?" asked the customer.

"Well, you just have to go out in the street to realize that God doesn't exist. Tell me, if God exists, would there be so many sick people? Would there be abandoned children? If God existed, there would be neither suffering nor pain. I can't imagine a loving God who would allow all of these things."

The customer thought for a moment, but didn't respond because he didn't want to start an argument.

The barber finished his job and the customer left the shop. Just after he left the barbershop, he saw a man in the street with long, stringy, dirty hair and an untrimmed beard. He looked dirty and unkempt. The customer turned back and entered the barbershop again and he said to the barber: "You know what? Barbers do not exist."

"How can you say that?" asked the surprised barber. "I am here, and I am a barber. And I just worked on you!"

"No!" the customer exclaimed. "Barbers don't exist because if they did, there would be no people with dirty long hair and untrimmed beards, like that man outside."

"Ah, but barbers DO exist! That's what happens when people do not come to me."

"Exactly!" affirmed the customer. "That's the point! God, too, DOES exist! That's what happens when people do not go to Him and don't look to Him for help. That's why there's so much pain and suffering in the world."

From 'SPAM' to BALONEY

(42) <u>Got to Love These Saskatchewan people!</u>

A young farm boy from Saskatchewan moved to Vancouver Island and went to a huge "everything-under-one roof-department-store" looking for a job.

The Manager says, "Do you have any sales experience?"

The kid says, "Yeah. I was a salesman back in Saskatchewan."

Well, the boss liked the kid and gave him the job. "You start tomorrow. I'll come down after we close and see how you did."

His first day on the job was rough, but he got through it. After the store was locked up, the boss came down. "How many customers bought something from you today?"

The kid says, "one."

The boss says, "Just one? Our salespeople average 20 to 30 customers a day. How much was the sale for?"

The kid says, "$101,237.65."

The boss says, "101 thousand dollars! What the heck did you sell?"

The kid says, "First, I sold him a small fish hook. Then I sold him a medium fish hook. Then I sold him a larger fish hook. Then I sold him a new fishing rod.

"Then I asked him where he was going fishing and he said down the coast, so I told him he was going to need a boat, so we went down to the boat department and I sold him a twin engine Chris Craft."

"Then he said he didn't think his Honda Civic would pull it, so I took him down to the automotive department and sold him that 4x4 Ford Expedition."

The boss astounded said, "You mean to tell me that a guy came in here to buy a fish hook and you sold him a BOAT and a TRUCK?"

The Saskatchewan farm boy said, "No, the guy came in here to buy tampons for his wife and I said, "<u>**Dude, your weekend's shot -- you should go fishing!**</u>

CHAPTER 19

Amazing facts

(1) <u>Properties of WATER</u>...

75% of Americans are dehydrated. Lack of water is the #1 trigger of daytime fatigue. Preliminary research indicates that 8-10 glasses of water a day could significantly ease back and joint pain for up to 80% of the sufferers. Drinking 5 glasses of water a day decreases the risk of colon cancer by 79% and you are 50% more likely to not develop bladder cancer.

. . . .

(2) <u>Properties of COKE (Cola)</u>...

In many states in America the highway patrol carries two gallons of coke in the truck to remove blood from the highway after a car accident. To clean a toilet: Pour a can of Coca-Cola into the toilet bowl and let 'the real thing' sit for one hour, then flush to clean. The citric acid in coke removes stains from vitreous china.

To clean corrosion from car battery terminals: Pour a can of Coca-Cola over the terminals to bubble away the corrosion.

To loosen a rusted bolt: Apply a cloth soaked in Coca-Cola to the rusted bolt for several minutes. To remove grease from clothes: Empty a can of Coke into a load of greasy clothes, add detergent, and run through a regular cycle. The Coke will help loosen grease stains. It will also clean road haze from your windshield. Yes, the distributors of coke have been using it to clean the engines of their own trucks for over twenty years now!

Now, the question is, "would you like a coke or a glass of water?"

. . . .

(3) GARDEN SNAKES CAN BE DANGEROUS...

Snakes also known as Garter Snakes can be dangerous. Yes, grass snakes, not rattlesnakes. Here's why. A couple in Sweetwater, Texas, had a lot of potted plants. During a recent cold spell, the wife was bringing a lot of them indoors to protect them from a possible freeze.

It turned out that a little green garden grass snake was hidden in one of the plants. When it had warmed up, it slithered out and the wife saw it go under the sofa.

She let out a very loud scream. The husband (who was taking a shower) ran out into the living room naked to see what the problem was. She told him there was a snake under the sofa. He got down on the floor on his hands and knees to look for it. About that time the family dog came and cold-nosed him on the behind. He thought the snake had bitten him, so he screamed and fell over on the floor. His wife thought he had had a heart attack, so she covered him up, told him to lie still and called an ambulance. The attendants rushed in, would not listen to his protests, loaded him on the stretcher, and started carrying him out.

About that time, the snake came out from under the sofa and the Emergency Medical Technician saw it and dropped his end of the stretcher. That's when the man broke his leg and why he is still in the hospital. The wife still had the problem of the snake in the house, so she called on a neighbor who volunteered to capture the snake. He armed himself with a rolled-up newspaper and began poking under the couch. Soon he decided it was gone and told the woman, who sat down on the sofa in relief.

But while relaxing, her hand dangled in between the cushions, where she felt the snake wriggling around. She screamed and fainted, the snake rushed back under the sofa. The neighbor man, seeing her lying there passed out, tried to use CPR to revive her. The neighbor's wife, who had just returned from shopping at the grocery store, saw her husband's mouth on the woman's mouth and slammed her husband in the back of the head with a bag of canned goods, knocking him out and cutting his scalp to a point where it needed stitches.

The noise woke the woman from her dead faint and she saw her neighbor lying on the floor with his wife bending over him, so she assumed that the snake had bitten him. She went to the kitchen and got a small bottle of whiskey, and began pouring it down the man's throat. By now, the police had arrived. They saw the unconscious man, smelled the whiskey, and assumed that a drunken fight had occurred. They were about to arrest them all, when the women tried to explain how it all happened over a little garden snake! The police called an ambulance, which took away the neighbor and his sobbing wife. Now, the little snake again crawled out from under the sofa and one of the police drew his gun and fired at it. He missed the snake and hit the leg of the end table. The table fell over, the lamp on it shattered and, as the bulb broke, it started a fire in the drapes.

The other policeman tried to beat out the flames, and fell through the window into the yard on top of the family dog who, startled, jumped out and raced into the street, where an oncoming car swerved to avoid it and smashed into the parked police car.

Meanwhile, neighbors saw the burning drapes and called in the fire department. The firemen had started raising the fire ladder when they were halfway down the street. The rising ladder tore out the overhead wires, put out the power, and disconnected the telephones in a ten-square city block area (but they did get the house fire out).

Time passed. Both men were discharged from the hospital, the house was repaired, the dog came home, the police acquired a new car and all was right with their world. A while later they were watching TV and the weatherman announced a cold snap for that night. The wife asked her husband if he thought they should bring in their plants for the night. And that's when he shot her!

. . . .

(4) <u>Subject: Romney's Character</u>

Unlike most urban legends, this one is 100% true.

In July 1996, the 14-year-old daughter of Robert Gay, a partner at Bain Capital, had disappeared. She had attended a rave party in New York City and gotten high on ecstasy. Three days later, her distraught father had no idea where she was. Romney took immediate action. He closed down the entire firm and asked all 30 partners and employees to fly to New York to help find Gay's daughter.

Romney set up a command center at the LaGuardia Marriott and hired a private detective firm to assist with the search. He established a toll-free number for tips, coordinating the effort with the NYPD, and went through his Rolodex and called everyone Bain did business with in New York, and asked them to help find his friend's missing daughter. Romney and the other

From 'SPAM' to BALONEY

Bain employees scoured every part of New York and talked with everyone they could: prostitutes, drug addicts, anyone.

That day, their hunt made the evening news, which featured photos of the girl and the Bain employees searching for her. As a result, a teenage boy phoned in, asked if there was a reward, and then hung up abruptly. The NYPD traced the call to a home in New Jersey, where they found the girl in the basement, shivering and experiencing withdrawal symptoms from a massive ecstasy dose. Doctors later said the girl might not have survived another day. Romney's former partner credits Mitt Romney with saving his daughter's life, saying, "It was the most amazing thing, and I'll never forget this to the day I die."

So, here's my epiphany: Mitt Romney simply can't help himself. He sees a problem, and his mind immediately sets to work solving it, sometimes consciously, and sometimes not-so-consciously. He doesn't do it for personal gain. He does it because that's just how he's wired.

Many people are unaware of the fact that when Romney was asked by his old employer, Bill Bain, to come back to Bain & Company as CEO to rescue the firm from bankruptcy, Romney left Bain Capital to work at Bain & Company for an annual salary of one dollar. When Romney went to the rescue of the 2002 Salt Lake Olympics, he accepted no salary for three years, and wouldn't use an expense account. He also accepted no salary as Governor of Massachusetts.

Character counts! The media and Obama re-election machine will focus on Romney's wealth and the immorality of it, as they see it, but Romney is a man who uses his wealth to bless and to make this world a better place. Let's get this message out because it is not likely that the media will do so!

(5) <u>Mathematical Viewpoint</u>

Ever wonder about those people who say they are giving More than 100% and how many times have you heard of giving 101%? This will help!

If A, B, C, D, etc (the whole alphabet) is represented as 1, 2, 3, 4 up to 26

Then <u>H-A-R-D-W-O-R-K</u> is
$8+1+18+4+23+15+18+11 = 98\%$ .....

and <u>K-N-O-W-L-E-D-G-E</u> is
$11+14+15+23+12+5+4+7+5 = 96\%$....

but, <u>A-T-T-I-T-U-D-E</u> is $1+20+20+9+20+21+4+5 = 100\%$ and look at how far the love of God will take you...

<u>L-O-V-E-O-F-G-O-D</u> will take you
$12+15+22+5+15+6+7+15+4 =$ <u>101%</u>

Therefore, one can conclude with mathematical certainty that: While Hard Work and Knowledge will get you close, and Attitude will get you there, it's the Love of God that will put you over the top!

. . . .

(6) <u>University of Miami – Football Player Entrance Exam</u>

* What language is spoken in France?

* What is the first name of Pierre Trudeau?

* Would you ask William Shakespeare to...

    (a) build a bridge (b) sail the ocean
    (c) lead an army OR (d) WRITE A PLAY

* What religion is the Pope?...

    (a) Jewish (b) Catholic (c) Hindu (d) Agnostic

* In Metric Conversion, how many feet is 0.0 meters?

From 'SPAM' to BALONEY

* What time is it when the big hand is on 12 and the little hand is on 5?

* How many commandments did Moses give? (Approximately).

* What are people in America from the North called?

    (a) Westerners (b) Southerners (c) Northerners

* Spell – Bush, Carter and Clinton

* Six kings of England have been called 'George', the last one being George the Sixth; name the previous five.

* Where does rain come from?

    (a) Macy's (b) a 7-11 (c) Canada (d) the sky.

* Can you explain Einstein's Theory of Relativity?

    (a) YES (b) NO

* What are coat hangers used for?

* The Star Spangled Banner is the National Anthem for what country?

* Where is the basement of a three-story house located?

* Which part of America produces the most oranges?

    (a) New York (b) Florida (c) Canada (d) Wisconsin

Chapter 20

Church' stories

(1) <u>The Greatest of These</u>...   Cor. 13:13

A mother said her day got off to a bad start when she saw her 6-year –old son breaking off a limb from her favorite azalea bush by the front side walk near the street. By the time she got to him he had it in his hand and asked if he could take it to school that day.

She agreed with a wave of her hand as she felt tears of disappointment swelling up inside her. She touched the bush as if to say to the bush, "I'm sorry."

She had already been angry with her husband when the washing machine had leaked on her brand new linoleum floor. She wondered why he hadn't fixed it the night before when she asked him; instead he sat and played checkers with their oldest son Jonathan all evening.

"What are his priorities anyway?" she thought as she was still mopping up the mess.

Jonathan walked into the kitchen and asked, "What's for breakfast, Mom?"

She opened the refrigerator and announced, "How about toast and jelly?" as she smeared the toast and set it in front of him. "Why am I so angry?" she thought as she tossed her husband's dishes into the sudsy water.

It was days like this that just made her want to quit. Well, she managed to lug the wet clothes to the Laundromat and spent most of the day washing and drying and thinking how love had but almost disappeared from her life.

As she finished hanging up the last of her husband's shirts she realized it was time to rush to the school to pick up the kids. She was out of breath as she knocked on the teacher's door and peered through the glass. The teacher motioned for her to wait a minute and she indicated they needed to talk.

"What now?" she thought.

The teacher said "I want to talk to you about Jonathan." She prepared for the worst as the teacher said, "Did you know Jonathan brought flowers to school today?"

The mother nodded that she did know that as she thought again of her once beautiful azalea bush.

"Let me tell you about yesterday," the teacher said. "See that little girl over there? Well, yesterday she was almost hysterical. Her mother and father are going through a divorce and that little girl told me and the class that she didn't want to live and would rather die. The teacher said, I watched that little girl bury her face in her hands and say loud enough for all the class to hear,"Nobody loves me! I tried to console her but all I did was to make things worse."

The mother interrupted by saying, "I thought you wanted to talk to me about my son."

"I do," said the teacher, "because today, your son walked straight over to that girl and handed her those pretty pink flowers and whispered, "I love you."

The mother said she felt her heart swell with pride for what her son had done. She smiled at the teacher and said, "Thank you, you've made my day!"

Later that evening as she was pulling weeds from around the lop-sided azalea bush, a verse from the Bible came running through her mind, *"...now these three remain, faith, hope, and love; But the greatest of these is love."* She thought that while her son was putting love into practice, she had only felt anger.

About that time she heard the familiar squeak of her husband's brakes as he pulled into the driveway. She stood up, put a smile on her face and snapped off a bristling bush of hot pink azaleas to give to her husband.

Her own words were, "I felt the seed of God's love beginning to bloom in me once again as my husband's eyes widened in surprise as **I handed him the flowers and said, 'I love you!'"**

· ·

(2) <u>I am grateful for...</u>
- The partner who hogs the covers every night, because I am not alone.
- The child who is not cleaning his room but is watching TV because he is home and not out walking the streets.
- The taxes I pay because it means I have a job.
- The mess to clean up after the party because it means I have been surrounded by friends.
- For the clothes that fit a little too snug because it means I have plenty to eat.
- For the lady behind me in church that sings off-key every Sunday because it means I can hear.
- For the pile of laundry and ironing because it means I have clothes to wear.
- For the alarm that goes off in the early morning hours because it means that I am alive.

(3) <u>How to plant your Garden</u>

    First, you come to the garden alone, while the dew is still on the roses.

1. <u>Plant three rows of peas</u> – peace of mind / peace of heart / peace of soul.
2. <u>Plant three rows of squash</u> – squash gossip / squash grumbling / squash selfishness.
3. <u>Plant three rows of lettuce.</u> – Let-us be faithful / let-us be kind / let-us love one another.
4. <u>Plant three rows of turnips.</u> – Turn-up for meetings / Turn up for service / Turn up to help one another!

. . . .

(4) <u>The Cracked Pot</u>…   <u>2 Cor. 4:7</u>

    A water carrier kept busy carrying two large pots on a pole behind his neck. It was his job as a slave on a remote estate. One of the pots, however, had a crack in it and while one pot always seemed full at the end of the long walk, the other pot was always only half full.

    For two years this was an every day job in order to supply the estate landlord with his daily water supply. Thus he carried one full pot and one half pot of water to his master.

    Well, the good pot was very proud to be of such splendid service while the cracked pot was ashamed of doing so poorly, being only able to do one-half of what he was intended to do.

    After two years of what he perceived to be a bitter failure, the cracked pot said to the slave, "Because of all my flaws, I think I am a dismal failure for all the work you have done."

    The slave worker felt sorry for the old cracked pot, and in his compassion said, "As we return to the master's house today, I want you to notice the beautiful flowers along the path."

    And sure enough, as they went up the long hill to the estate the old cracked pot noticed the beautiful flowers along the trail and he seemed to feel a bit better. But at the end of the trail, he again felt like such a failure because he only could deliver a half pail of water, and once again began to apologize for being such a failure.

The slave said to the old cracked pot, "Did you notice that there were flowers only on your side of the path, and no flowers on the other pots side? Well, that's because I have always known about your flaw, and I took advantage of it. I planted flower seeds on your side of the path and every while we walked back from the stream, you've watered them. For two years I have been able to pick these beautiful flowers to decorate my master's table. Without you being just the way you are, he would not have this beauty to grace his table."

The moral is that each of us has our own unique flaws. We're all cracked pots. But if we allow it the Lord will use our flaws to grace His Father's table. In God's great economy, nothing goes to waste. Don't be afraid of your flaws. Acknowledge them and you too can be the cause of beauty!

. . . .

(5) <u>A wealthy man</u> decided to go on a safari in Africa. He took his faithful pet dog along for company. One day the dog starts chasing butterflies and before long he discovers that he is lost. So, wandering about he notices a leopard heading rapidly in his direction with the obvious intention of having lunch.

The dog thinks, "Boy am I in big trouble now!" Then he noticed some bones on the ground close by and immediately settles down to chew on the bones with his back to the approaching cat.

Just as the leopard is about to leap, the dog exclaims loudly, "Man, that was one delicious leopard. I wonder if there are any more leopards around here."

Hearing that, the leopard stops in mid-stride as a look of terror comes over him and he slinks away into the trees. "Whew," says the leopard, "that was close. That dog nearly had me."

Meanwhile, a monkey who had been watching the whole scene from a nearby tree figures he can put this knowledge to good use and trade it for protection from the leopard. So off he goes. But the dog saw him heading after the leopard, and figures that something is up.

The monkey soon catches up with the leopard, spills the beans and strikes up a deal with the leopard. The cat is furious at being made a fool of and says, "Here monkey, hop on my back and I'll show you what's going to happen to that conniving canine."

Now the dog sees the leopard coming with the monkey on his back and thinks, "What am I going to do now?" But instead of running, the dog sits down with his back to his would-be attackers pretending he hasn't seen them yet. And just when they get close enough to hear, the dog says, "Where's that monkey? I sent him off an hour ago to bring me back another leopard, and he's still not back!" **And being smart wins out again!**

. . . .

(6) Ben Stein: (CBS Sunday Morning Commentary)...
*"**We reap what we sow.**"*

I have no idea where the concept came from, that America is an explicitly atheist country. I can't find it in the Constitution and I don't like it being shoved down my throat.

Or maybe, I can put it another way; where did the idea come from that we should worship celebrities and we aren't allowed to worship God. I guess that's a sign that I'm getting old!

But there are a lot of us who are wondering where these celebrities came from and where the America we knew went to...

Now we're asking ourselves why our children have no conscience, why they don't know right from wrong, and why it doesn't bother them to kill strangers, their classmates, and themselves.

Probably, if we think about it long enough, we can figure it out. I think it has a great deal to do with... *"We reap what we sow!"*

• •

(7) <u>7 wonders of the world</u>...

A group of students were studying geography and they were asked to list what they considered to be the 'Seven Wonders of the World.' Though there was some disagreement, the following got the most votes...

1. Egypt's Great Pyramids / 2. Taj mahal / 3. Grand Canyon / 4. Panama Canal / 5. Empire State Building / 6. St. Peter's Basilica/ 7. China's Great Wall.

While gathering the votes, the teacher noted that one quiet little girl hadn't turned in her paper yet. She asked the girl if she was having trouble with her list. The girl replied, "Yes, there are so many."

The teacher said, "Well, let me look at what you have, perhaps I can help." The girl hesitated, and then read, "I think the 7 wonders of the world are...

1. to touch / 2. to taste / 3. to see / 4. to hear / 5. to run / 6. to laugh / 7. to love.......... Yes, it's too easy to look at man's achievements and overlook what we call ordinary.

May we be reminded of those things which are truly wondrous!

(8) <u>The Circus</u>...

Once, when I was a teenager, my father and I were standing **in line to buy tickets for the circus.** There was one family ahead of us. There were eight kids in two rows with the mother and father at the counter window. We could tell they were quite poor yet very excited about getting to come to the circus.

The ticket lady said' "How many?" then quoted the price. The mother dropped her head and her lip began to quiver; we knew they didn't have enough money.

My father, seeing what was going on, put his hand in his pocket and pulled out a $20 bill then dropped it on the ground. Then my father reached down and picked up the bill, tapped the man on the shoulder and said, "Excuse me sir, this fell out of your pocket."

The man knew what was going on. He wasn't begging for a handout but certainly appreciated the help in a desperate situation. He looked straight into my father's eyes, took my dad's hands in both of his, and squeezed tightly the twenty dollar bill. With tears on his cheek he said to my dad, "Thank you, thank you sir, this really means a lot to me and my family." My father and I then turned and slowly walked back to our car and drove home. We didn't go to the circus that night, but we didn't go without either! *"It is more blessed to give than receive."*

• •

(9) <u>TV Interview with Billy Graham's daughter</u>...

Bryant Gumbel recently interviewed Billy Graham's daughter when Gumbel said, "Why didn't God stop this or do something about this?"

Billy Graham's daughter said, "For years we have told God we didn't want Him in our schools. We didn't want Him in our government and we didn't want Him in our finances and God, being a Perfect Gentleman, is doing just what we asked Him to do. We need to make up our mind; do we want God or do we not want Him? We cannot just ask Him in when disaster strikes." Bryant Gumble was silent.

· ·

(10) Cheeter the Greeter...

Greenwood United Methodist Church sits at the edge of the woods in Butler County, PA. next to a farm where the church greeter lives. Sunday mornings, as soon as he hears the pastor's tires crunching the gravel in the parking lot, the greeter, a rugged sort with thick blond hair, leaves his house and cuts across a field and through the woods. It's the fastest way to the church door.

By the time the first parishioners drive up, he's ready to welcome them. He hasn't missed a service in four years, not to mention church dinners, meetings, and the occasional wedding or funeral.

He stays at his post until the last car pulls out of the lot, then he hikes back through the woods and back to the farm. Like any church volunteer, he's a little protective of his turf. The only one he's been known to share it with is a cat who will sometimes sit next to him at the door.

This greeter has a good voice. When the bells toll at the start of the worship service, he raises his head and adds his rich baritone voice. He has his favorite hymn too, called, "All creatures great and small." Yes, indeed...

Cheeter the Golden Retriever has found his calling! Have you found yours?

(11) Church Bulletins!
- The 'Fasting & Prayer Conference' includes meals.
- The sermon this morning is entitled; 'Jesus walks On the Water'; the sermon tonight is 'Searching for Jesus'.
- Remember in prayer the many that are sick of our community.
- Smile at someone who is hard to love; say 'Hell' to someone who doesn't care much about you.

. . . .

(12) Love Is Action…   1 Cor. 13:4-17

I took my 8-year-old Helen and my 5-year-old Brandon to the mall to go shopping. In the mall parking lot was a 'Petting Zoo.' My kids began jumping and begging to go to the petting zoo. I thought "why not" and gave them each 50 cents and said, "meet me later in the Sears hardware dept."

A few minutes later I noticed my oldest, Helen, came in and so I said to her, "What are you doing in here? I thought you wanted to go to the Petting Zoo." She said to me, "It cost $1.00 and so I gave my 50 cents to Brandon so he could go."

"Well," I thought, "that's about the sweetest thing I could have heard her say." She was really getting our family motto, *love is action*.

What do you think I did? Well, it's probably not what you think. As soon as I finished my shopping, Helen and I went back out to the Petting Zoo. We stood by the fence and watched Brandon going crazy petting and feeding the animals.

I had another dollar burning a hole in my pocket but I never offered it to Helen and she never asked for it. The reason was our family motto stood for 'Love is sacrificial action!' Real love always costs you something.

Love is expensive. Love gives, and expects nothing in return. Helen gave her money to her younger brother so he could enjoy the Petting Zoo and she knew that meant she would sacrifice her pleasure in order to be a blessing to someone else. She knew she would have to feel a sacrifice if she really wanted to experience ***love is a sacrificial action!***

. . . .

<u>(13) Taking Aim</u>…*"in as much…"*

A young man **in Seminary class** tells of the time when his professor gave the class an object lesson. One day as the students walked into class, they noticed a big target tacked to the wall near each student's desk.

The professor asked the students to draw a picture on the target of someone they disliked or someone who made them angry. He then suggested that each student relieve their frustration by throwing darts at the picture they had drawn on the target.

This young man drew a picture of a former friend who had double-crossed him in a business deal and laughed all the way to the bank. Other students furiously drew pictures of people who had betrayed them or misused them in some way.

The class lined up and began throwing darts with much laughter and hilarity. Some of the students threw their darts with such force that their targets began to rip apart. Eventually, the students returned to their seats.

The seminary professor calmed down the students and preceded with his lesson by removing the targets from the wall, and underneath each target was a picture of Jesus! A complete hush fell over the room as each student looked at the mangled picture of their Lord with holes and jagged marks all over His face and form. All the professor said was, *"In as much as you have done it unto the least of these My brethren, you have done it unto Me."*

(14) <u>The Judge Said to the Mexican Witness</u>:
"Now you must tell us only what you yourself actually saw; not what you think, or assumed, or heard someone else tell you. Do you understand that?"

"Si," said the witness.

"Very well," said the Judge, as the prosecuting attorney approached to examine the witness. "Give us your full name" said the attorney.

"Full name is Rafael Miguel Escudorzi Cortille."

"And what is your profession?"

"I am a plumber" said the witness.

"Good" said the lawyer, "And how old are you Mr. Cortille?"

"Ah...Ah...Ah" sighed Cortille, then he said, "I no can answer, Judge."

"You can't tell us how old you are?" asked the Judge.

"No," said the witness, "My age depend on when I was born. Si? And I no can say that. Yes, I was there, but like you tell me judge, **all I know is hearsay, Si?**

. . . .

(15) <u>Are You Jesus?</u>...

A few years ago a group of salesmen went to a regional convention in Chicago. They had assured their wives that they would be home in plenty of time for Friday's night dinner.

In their rush, with tickets and brief cases, one of the salesmen inadvertently kicked the leg of a table which held a display of baskets of apples. Apples flew everywhere! Without stopping or looking back, they all managed to reach their plane in time for their nearly missed boarding.

All but one, that is. He paused, took a deep breath, got in touch with his feelings, and experienced a twinge of compassion for the girl whose apple stand had been over-turned.

He told his buddies to go on without him, waved goodbye, told one of them to call his wife and let her know he'd be on the next flight. Then he returned to help clean up the apple mess. He was glad he did. There on the floor was a 16-year old girl, who was totally blind, crying in frustration as she tried to gather up the apples. Crowds were all around rushing to get on their way but no one stopped to help.

The salesman knelt on the floor with her, gathered up the apples, put them in the baskets and helped reconstruct the display. As he did this, he noticed that many of the apples had become battered and bruised; these he set aside in another basket.

When he had finished, he pulled out his wallet and said to the girl, "Here, please take this $20 for the damage we did. Are you OK? She nodded through her tears. He continued on with, "I hope we didn't spoil your day too badly."

As the salesman started to walk away, the bewildered blind girl called out to him, "Mister." He paused, turned around to look into those blind eyes again as she continued, "Are you Jesus?"

He stopped in mid-stride, and he wondered. Then slowly he made his way to catch the later flight with that question burning in his soul, "Are you Jesus?"

Do people mistake you for Jesus? If we claim to know Him, we should live, walk and act as He would. We are the 'apple of His eye.' He stopped what He was doing, picked you and me up, and took us to a hill called Calvary and paid in full for our damaged fruit. Let's start living like we are worth the price He paid!

. . . .

(16) Making Pancakes…

Six year old Brandon decided one Saturday morning to fix pancakes for his parents. He found a big bowl and spoon, pulled a chair to the counter, opened the cupboard and pulled out the heavy flower canister, spilling it on the floor. He scooped some of the flour into the bowl with his hands, mixed in most of a cup of milk and added some sugar, leaving a floury trail on the floor which by now had a few tracks left by his kitten.

As Brandon was wondering what to do next, he suddenly noticed his kitten licking from the bowl of mix and reached to push her away, knocking the egg carton to the floor. Frantically he tried to clean up the mess but slipped on the eggs, getting his pajamas white and sticky.

And just then he saw dad standing in the doorway. Big tears welled up in Brandon's eyes. He knew he was in trouble and yet all he wanted to do was surprise his parents with a pancake breakfast.

He was sure he was in for a good scolding and maybe even a spanking. But, walking thru the mess, coming toward him, was his dad. Dad picked up his crying son, hugged him while at the same time getting his own pajamas white and sticky in the process.

That's how God deals with us. We try to do something good in life, but it often turns out to be a mess. Our marriage gets all sticky, or we insult a friend by saying the wrong thing, or we can't stand our job and our health goes sour.

Often all we can do it seems is stand there in tears because we cannot think of anything else to do. That's when God picks us up, and loves us and forgives us, even the mess we've made of our life.

But, we still ought not to stop trying to make pancakes. We may never get it all right but we'll never accomplish anything unless we try and one day we will be glad we tried.

From 'SPAM' to BALONEY

(17) <u>Someone is raising their kid right...</u>

One day a 6-year-old girl was sitting in a classroom when the teacher was trying to explain evolution to the class.

The teacher said to a little boy, "Tommy, do you see the grass outside?"

Tommy said, "Yes."

The teacher said, "Tommy, go outside and look up and tell the class if you can see the sky."

A few minutes later Tommy comes back in and the teacher says, "Tommy, did you see the sky?"

Tommy says, "Yes teacher, I saw the sky".

The teacher said, "Tommy, did you see God?"

Tommy said, "No, I did not see God."

The teacher then replied, "That's my point. We can't see God because He isn't there. He just does not exist."

A little girl spoke up and wanted to ask Tommy some questions and was given permission to do so.

She said, "Tommy, do you see the grass?"

Tommy said, "Yes."

The little girl said, "Tommy, did you see the sky?"

Tommy said, "Yes."

Then the little girl said, "Tommy, do you see the teacher?"

Again Tommy said, "Yes I do."

Then the little girl asked, "Tommy, do you see the teacher's brain?"

Tommy said emphatically, "NO!"

The little girl then said, "According to what we were taught in school today**, the teacher must not have one**!"

. . . .

(18) <u>The Wicker Basket</u>

Each morning, Grandpa was up early sitting at the kitchen table reading from his old worn-out Bible. His grandson who wanted to be just like him tried to imitate him in any way he could.

One day the grandson asked, "Papa, I try to read the Bible just like you, but I don't understand it, and what I do understand, I forget as soon as I close the book. What good does reading the Bible do?"

The Grandfather quietly turned from putting coal in the stove and said, "Take this old wicker coal basket down to the river and bring back a basket of water."

The boy did as he was told, even though all the water leaked out before he could get back to the house.

The grandfather laughed and said, "You will have to move a little faster next time," and sent him back to the river with the basket to try again.

This time the boy ran faster, but again the old wicker basket was empty before he returned home.

Out of breath, he told his grandfather that it was impossible to carry water in a basket, and he went to get a bucket instead.

The old man said, "I don't want a bucket of water, I want a basket of water. You can do this. You're just not trying hard enough," and he went out the door to watch the boy try again.

At this point, the boy knew it was impossible, but he wanted to show his grandfather that even if he ran as fast as he could, the water would leak out before he got far at all.

The boy scooped the water and ran hard, but when he reached his grandfather the basket was again empty.

Out of breath, he said, "See Papa, it's useless!"

"So you think it is useless?" the old man said.

"Look at the basket."

The boy looked at the basket and for the first time he realized that the basket looked different. Instead of a dirty old wicker coal basket, it was clean.

"Son, that's what happens when you read the Bible. You might not understand or remember everything, but when you read it, it will change you from the inside out."

Moral of the wicker basket story:

Take time to read a portion of God's word each day; it will affect you for good even if you don't retain a word.

• •

(19) <u>Daddy's Empty Chair</u>...

A man's daughter had asked the local minister to come and pray with her father. When the minister arrived, he found the man lying in bed with his head propped up on two pillows. An empty chair sat beside his bed.

The minister assumed that the old fellow had been informed of his visit. "I guess you were expecting me," he said. The old man replied, "No, who are you?"

The minister told him his name and then remarked, "I saw the empty chair and I just figured you knew I was going to show up."

"Oh yeah, the chair," said the bedridden man. "Would you mind closing the door?" The minister was a bit puzzled, but he did close the door and the old man said, "I've never told anyone this, not even my daughter. But all of my life I have never known how to pray. At church I used to hear the preacher talk about prayer, but I guess it went right over my head. I just about gave up any attempt at prayer."

The minister remained silent and old man continued, "Well, one day, about four years ago, my best friend said to me, 'Johnny, prayer is just a simple matter of having a conversation with Jesus. Here is what I suggest. Sit down in a chair and put an empty chair in front of you and in faith see Jesus sitting on that other chair. Then speak to Him just like you would talk to me.'"

"So," the old man continued, "I tried it and I liked it. I liked it so much that I try to do it every day, sometimes, several times a day."

The minister was greatly moved as he listened to the old man tell his story and he encouraged him to continue as he had been doing. The minister then prayed for the old man and anointed him with oil and went on back to his church.

Two nights later the daughter called to tell the minister that her daddy had died that afternoon. "Did he die in peace?" the minister asked.

"Yes," she said, "when I left the house about two o'clock, he called me over to his bedside. He told me he loved me and kissed me on the cheek. When I got back from the store and hour or so later, I found him dead."

"But," she said, "there was something strange about his death. Apparently, just before daddy died, he leaned over and rested his head on the chair beside the bed. What on earth do you make of that?"

The minister wiped a tear from his eye and said, "I wish we could all go like that!"

. . . .

(20) <u>Allah or Jesus?</u>

(A true story given by a prison guard, Rick Mathews)

Last month I attended my annual training session that's required for maintaining my state prison security clearance. During the training session there was a presentation by three speakers representing the Roman Catholic faith, the Protestant faith, and the Muslim faith, each explaining their belief systems.

I was particularly interested in what the Islamic Imam had to say. The Imam gave a great presentation of the basics of Islam, complete with a video. After the presentation, time was provided for questions and answers.

When it was my turn, I directed my question to the Imam and asked, "Please sir, correct me if I'm wrong, but I understand that most Imams and clerics of Islam have declared a jihad, a holy war, against the infidels of the world. And, that by killing an infidel, which is a command to all Muslims, they are assured of a place in heaven. If that's the case, can you give me the definition of an infidel?"

There was no disagreement with my statements and without hesitation, he replied, "Non-believers."

I responded, "So let me make sure I have this straight. All followers of Allah have been commanded to kill everyone who is not of your faith so they can go to heaven, is that correct?"

The expression on his face changed from one of authority to that of a little boy who had just gotten caught with his hand in the cookie jar. He sheepishly replied, "'Yes.'"

I then stated, "Well sir, I have a real problem trying to imagine the Pope commanding all Catholics to kill those of your faith, or of Dr. Stanley ordering all Protestants to do the same in order to go to heaven."

The Imam was speechless.

I concluded by saying, "I also have a problem with being your friend when you and your brother clerics are telling your followers to kill me. Let me ask you a question. Would you rather have your Allah who tells you to kill me in order to go to heaven or my Jesus who tells me to love you because I am going to heaven and He wants you to be with me?"

You could have heard a pin drop as the Imam hung his head in shame.

· ·

(21) Our Church Needs No Money!

We have discovered a way for a church to function without money. Will you cooperate?

Each member will come to church during the week with a broom and mop to keep their area of the church presentable. Then a paid janitor will not be needed.

Each member will bring materials and tools to repair and remodel the building. Here we can really save money.

Each one must agree to spend at least a year as a missionary at his own expense on some foreign field; thus no missionary offerings will be necessary.

Each member will go to school for the required years and fulfill all the required qualifications to become a pastor. Then he will take his turn preaching, leading the service, conducting the funerals and weddings, visiting the sick and keeping up with the office work. Thus, there would be no need for paying a preacher.

Isn't that a great idea? But, would you really want it that way?

Yes, the church needs no money, but the church does need you! You are the one who uses the lights, the heat, the water and the music and so on. Perhaps it is better to do it God's way; by giving God your tithe, your 10% and the church can operate in the scriptural way. So, which will it be?

. . . .

(22) <u>A little two-letter word 'UP!'</u>

There is a two-letter word that perhaps has more meaning than any other two-letter word, and that is 'U-P.' It's easy to understand 'UP,' meaning toward the sky or at the top of the list, but ...

* when we waken in the morning, why do we 'wake UP?' And at a meeting, why does a topic 'come UP?' And why do we 'speak UP?' and why are officers 'UP for election?' And why is it 'UP to the secretary' to 'write UP' a report?

We 'call UP' our friends, we use it to 'brighten UP' a room, 'polish UP' the silver, we 'warm UP' the leftovers, and 'clean UP' the kitchen.

From 'SPAM' to BALONEY

And at other times this little word has a special meaning. People 'stir UP' trouble, 'line UP' for tickets; 'work UP' an appetite, and 'think UP' excuses.
And to be dressed is one thing, but to be 'dressed UP' is something special.

And this is confusing...A drain must be 'opened UP' because it is 'stopped UP.' We 'open UP' a store in the morning but we 'close it UP' at night. To be knowledgeable of the proper use of 'UP' we need to 'look UP' the word in the dictionary. This little word 'UP' takes 'UP' about ¼ of a page and the definitions 'add UP' to about thirty.

- if you are 'UP to it' you might try 'building UP' a list of the many ways 'UP' is used. It will 'take UP' a lot of your time, but if you don't 'give UP' you may 'wind UP' with a hundred or more. And finally, when it threatens to rain, we say it is 'clouding UP;' when the sun comes out we say it is 'clearing UP' but when it rains it 'wets UP' the earth. When it doesn't rain for awhile, things 'dry UP'...we could go on and on but I think I'll 'wrap it UP' for now because my 'time is UP' so I'll just 'SHUT-UP!'

CHAPTER 21

HOLIDAY stories

(1) <u>Thanksgiving at Christmas...</u>

If you have food in the refrigerator, clothes on your back, a roof overhead and a place to sleep... you are richer than 75% of the people in this world.

If you have money in the bank, money in your wallet and spare change in a dish someplace... you are among the top 8% of the world's wealthy.

If you woke up this morning with more health than illness...you are more blessed than the million who will not survive this week.

If you have never experienced the danger of battle, the loneliness of imprisonment, the agony of torture or the pangs of starvation... you are ahead of 500 million people in the world.

If you can attend a church meeting without fear of harassment, arrest, torture or death... you are more blessed than 3 billion people in the world.

If you can hold someone's hand, hug them or even touch them on the shoulder... you are blessed because you can offer a healing touch.

(2) Independence Day…The Fourth of July

Have you ever wondered what happened to the 56 men who signed the Declaration of Independence?

- Five signers were captured by the British as traitors and tortured before they died.
- Twelve had their homes ransacked and burned.
- Two lost their sons serving in the Revolutionary Army, and another had two sons captured.
- Nine of the 56 fought and died from wounds or hardships of the Revolutionary War. They signed and they pledged their lives, their fortunes, and their sacred honor. What kind of men were they?
- Twenty-four were lawyers and jurists, eleven were merchants, nine were farmers and large plantation owners. They were men of means and well educated, yet, they signed the Declaration of Independence knowing full well that the penalty would be death if they were captured.

Carl Braxton of Virginia sold his home and property to pay his debt and died in rags.
Thomas McKean was forced to move his family almost constantly, serving in Congress without pay while his family was kept in hiding.
Nelson's home was destroyed and he died bankrupt.
Francis Lewis had his home and property destroyed, his wife was jailed and died within a few months.
Eight other signers had their properties looted by soldiers or vandals.
John Hart was driven from his wife's bedside as she was dying and their 13 children fled for their lives. For more than a year he lived in forests and caves as his fields and gristmill were laid waste. Upon returning home, he found his wife dead and his children had vanished. A few weeks later John died from exhaustion and a broken heart.

And there are many other stories of sacrifice that can be told about the American Revolution. These men mentioned were not wild-eyed rabble-rousing ruffians. They were soft-spoken men of means and education. They had security, but they valued liberty more.

They gave you and me a free and independent America. Yes, so many of us take our liberties so much for granted, but we shouldn't. So, let's take a few minutes while we are enjoying our 4th of July holiday and silently thank these patriots; it's not too much to ask considering the price they paid. And never forget:

The Fourth of July means more than beer, picnics and baseball games!

• •

(3) The folded napkin meant 'I'm coming back'...   John 20:1-7

In the dark of the first Easter Sunday morning, Mary Magdalene came to the tomb and found the stone rolled away from the entrance. Later on in the account it says, *"She also noticed the linen wrappings lying there, while the cloth that had covered Jesus' head was folded up and lying to the side."* Is that important? It certainly is.

In order to understand the significance of the folded napkin, you have to know a little bit about the Hebrew tradition of that day. The folded napkin dealt with the Master and Servant and every Jewish boy knew this tradition. When the servant set the dinner table for the master, he made sure that it was exactly the way the master wanted it. The table was furnished perfectly and then the servant would wait, just out of sight, until the master had finished eating. The servant would not dare touch the table until the master was finished.

Now, when the master was done eating, he would rise, wipe his hands and mouth with the napkin and toss it on to the table. The servant would then know it was time to clear the table. In those days, the wadded napkin meant, "*I'm done.*" But if the master got up from the table, folded his napkin and laid it beside his plate, the servant knew that the folded napkin meant, *"I'm not finished yet."* The folded napkin meant, *"I'm coming back!"*

And so He is!

· ·

(4) <u>I Remember Nancy</u>... (Easter story)

I remember Nancy Flurrie. It was 1953 and we were both in the 2nd grade. I was the 'smart' one, and she was the 'dumb' one - or so I thought. I made life a living hell for that poor girl and she just took it.

Gentle and shy, Nancy was about 11-years-old because it had taken her a few years to reach the 2nd grade. She had difficulty reading and writing. All the kids made fun of her, especially me. Nancy would just stand there, avoid making eye contact with me and the tears would roll down her cheeks. Cruel and clever, I was able to manipulate the crowd so that the taunts of the audience would increase Nancy's misery and shame. We called her stupid, ugly, smelly, dirty but Nancy never fought back. This was a riot to her tormentors.

Then one day something changed. I went to a Bible class and Nancy was there, sitting by herself in the back of the room. The Bible story was about the trial of Jesus, who had been sent to King Herod. The story was being told by Father McKeever, teacher of the class. He became quite animated in his wonderful Irish fashion. He told us how the Son of God was spat on, beaten and kicked.

Then Father McKeever made us wince as he described the crown of thorns being pushed and pounded into the flesh and bone of our Lord's skull. I could feel the nails, piercing His wrists and feet. Our teacher repeated the mocking words that had been hurled at the 'Holy One.' He paused for a moment, his eyes filled with tears, and he looked at Nancy, in the back of the room, all alone with her head bowed. A look of intense sorrow passed over his features. And then his steel blue eyes focused on me.

I felt like I was the only one in the room and this decent, kind man of God was speaking ... only to me. *"How would it feel to be all alone and innocent?"* he asked softly, in his rich Irish accent. *"How would it feel to be hauled in front of your enemies, dirty, unloved and with no one to protect you?"*

My eyes welled up with tears because when I was 7-years-old, I loved Jesus only a little more than I loved Father McKeever. I understood the message immediately! I was overwhelmed. I looked back at Nancy, in her dirty clothes that I helped smear and I felt so ashamed. It seemed as though everyone had missed the point that pierced my heart that day. I suddenly saw myself as a seven-years-old in Herod's courtyard, mocking and striking Jesus. In my mind's eye, I saw Jesus lift His head and look at me - my 7-year-old heart broke.

As I sat there stunned, I knew I would never be the same again. Then I gathered my things, stood up and walked to the back of the room. I pulled a chair up next to Nancy and sat down. With hands shaking and incredible sorrow in my heart, I reached over and took Nancy's hand. She looked at me with her eyes, her big eyes that were perfectly round, and her mouth was in the shape of an 'o.'

"Nancy", I began with a trembling voice. *"I want you to be my friend, my very best friend!"* Nancy looked at me for what seemed a very long time. The room was silent. I noticed that Nancy's eyes were an incredibly beautiful shade of blue, framed with lovely dark lashes. Her lips moved and she smiled, framing white, perfect teeth. For the very first time, I noticed how pretty she really was!

After that day, I tripped over myself to become Nancy's friend and protector. I spent the rest of that year with skinned knees, bruises and a few bloody noses. My family moved away the next summer and I never saw Nancy or Father McKeever again. But both of them have lived in my heart ever since. Nancy taught me about forgiveness and Father McKever taught me about redemption. *Wherever you both are, I thank God for putting you in my life!*

. . . .

(5) <u>Bad Parrot</u>:

    A young preacher man received a parrot as a gift. The parrot had a bad attitude and an equally bad vocabulary. The young preacher man tried and tried to change the bird's attitude by continually quoting scripture and speaking nicely to people.

    After quite some time and feeling quite exasperated, the preacher yelled very loudly at the parrot and the parrot yelled very loudly back at him. As he continued to yell and shake the parrot the bird became angrier and ruder. In desperation, he grabbed the bird by the neck and threw it into the freezer. For a few minutes the bird squawked, kicked and screamed. Then suddenly there was total silence; not even a peep.

    Fearing he had done serious damage to the parrot, the young preacher man quickly opened the freezer door as the bird stepped out to the welcoming hand. The parrot apologetically began, *"Sir,* the parrot said, *"if I have offended you by my rude language, I am truly sorry and repent of my sinful actions and I will do everything I can to correct my terrible behavior."*

    The preacher man was stunned at the change in the bird's behavior. He was about to ask the parrot what had made such a dramatic change in his behavior when the bird said, *"Would you mind telling me what that turkey did?"*

Happy Thanksgiving

(6) The 'W' in Christmas

Every December, I vow to make Christmas a calm and peaceful experience. I cut back on non-essential obligations such as extensive card writing, endless baking, decorating and even over spending on presents. Yet I still found myself exhausted, unable to appreciate family moments and, of course, the true meaning of Christmas.

My son, Nicky, was in kindergarten that year and it was an exciting season for a six-year-old. For weeks he'd been memorizing songs for his school's *'winter pageant.'* I didn't have the heart to tell him I'd be working the night of the production. Unwilling to miss his shining moment, I spoke with his teacher who assured me there'd be a dress rehearsal the morning of the presentation. All parents unable to attend that evening were welcome to come then. Fortunately, Nicky seemed happy with the compromise.

The morning of the dress rehearsal came and I arrived ten minutes early. I found a spot on the cafeteria floor and sat down. I saw several other parents in the room quietly scampering to their seats. As I waited, the students were led into the room by their teacher and sat cross-legged on the floor. Each group, one by one, rose to perform their song.

Year ago, the public school system stopped referring to the winter holiday as *'Christmas.'* I didn't expect anything other than fun, commercial entertainment, songs of reindeer, Santa Claus, snowflakes and good cheer. Therefore, when my son's class rose to sing, *'Christmas Love,'* I was slightly surprised by its bold title. My Nicky was aglow, as were all of his classmates, adorned in fuzzy mittens, red sweaters and bright snowcaps upon their heads. Classmates in the front row center stage held up large letters, one by one, to spell out the title of the song. As the class would sing ... *'C' is for Christmas,* a child would hold up the letter 'C' Then *'H' is for happy* and on and on until each child held a letter that presented the complete message, *'CHRISTMAS LOVE.'*

The performance was going smoothly until we noticed a small quiet girl in the front row holding the letter 'M' upside down. She was totally unaware that the letter 'W' appeared instead of a 'M'. The audience of 1st thru 6th graders snickered at the little girls' mistake. But, she had no idea they were laughing at her, so she stood tall and proud holding her 'M' upside down.

Although many teachers tried to hush the children, the laughter continued until the last letter was raised. And then we all saw it together. A hush then came over the audience and eyes began to moisten. In that instant, we understood the reason we were there. We understood again why we celebrate the holiday in the first place; we understood *"the reason for the season."*

For when the last letter was held high, the message read loud and clear; *'CHRIST WAS LOVE'* and I believe He still is!

. . . .

(7) Christmas Miracle at the 'Big-Wheel' Truck Stories

In September 1960, I woke up one morning with six hungry babies and just a couple of dollars in my pocket. The boys ranged from 3 months to 7 years and their sister was two. Their father was gone; he had never been much more than a presence they feared. Whenever they heard his tires crunch on the gravel driveway, they would scramble to hide under their beds. He did manage to leave a few dollars each week to buy groceries. Now that he had decided to leave, there would be no more beatings, but no food either. If there was a welfare system in effect in southern Indiana at that time, I certainly knew nothing about it. I scrubbed the kids and loaded them into the rusty old '51 Chevy and drove off to find a job. The seven of us went to every factory, store and restaurant in our small town. The last place we went to was a truck stop called *'The Big Wheel.'* An old lady named *'Granny'* owned the place and she peeked out of the window from time to time at all those kids. She needed someone on the 'graveyard

From 'SPAM' to BALONEY

shift'- 11 o'clock at night till seven in the morning. She paid $2.00 an hour and I could start right away.

That night when the little ones and I knelt to say our prayers, we all thanked God for finding mommy a job. And so I started working at *The Big Wheel.*' As the weeks went by, heating bills added a strain to my meager wage and the tires on my old Chevy had begun to leak. I had to fill them with air on the way to work and fill them again every morning before I could go home. One bleak fall morning, I dragged myself to the car to go home and found four tires in the back seat. New tires! There was no note, no nothing; just those beautiful brand new tires. Had angels taken up residence in Indiana? I wondered.

I was now working six nights instead of five and it still wasn't enough. Christmas was coming and I knew there wouldn't be money to buy toys for the kids. I found a can of red paint and started repairing and painting some of the old toys. Then I hid them in the basement so there would be something for Santa to deliver on Christmas morning.

On Christmas Eve, the usual customers were drinking coffee at *'The Big Wheel.'* There were some truckers, Les, Frank and Jim and a state trooper named Joe. A few musicians were hanging around after a gig at the Legion and were dropping coins in the pinball machine. The regulars all just sat around and talked through the wee hours of the morning and then departed for home before the sunrise.

When seven o'clock arrived Christmas morning, it was time for me to leave and I hurried to the car. I was hoping to get home before the kids would wake up so I could bring the presents from the basement to place under the tree. While getting my car keys, I glanced into a side window and my jaw dropped in amazement and wonder. My old battered Chevy was filled to the top with gift boxes in all shapes and sizes. I quickly opened the driver's door and bowed my head in a prayer of thanksgiving. I drove back through empty streets as the sun slowly rose on the most amazing Christmas

Day of my life. I was sobbing with gratitude and I will never forget the joy on the faces of my little ones that precious morning.

Yes, there were angels in Indiana that long-ago December and they all hung out at *'The Big Wheel'* Truck Stop!

. . . .

(8) <u>Our God Is Awesome</u>! For example...
- the eggs of a potato bug hatch in 7 days.
- those of a canary in 14 days.
- those of a barnyard hen in 21 days.

And the eggs of ducks and geese hatch in 28 days, except those of the Mallard Duck which happens to be 35 days!

- the eggs of the parrot and the ostrich hatch in 42 days. (And notice all are divisible by 7, the number of days in a week)
- Wrinkled was not one of the things I wanted to Be when I grew up.
- Procrastinate Now!
- Stupidity is not a handicap; park elsewhere!
- He who dies with the most toys is nonetheless DEAD.
- A picture is worth a thousand words, but it uses up three thousand times the memory

. . . .

(9) <u>Think you are having a Bad Day?</u>

A woman came home to find her husband in the kitchen shaking frantically, almost in a dancing frenzy, with some kind of wire running from his waist towards the electric kettle. Intending to jolt him away from the deadly current, she ran outside and grabbed a handy plank of wood. She then smacked him with it breaking his arm in two places. Up to that moment, he had been happily listening to his iPod.

Are You OK Now? - No?
Two animal rights defenders were protesting the cruelty of sending pigs to a slaughterhouse in Bonn, Germany. Suddenly, all two thousand pigs broke loose and escaped through a broken fence. A maddening stampede ensued and the two helpless protesters were trampled to death.

What? STILL having a Bad Day?
Iraqi terrorist Khay Rahnajet didn't pay enough postage on a letter bomb. It came back with 'Return to Sender' stamped on it. Forgetting it was the bomb; he opened it and was blown to bits. God is good!

. . . .

(10) <u>If God Should Go On Strike</u>*('Thanksgiving')*

How good it is that God above has never gone on strike,
Because He was not treated fair in things He didn't like.
If only once He'd given up and said, "That's it! I'm through!
I've had enough of those on earth, so this is what I'll do.

I'll give My orders to the sun – cut off the heat supply!
And to the moon, give no more light and run the oceans dry.
Then just to make things really rough and put the pressure on,
Turn off the vital oxygen, till every breath is gone."

You know He would be justified if fairness was the game,
For no one has been more abused or met with more distain
Than God, and yet He carries on, supplying you and me,
With all the factors of His grace and everything for free.

Men say they want a better deal and so on strike they go,
But what a deal we've given God to whom all things we owe.
We don't care who we hurt to gain the things we like,
But what a mess we'd all be in if God should go on strike!

· ·

(11) <u>Good Friday in the Garden</u> (Easter)

    My husband, John, said to me, as he left to go to work at his barber shop, *"Freda, this looks like a good day to plant those seeds."* So, that afternoon, in the warmth of the sunshine, I knelt in the garden planting sweet-pea seeds.

    It was Good Friday and the hour when a lot of people from town were at church. I was still recovering from a serious operation. The doctor didn't think I would walk again. However, I could get around with the help of a walker but I felt slow, awkward and frustrated. My complete recovery seemed so slow and so very far away.

    "Why is it called 'Good Friday?' I mused. For Jesus, it had been a day of sadness and pain. Crawling slowly on my knees, I poked a finger into the earth, dropped in a seed and then covered it. *"Soon shoots will be popping through the dirt,"* I told myself. I pictured them in full bloom and could almost smell their fragrance.

    In my garden I felt very near to God. I thought of Christ praying in the Garden of Gethsemane. As I struggled on my knees, my thoughts travelled with Jesus to His trial and then to Golgotha where He suffered on the cross. I remembered His cry, *"It is finished!"* I, too, had suffered and lingered near death after brain surgery.

Only my faith and my family had sustained me. I felt at peace working in the soil and strengthened by it all. Tucking in the last seed, I stood and gazed proudly at my neat row and said, *'It is finished.'*

My thoughts remained on Good Friday as I walked to the house. At the porch, I glanced back at my garden. Then I saw… standing among the rows…was my walker. I gasped. I had walked without it and I haven't needed it since…Yes, GOOD FRIDAY!

Chapter 22

Inspirational Stories

(1) God's Hall of Fame (Heb. Ch. 11)

> Your name may not appear down here in this world's Hall of Fame,
> In fact, you may be so unknown that no one knows your name.
> The Oscars here may pass you by and neon lights of blue,
> But if you love and serve the Lord then I have news for you!
> This Hall of Fame is only good as long as time shall be,
> But keep in mind, God's Hall of Fame is for eternity!
> To have your name inscribed up there is greater, yes, by far,
> Than all the Halls of Fame down here and every man-made star.
> Here on earth they soon forget the heroes of the past;
> They cheer like mad until you fall and that's how long you last.
> But God, He never does forget for in His Hall of Fame,
> By just believing in His Son, inscribed you'll find your name.
> I tell you friend, I wouldn't trade my name however small,
> For one that's written beyond the stars, in God's celestial Hall,
> Nor for every famous name on earth or glory that they share,
> I'd rather be an unknown here and have my name up there!

(2) <u>A Reason for Life</u>…
>I don't know how to say it but somehow it seems to me,
>That maybe we are stationed where God wants us to be.
>This little place I'm filling is the reason for my birth,
>And when I do just what I do is my reason on this earth.
>
>If God wanted otherwise I reckon He'd have made
>Me just a little different of a worse or better grade.
>And since God knows and understands everything you see,
>I fancy that He placed me here just where He wanted me!
>
>Sometimes I get to thinkin' as my labors I review,
>That I would like a higher place with greater things to do.
>But I came to the conclusion when the envying is stilled,
>The place to which God sent me is the place He wanted filled.
>
>So I plod along and struggle in the hope when day is through,
>That I have been really necessary in the things God wants to do.
>And there isn't any service I've been given that I can scorn,
>For it may be just the reason God allowed me to be born!

. . . .

(3) <u>God's wife?</u>

A little boy was standing in front of a shoe store, barefoot, shivering and very cold. A certain lady came by and said to him, "My little fellow, why are you staring so intently in the window?"

The little boy said, "I was asking God to give me a pair of those warm boots." The lady took the boy inside and purchased a pair of boots and some socks for the boy. Then she asked the clerk for a basin of water and a towel. She took the boy to the back of the store, removed her own hat and gloves, and washed and dried the little feet.

By this time the clerk returned with the boots and socks which she put on those little feet. She then patted him on the head and said, "No doubt, little fellow, you will be more comfortable now!"

As the little guy turned to go, he took the lady by the hand, looked up into her face and said to her... **Are you God's wife?**

. . . .

(4) <u>The Bird Cage</u>...

There once was a man named George Thomas who was pastoring in a small New England town. One Easter Sunday morning he came to the church carrying a rusty, bent, old bird cage and set it on the pulpit. Several eyebrows were raised and, as if in response, the pastor began to speak. "I was walking through town yesterday when I saw a young boy coming toward me, swinging this bird cage. On the bottom of the cage were three little wild birds, shivering with cold and fright."

The pastor said, "I stopped the lad and asked, what you got there, son?"

The boy said, "Just some old birds."

Then I said to him, "What will you do with them?" The boy said he would take them home, tease them a bit, pull out some of their feathers and make them fight with each other; just for fun, you know.

Then I said, "But you'll get tired of those birds sooner or later, and what will you do then?"

He said, "I got cats and they like birds so I'll feed them to them."

The pastor continued by saying he offered to buy the birds and after some dickering they struck up a deal for $25 and off the boy ran with the money. Then the pastor told how he walked over to the edge of the field and opened the cage door and coaxed the birds out to freedom. Off they flew to freedom.

Then he began his sermon... "One day Satan and Jesus were having a conversation. Satan had just come from the Garden of

Eden, and he was gloating and boasting. "Yes sir", he said, "I just caught the world full of people down there. Set me a trap; used bait I knew they couldn't resist and got them all!"

"Well, what are you going to do with them?" Jesus asked.

"Oh, I'm gonna have fun with 'em; gonna teach 'em how to marry and divorce each other, to hate and abuse each other, to invent guns and bombs and kill each other. I'm really gonna have fun with them!"

"And what are you gonna do with them then?" Jesus asked. And Satan replied, "Then I'll kill them."

Jesus then said to Satan, "Well, how much do you want for them?"

Satan answered, "Oh, you don't want those people. They ain't no good! They'll just hate you; they'll spit on you, curse you and kill you. You don't want those people."

"How much?" Satan looked at Jesus and sneered, "All your tears and all your blood." So, Jesus went to the cross and paid the price. The pastor picked up the cage and opened the door for the congregation to see. He then said, "And purchased our redemption so we can go free!"

. . . .

(5) A Lesson in heart...

My little 10-year-old Sarah was born with a muscle missing in her foot so she wears a brace all the time. She came home one day to tell me she had competed in *'field day.'* That's where they have lots of races and other competitive events.

Because of her leg support, my mind raced as I tried to think of words to encourage Sarah, something I could say to her about not let this get her down. But before I could get a word out, she said, "Daddy, I won two of the races!" I couldn't believe it! And then Sarah said, "But I had an advantage." Ah, I knew it. I thought she must have been given a head start or some other physical advantage. But before I could say anything, she said, "Daddy, I didn't get a head start. **My advantage was I had to try harder, and I did, and I won!**

. . . .

(6) <u>Wesley Tip</u>...**Did you know?** John Wesley stood only 5'3" all and weighed 128 pounds. (1 Samuel 16:7)
<u>Life Tip</u>... If at first you do succeed, try something harder.
<u>Student Tip</u>... There are times when silence is golden, other times it is just plain cowardly.(Read Ecc. 3:1 / 7b)
<u>Funny Bone</u>... A boy was watching his father, a pastor, write a sermon. The young lad asked, "Dad, how do you know what to write?" His father replied, "Why son, God tells me what to write." The boy answered, "Then why do you keep crossing things out?"

. . . .

(7) <u>Don't quit!</u>...

    When things go wrong as they sometimes will,
    When the road you're trudging seems all uphill,
    When the funds are low and the debts are high,
    And you want to smile, but you have to sigh,
    When care is pressing you down a bit,
    Rest if you must, but don't you quit!

    And you never can tell how close you are;
    Eternity may be near when it seems so far.
    And many a failure is turned about,
    When you don't quit, but stick it out.
    So stick to the fight when you're hardest hit.
    It's when things seem worse that you must not quit!
    When care is pressing you down a bit,
    Rest if you must but don't you quit!

(8) <u>A TRUE STORY</u> by Malcolm Forbes
The will of God will never take you where the Grace of God will not protect you.

There are **five things that you cannot recover in life:**
1. The Stone................after it's thrown,
2. The Word...............after it's said,
3. The Occasion..........after it's missed, and
4. The Time................after it's gone.
5. A Person................after they die

. . . .

(9) <u>Irish Friendship Week</u>...

His name was 'Fleming' and he was a poor Scottish farmer. One day while tending to his farm chores, he heard a cry for help coming from a nearby swamp. He immediately dropped his tools and ran to see if he could help. There he saw a young lad mired in muck up to his waste and sinking. He was screaming for help as Farmer Fleming saved the young lad from certain death.

The next day, a fancy carriage pulled up to the Scotsman's humble farm house. Out stepped an elegantly dressed nobleman and introduced himself as the father of the lad that farmer Fleming had saved. "I want to repay you," said the nobleman, "You saved my son's life."

The Scottish farmer replied, "No, I can't accept payment for what I did," and waved the Nobleman off.

About that time the farmer's own son came to the door of the humble abode and the Nobleman said, "Is that your son?"

"Yes," the farmer proudly replied.

"Well then" said the Nobleman, "I'll make you a deal. Let me provide him with the level of education my own son will enjoy. And, I'm sure if the lad is anything like his father, he'll no doubt grow to be a man of whom we'll both be proud." And that he did!

In time, farmer Fleming's son attended the very best schools and soon he graduated from St. Mary' Hospital Medical school in London. He went on to become known throughout the world as the noted Sir Alexander Fleming and the discoverer of penicillin.

Years later, the same Nobleman's son who was saved from the swamp, was stricken with pneumonia. What save his life this time was penicillin. The name of the Nobleman was Lord Randolph Churchill and **the son was Sir Winston Churchill**.

Now you know the rest of the story!

• •

(10) **Carl was a quiet man** who didn't talk much. He always greeted you with a big smile and a firm handshake. But after living in our neighborhood for over 50 years, no one could really say they knew him very well.

Before his retirement, he took the bus to work each morning. The lone sight of him walking down the street often worried us. He had a slight limp from a bullet wound received in WWII. Watching him, we worried that although he had survived WWII, he may not make it through our changing uptown neighborhood with its ever-increasing random violence, gangs, and drug activity. When he saw the flyer at our local church asking for volunteers to care for the gardens behind the minister's residence, he responded in his characteristically unassuming manner. Without fanfare, he quickly volunteered.

Carl was well into his 87th year when the very thing we always feared finally happened. He had just finished watering the garden when three gang members approached him. Ignoring their attempt to intimidate him, Carl simply asked, "Would you like a drink from the hose?"

The tallest and toughest-looking of the three said, "Yeah, sure," with a malevolent little smile. As Carl offered the hose to him, the other two men grabbed Carl's arm and threw him to the ground. As the hose snaked crazily over the ground, dousing everything in its way, Carl's assailants stole his retirement watch and wallet and then fled. Carl tried to get up but he had landed on his bad leg. He lay there trying to gather himself as the minister came running to help him. Although the minister had witnessed the attack from his window, he couldn't get there fast enough to stop the attack.

"Carl, are you okay? Are you hurt?" the minister kept asking as he helped Carl to his feet.

Carl just passed a hand over his brow and sighed, shaking his head. "Just some punk kids. I hope they'll wise-up someday."

His wet clothes clung to his slight frame as he bent to pick up the hose. He adjusted the nozzle again and started to water. Confused and a little concerned, the minister asked, "Carl, what are you doing?"

"I've got to finish my watering. It's been very dry lately," was the calm reply. Satisfied that Carl was all right, the minister could only marvel. Carl was a man from a different time and place.

A few weeks later the three men returned. Just like before, their threats went unchallenged. Carl again offered them a drink from his hose. This time they didn't rob him. They wrenched the hose from his hand and drenched him head to foot in the icy water. When they finished humiliating him, they sauntered off down the street and made catcalls and cursed at him. Laughing so hard, they even fell over one another at the hilarityy of what they had just done. Carl just watched them awhile and then turned towards the warmth giving sun, picked up the hose and continued watering.

The summer was quickly fading into fall. Carl was doing some tilling when he was startled by the sudden approach of someone behind him. He stumbled and fell into some evergreen branches. As he struggled to regain his footing, Carl turned to see the tall leader of his tormentors reaching down for him. He braced himself for the expected attack. "Don't worry old man, I'm not gonna hurt you this time."

The young man spoke softly, still offering the tattooed and scarred hand to Carl. As he helped Carl get up, the man pulled a crumpled bag from his pocket and handed it to Carl.

"What's this?" Carl asked.

"It's your stuff," the man explained. "It's your stuff back, even the money in your wallet."

"I don't understand," Carl said. "Why would you help me now?"

The man shifted his feet, seemingly embarrassed and ill at ease. "I learned something from you," he said. "I ran with that gang and hurt people like you. We picked you because you were old and we knew we could do it. But every time we came and did something to you, instead of yelling and fighting back, you tried to give us a drink. You didn't hate us for hating you but kept showing love against our hate."

He stopped for a moment. "I couldn't sleep after we stole your stuff, so here it is back." He paused for another awkward moment not knowing what more there was to say. "That bag's my way of saying thanks for straightening me out, I guess." And with that, he walked off down the street.

Carl looked down at the sack in his hands and gingerly opened it. He took out his retirement watch and put it back on his wrist. Opening his wallet, he checked for his wedding photo. He gazed for a moment at the young bride that still smiled back at him from all those years ago.

He died one cold day after Christmas that winter. Many people attended his funeral in spite of the weather. The minister noticed one particular tall, young man that he didn't know sitting quietly in a distant corner of the church. The minister spoke of Carl's garden as a lesson in life. In a voice made thick with unshed tears, he said, "Do your best and make your garden as beautiful as you can. We will never forget Carl and his garden."

The following spring another flyer was posted. It read: "Person needed to care for Carl's garden." The flyer went unnoticed by the busy parishioners until one day when a knock was heard at the minister's office door.

Opening the door, the minister saw a pair of scarred and tattooed hands holding the flyer. "I believe this is my job, if you'll have me," the young man said. The minister recognized him as the same young man who had returned the stolen watch and wallet to Carl. He knew that Carl's kindness had turned this man's life around.

As the minister handed him the keys to the garden shed, he said, "Yes, go take care of Carl's garden and honor him." The man went to work and, over the next several years, he tended the flowers and vegetables just as Carl had done. During that time, he went to college, married and became a prominent member of the community. But he never forgot his promise to Carl's memory and kept the garden as beautiful as he thought Carl would have kept it.

One day he approached the new minister and told him that he couldn't care for the garden any longer. He explained with a shy and happy smile, "My wife just had a baby boy last night and she's bringing him home on Saturday."

"Well, congratulations!" said the minister, as he was handed the garden shed keys. "That's wonderful! What's the baby's name?"

"Carl," he replied. That's the whole gospel simply stated.

· ·

(11) <u>Love people and use things; not love things and use people!</u>

A loving wife and mother of three children had recently completed her college degree. The last class she had to take was Sociology. She was so thankful to God for having such a tremendously inspiring Christian teacher.

From 'SPAM' to BALONEY

Her teacher's last assignment was called 'Smile'; go out and smile at three unusual people and document their reactions. This will be easy she said to herself and kept watching for the right moment.

Shortly thereafter, she was standing in line at McDonalds with her husband and oldest son. Suddenly she noticed that everyone in line began to back away, even her husband. She did not move but turned to see why they had moved.

As she turned around she was looking into the eyes of a horribly bad smelling little man who smiled at her and she smiled back. The first thing she noticed was the beautiful sky-blue color of his eyes and then noticed in his eyes, 'God's light' as he seemed to search for acceptance. She thought this was certainly an unusual opportunity for her class assignment.

The little man said to her 'Good-day' as he counted in his hands a few coins for a coffee. She watched silently as tears of God's love overpowered her with compassion. She knew he could only afford the coffee but it was a place to be inside where it was warm. She just wanted to reach out and hug the little man as God's love came over her but by now all eyes in the restaurant were on her and judging her every action.

In her report she wrote as follows. "I smiled at the young lady behind the counter and ordered an extra breakfast on a separate tray. I took the tray around the corner to the table where the little man was sitting. I placed the tray on his table and then placed my hand on top of his cold, shriveled hand. 'I did not do this for you; this is God's gift to you, to give you hope for today,' she told him."

"I was crying" she wrote, "as I walked over to the table where my husband and son were sitting. We held hands for a moment and we both knew that we had just witnessed God's amazing love and power that comes to us through the Gospel message."

She returned to college for her last class and handed in her report. The instructor read it and asked to share it with the whole class. It touched the people at McDonald's, her husband and son, her instructor and you and me.

Thus, this powerful message of God's love is available to all who are a member of God's family because His Holy Spirit abides within us. It is His *'Unconditional Acceptance'* that He has so graciously extended to us, that we are able to share with others... Life is short at best. Let us use our time wisely, and may we always remember to..

Love People and use things; not love things and use people!

....

(12) TWO HEROES IN ONE FAMILY

A half a century ago, the world has applauded John Glenn as a heart-stirring American hero. He lifted the nation's spirits when, as one of the original Mercury 7 astronauts, he was blasted alone into orbit around the Earth. The enduring affection for Mr. Glenn is so powerful that even today, people find themselves misting up at the sight of his face or the sound of his voice.

Recently there has been news coverage of the 50th anniversary of Glenn's flight into orbit. We are reminded that he remains America's unforgettable hero but John has never really bought that. Because the heroism he most cherishes is one that is seldom cheered. It belongs to the person he has known longer than anyone else in the world. That person is Annie Glenn, his wife for more than 68 years. He is 90 years old; she turned 92 on Friday.

John Glenn and Annie Castor first knew each other when, literally they shared a playpen. In New Concord, Ohio, their parents were good friends. And, of course, whenever the families were together, all the children played. John - the future Marine fighter pilot, the future test-pilot ace, the future astronaut - was pure gold from the start. He had what it takes to rise to the absolute pinnacle of American hero during the space race. Imagine what it meant to be the young John Glenn in the small confines of New Concord. Three-sport varsity athlete, most admired boy in town, Mr. Everything.

Annie Castor was bright, caring, talented, and possessed a generous of spirit. But she could talk only with the most excruciating of difficulty; it haunted her. She severe stuttering was categorized as an 85% disability - 85% of the time she could not manage to make words come out. When she tried to recite a poem in elementary school, Annie was laughed at. She was not able to speak on the telephone. She could not have a regular conversation with a friend yet John Glenn loved her. Even as a boy he was wise enough to understand that people who couldn't see past her stutter, were missing out on knowing a rare and wonderful girl. They married on April 6, 1943. As a military wife, she found that life could be quite hurtful as they moved around the country. She wrote: "I can remember some very painful experiences -- especially the ridicule."

In department stores, she wandered unfamiliar aisles trying to find the right section, embarrassed to ask salesclerks for help. In taxis, she would write destinations requests to the driver and she would point to menu items at restaurants. Being a fine musician, Annie would play the church organ as a way to make new friends in every community they lived.

She wrote: "Can you imagine living in the modern world and being afraid to use the telephone? Hello used to be so hard for me to say. I worried that my children would be injured and needing a doctor. Could I somehow find the words to get the right information conveyed on the phone?"

John, as a Marine aviator, flew 59 combat missions in World War II and 90 during the Korean War. Every time he was deployed, he said goodbye to Annie the same way. His last words would be: "I'm just going down to the corner store to get a pack of gum." Her reply would always be: "Don't be long."

On that February day in 1962 when the world held its breath and the Atlas rocket was about to propel him toward space, those were the words exchanged once again. And in 1998, when John went back to space aboard the shuttle Discovery, it was an understandably tense time for them. What if something happened to end their life together? Annie knew what he would say to her before boarding the shuttle. He did -- and this time John gave her a present to hold onto: A pack of gum. She carried it in a pocket next to her heart until he was safely home.

Many times she tried various treatments to cure her stuttering problem but none worked. But in 1973, she found a doctor in Virginia who ran an intensive program that could help her. Annie enrolled in the program and gave it her best effort. The miracle she and John had always wanted had finally arrived. At age 53, she was able to talk fluidly; not in brief, anxiety-ridden, agonizing bursts.

John has said that on the first day he heard her speak to him with confidence and clarity, he dropped to his knees to offer a prayer of gratitude. He wrote: "I saw Annie's perseverance and strength through the years and it just made me admire her and love her even more." He has heard thunderous ovations in countries around the globe for his own valor but his awe is reserved for Annie, and what she accomplished. "I don't know if I would have had the courage."

Annie's voice is so clear and steady, that now she regularly gives public talks. If you are fortunate enough to know the Glenn's, the sight and sound of them bantering and joking with each other and playfully finishing each others sentences is something that warms your heart and makes you thankful just to be in the same room.

Soon it will be the anniversary of the Mercury space shot and once again people will remember and will speak of the heroism of Glenn the astronaut. But if you ever find yourself at an event where the Glenn's are appearing and you want to see someone so brimming with pride and love that you may feel your own tears start to well up, wait until the moment that Annie stands to say a few words to the audience.

And as she begins, take a look at her husband's eyes.

· ·

(13) <u>THE GINGHAM DRESS</u>

<u>A lady in</u> a faded gingham dress and her husband wearing a homespun, threadbare suit stepped off the train in Boston. Without an appointment, they walked timidly into the Harvard University President's outer office. The secretary could tell in a moment that such backwoods, country hicks had no business at Harvard & probably didn't even deserve to be in Cambridge.

"We'd like to see the president," the man said softly.

"He'll be busy all day," the secretary snapped.

"We'll wait," the lady replied. For hours the secretary ignored them, hoping that the couple would finally become discouraged and go away. They didn't and the secretary grew frustrated and finally decided to disturb the president even though it was a chore she always regretted.

"Maybe if you see them for a few minutes, they'll leave," she said to him! He sighed in exasperation and nodded. Someone of his importance obviously didn't have the time to spend with them and he detested gingham dresses and homespun suits cluttering up his outer office.

The president, stern faced and with dignity, strutted toward the couple. The lady told him, "We had a son who attended Harvard for one year. He loved Harvard. He was happy here. But about a year ago, he was accidentally killed. My husband and I would like to erect a memorial to him somewhere on campus."

The president wasn't touched; he was shocked. "Madam," he said, gruffly, "we can't put up a statue for every person who attended Harvard and died. If we did, this place would look like a cemetery."

"Oh, no," the lady explained quickly. "We don't want to erect a statue. We thought we would like to give a building to Harvard."

The president rolled his eyes. He glanced at the gingham dress and homespun suit and then exclaimed, "A building! Do you have any earthly idea how much a building costs? We have over seven and a half million dollars in the physical buildings here at Harvard."

For a moment the lady was silent. The president was pleased. Maybe he could get rid of them now. The lady turned to her husband and said quietly, "Is that all it cost to start a university? Why don't we just start our own?" Her husband nodded. The president's face wilted in confusion and bewilderment.

Mr. and Mrs. Leland Stanford got up and walked away, traveling to Palo Alto, California where they established the university that bears their name, Stanford University, a memorial to a son that Harvard no longer cared about.

You can easily judge the character of others by how they treat those who they think can do nothing for them.

. . . .

(14) A Girl With An Apple

(This is a true story by Googling Herman Rosenblat. August 1942. Piotrkow, Poland)

The sky was gloomy that morning as we waited anxiously. All the men, women and children of Piotrkow's Jewish ghetto had been herded into a square as there was talk that they were being moved. My father had only recently died from typhus which had run rampant through the crowded ghetto. My greatest fear was that our family would be separated.

"Whatever you do," Isidore, my eldest brother, whispered to me, "don't tell them your age; say you're sixteen." I was tall for a boy of 11 so I could pull it off. That way I might be deemed valuable as a worker.

An SS man approached me, his boots clicking against the cobblestones. He looked me up and down and then asked my age. "Sixteen," I said. He directed me to the left where my three brothers and other healthy young men already stood. My mother was motioned to the right with the other women, children, sick and elderly people. I whispered to Isidore, "Why?" He didn't answer.

I ran to Mama's side and said I wanted to stay with her. "No," she said sternly. "Get away. Don't be a nuisance. Go with your brothers. "She had never spoken so harshly before. But I understood - she was protecting me. She loved me so much that, just this once, she pretended not to. It was the last I ever saw of her.

My brothers and I were transported in a cattle car to Germany. We arrived at the Buchenwald concentration camp one night later and were led into a crowded barrack. The next day, we were issued uniforms and identification numbers. "Don't call me Herman anymore," I said to my brothers, "Call me 94983."

I was put to work in the camp's crematorium, loading the dead into a hand-cranked elevator. I, too, felt dead. Hardened, I had become a number. Soon, my brothers and I were sent to Schlieben, one of Buchenwald's sub-camps near Berlin. One morning I thought I heard my mother's voice. "Son," she said softly but clearly, "I am going to send you an angel." Then I woke up. It was just a dream; a beautiful dream.

But in this place there could be no angels. There was only work. And hunger. And fear. A few days later, I was walking around the camp and around the barracks. I found myself alone near the barbed-wire fence where the guards could not easily see. On the other side of the fence, I spotted someone: a little girl with light, almost luminous curls. She was half-hidden behind a birch tree. I glanced around to make sure no one saw me. I called to her softly in German, "Do you have something to eat?" She didn't understand so I inched closer to the fence and repeated the question in Polish. She stepped forward. I was thin and gaunt, with rags wrapped around my feet but the girl looked unafraid. In her eyes, I saw life. She pulled an apple from her woolen jacket and threw it over the fence. I grabbed the fruit and as I started to run away, I heard her say faintly, "I'll see you tomorrow."

I returned to the same spot by the fence at the same time every day. She was always there with something for me to eat - a hunk of bread or, better yet, an apple. We didn't dare speak or linger. To be caught would mean death for us both. We didn't know anything about her, just a kind farm girl, except that she understood Polish. What was her name? Why was she risking her life for me? Hope was in such short supply and this girl on the other side of the fence gave me some, as nourishing in its way as the bread and apples.

Nearly seven months later, my brothers and I were crammed into a coal car and shipped to Theresienstadt camp in Czechoslovakia. "Don't return," I told the girl that day. "We're leaving." I turned toward the barracks and didn't look back, didn't even say good-bye to the little girl whose name I'd never learned, the girl with the apples.

We were in Theresienstadt for three months. The war was winding down and Allied forces were closing in, yet my fate seemed sealed. On May 10, 1945, I was scheduled to die in the gas chamber at 10:00 AM. In the quiet of dawn, I tried to prepare myself. So many times death seemed ready to claim me but somehow I'd survived. Now, it was over.

I thought of my parents. At least, I thought, we will be reunited. But at 8 A.M. there was a commotion. I heard shouts, and saw people running every which way through camp. I caught up with my brothers. Russian troops had liberated the camp! The gates swung open. Everyone was running, so I did also. Amazingly, all of my brothers had survived; I'm not sure how. But I knew that the girl with the apples had been the key to my survival.

In a place where evil seemed triumphant, one person's goodness had saved my life, had given me hope in a place where there was none. My mother had promised to send me an angel, and the angel had come.

Eventually I made my way to England where I was sponsored by a Jewish charity, put up in a hostel with other boys who had survived the Holocaust and trained in electronics. Then I came to America, where my brother Sam had already moved. I served in the U.S. Army during the Korean War and returned to New York City after two years.

By August 1957 I'd opened my own electronics repair shop. I was starting to settle in.

One day, my friend Sid who I knew from England called me; "I've got a date. She's got a Polish friend. Let's double date." A blind date? Nah, that wasn't for me. But Sid kept pestering me, and a few days later we headed up to the Bronx to pick up his date and her friend Roma. I had to admit, for a blind date this wasn't too bad. Roma was a nurse at a Bronx hospital. She was kind, smart and beautiful, too, with swirling brown curls and green, almond-shaped eyes that sparkled with life.

The four of us drove out to Coney Island. Roma was easy to talk to, easy to be with. Turned out she was wary of blind dates too! We were both just doing our friends a favor. We took a stroll on the boardwalk, enjoying the salty Atlantic breeze and then had dinner by the shore. I couldn't remember having a better time.

We piled back into Sid's car, Roma and I sharing the backseat. As European Jews who had survived the war, we were aware that much had been left unsaid between us. She broached the subject, "Where were you," she asked softly, "during the war?"

"The camps," I said, the terrible memories were still vivid, the irreparable loss. I had tried to forget. But you can never forget. She nodded. "My family was hiding on a farm in Germany, not far from Berlin," she told me. "My father knew a priest and he got us Aryan papers. "I imagined how she must have suffered too, fear, a constant companion. And yet here we were both survivors in a new world.

"There was a camp next to the farm," Roma continued. "I saw a boy there and I would throw him apples every day." What an amazing coincidence that she had helped some other boy. "What did he look like?" I asked.

"He was tall, skinny, and hungry. I must have seen him every day for six months." My heart was racing. I couldn't believe it. This couldn't be.

"Did he tell you one day not to come back because he was leaving Schlieben?" Roma looked at me in amazement. "Yes!" "That was me!" I was ready to burst with joy and awe, flooded with emotions. I couldn't believe it, my angel! "I'm not letting you go," I said to Roma. And in the back of the car on that blind date, I proposed to her. I didn't want to wait.

"You're crazy!" she said. But she invited me to meet her parents for Shabbat dinner the following week.

There was so much I looked forward to learning about Roma, but the most important things I always knew: her steadfastness, her goodness. For many months, in the worst of circumstances, she had come to the fence and given me hope. Now that I'd found her again, I could never let her go.

That day, she said yes. And I kept my word. After nearly 50 years of marriage, two children and three grandchildren, I have never let her go.

Herman Rosenblat of Miami Beach, Florida

This story is being made into a movie called The Fence.

(15) <u>The Red Umbrella</u>

As the drought continued for what seemed an eternity, a small community of Midwest farmers was in a quandary as to what to do. The rain was important not only in order to keep the crops healthy but also to sustain the townspeople's very way of living. As the problem became more urgent, the local church felt it was time to get involved. They planned a prayer meeting in order to ask for rain.

In what seemed a vague remembrance of an old Native American ritual, the people began to show up. The pastor soon arrived and watched as the congregation continued to file in. He slowly circulated from group to group as he made his way to the front in order to officially begin the meeting. Everyone he encountered was visiting across the aisle and enjoyed the opportunity to socialize with their friends. As the pastor finally secured his place in front of the flock, his thoughts were on the importance of quieting the crowd and starting the meting.

Just as he began asking for quiet, he noticed an eleven year old girl sitting in the front. She was angelically beaming with excitement and lying next to her was a bright red umbrella, ready for use. The beauty and innocence of this sight made the pastor smile to himself as he realized the faith this young girl possessed which the rest of the people in the room seemed to have forgotten. For the rest had come just to pray for rain, she had come to see God answer.

· ·

(16) <u>Who's Packing Your Parachute?</u>

Charles Plumb, a U.S. Naval Academy graduate, was a jet pilot in Vietnam. After flying more than 75 combat missions, his plane was shot down and he parachuted safely into enemy hands. He was captured and spent 6 years in a communist prison. He survived the ordeal and now lectures on lessons he learned from that experience.

One day, Charles Plumb and his wife were sitting in a restaurant when a man at another table came over to him. He said, "You're Plumb! You flew a jet fighter in Vietnam from the aircraft Kitty Hawk. You were shot down!" The surprised pilot said, "How in the world did you know that?" The man pumped his hand with a hearty handshake and said, "I packed your parachute and I guess it worked!" Mr. Plumb assured him, "It sure did! If you didn't do a good job, I wouldn't be here today!"

Charles Plumb couldn't sleep very well that night. He kept thinking about that man who packed his parachute. He kept wondering what he might have looked like in a Navy uniform: a white hat, a bib in the back and bell-bottom trousers. He wondered how many times he might have seen him and not even said, "Good Morning" or if he even spoke to him at all because he was just a sailor and I was a fighter pilot. He thought of the many hours that sailor must have spent at a long wooden table in the bowel of the ship, carefully folding the silk and knowing that in his hands he held the fate of someone he didn't know. Now Mr. Plumb asks his audience, "Who's packing your Parachute?"

Everyone has someone who provides what they need to make it through the day. Plumb also points out that he needed many kinds of parachutes when his plane was shot down over enemy territory. He needed his <u>physical</u> parachute, his <u>emotional</u> parachute, and his <u>spiritual</u> parachute. He needed them all as support before he was able to be rescued. "Sometimes," he tells his audiences, "in the daily challenges of life, we miss what is really important. So often we fail to say 'Hello' or 'Good-Morning' or 'Please' and 'Thank-You' or to congratulate someone on a job well done, or just do something nice for no reason at all."

As you go through this week, this month, this year, be sure to recognize the people who *'pack your parachute!'*

17) <u>An Incredible Missionary Testimony</u>

At one particular service, a missionary gave this personal testimony...

I was serving as a missionary at a small field hospital in Africa. Every two weeks I would travel by bicycle through the jungle to a nearby city for supplies. This was a two-day journey and required camping overnight at the half-way point. On one of these journeys, I arrived in the city where I planned to collect money from the bank to purchase my medicine and other supplies. I would then proceed with my two-day journey back to the field hospital.

When I came back near the hospital, I noticed two men fighting and one of them was seriously injured. I stopped and treated the injured man and all the while I talked to him about the Lord. Two weeks later I made the trip again when this time I was approached by the young man I had previously treated. He knew I carried money and medicine and said, "Some friends and I followed you into the jungle. We knew you camped overnight and we planned to kill you and take your money and drugs. But, just as you were about to set up your camp, we saw that you were surrounded by 26 armed guards."

At that, I laughed and said that I was certainly all alone. However, the young man pressed the point and said, "No sir, I was not the only person to see the guards. My five friends also saw them and we all counted them. It was because of those guards that we were afraid and left you alone."

At this point in the testimony, one of the men in the congregation jumped to his feet and interrupted the missionary and asked if he could tell the exact day this happened. The missionary told the congregation the date and the man who interrupted told him this story.

"On the night of your incident in Africa, it was morning here and I was preparing to go play golf. I was about to putt when I felt the urge to pray for you. In fact, the urging of the Lord was so strong that I called men in this church to meet with me here in the sanctuary to pray for you. Would all of those men who met with me on that day stand up?

The men who met together to pray that day stood up. The missionary wasn't concerned with who they were, he was too busy counting how many men he saw. He counted exactly 26 men! This is an incredible story of how the Spirit of the Lord moves in mysterious ways.

• •

(18) <u>The Wooden Bowl</u>

A frail old man went to live with his son, daughter-in-law and 4-year- old grandson. The old man's hands trembled, his eyesight was blurred and his steps faltered. The family ate together at the table but the elderly grandfather's shaky hands and failing sight made eating difficult. Peas rolled off his spoon onto the floor and when he took hold of his glass, milk spilled on the tablecloth.

The son and daughter-in-law became irritated with the mess. "We must do something about father," said the son. "I've had enough of his spilled milk, noisy eating, and food on the floor."

So, the husband and wife set a small table in the corner. There, grandfather ate alone while the rest of the family enjoyed dinner. Since grandfather had broken a dish or two, his food was served in a wooden bowl. When the family glanced in grandfather's direction, sometimes he had a tear in his eye as he sat alone. Still the only words the couple had for him were sharp admonitions when he dropped a fork or spilled food.

The four-year-old watched it all in silence. One evening before supper, the father noticed his son playing with wood scraps on the floor. He asked the child, "What are you making?"

The four-year-old said, "I am making a little bowl for you and mama to eat your food in when I grow up." The four-year-old smiled and went back to work.

These words so struck the parents so hard they were speechless and tears started to stream down their cheeks. Though no word was spoken, both knew what must be done.

That evening the husband took grandfather's hand and gently led him back to the family table. For the remainder of his days he ate every meal with the family.

And for some reason, neither husband nor wife seemed to care any longer when a fork was dropped, when milk was spilled or when the tablecloth was soiled.

• •

(19) <u>The Old Phone</u>

When I was quite young, my father had one of the first telephones in our neighborhood. I remember the polished, old case fastened to the wall. The shiny receiver hung on the side of the box. I was too little to reach the telephone, but used to listen with fascination when my mother talked to it.

Then I discovered that somewhere inside that wonderful device lived an amazing person. Her name was *'Information Please'* and there was nothing she did not know.

'Information Please' could supply anyone's number and the correct time of the day or night. My personal experience with *'Information Please'* began one day when I was home alone and wacked my finger with the hammer. The pain was terrible, but there seemed no point in crying because there was no one home to give me sympathy.

I walked around the house sucking my throbbing finger, until finally I spotted the telephone hanging there on the parlor wall. I climbed up on a stool and got the receiver to my ear and said *'Information Please.'* In no time a cheerful woman's voice spoke in my ear, *'Information!'* I wailed in the phone, and my tears began to flow now that I had an audience, "I hurt my finger," I wailed.

Then I heard, "Isn't your mother home?"

"Nobody's home but me," I blubbered.

"Are you bleeding?" I heard her say.

"No but I hit my finger with the hammer and it hurts," I said.

"Can you open the icebox?" she asked.

I said I could. "Then," she said, "chip off a little bit of ice and hold it on your finger."

After that, I called *'Information Please'* for everything. I asked her for help with my geography, and she told me where to find Philadelphia. She helped me with my math. She told me my pet chipmunk that I had caught in the park that day, would eat fruit and nuts.

Then there was the time Petey, our pet canary, died. I called *'Information Please'* and told her the sad story. I asked her "Why is it that birds, that sing so beautifully and bring so much joy to families, end up as a heap of feathers on the bottom of a cage?"

She must have sensed my deep concern, for she said quietly, "Lenny, always remember that there is another world to sing in." Well, somehow, I seemed to feel better.

On another occasion I was on the telephone with *'Information Please'* and I said, "How do I spell fix?" All this took place in a small town in the Atlantic Northeast.

When I grew older and moved South, I missed my friend *'Information Please'* who lived in that old wooden box on the wall.

I now had a shiny new phone but it wasn't quite the same. I often thought how patient, understanding and kind she was to a little boy.

A few years later I was passing thru my old home town and had a few minutes to spare so I dialed my hometown operator and said, *'Information please.'* I again heard that sweet familiar voice on the other end of the line, and I said, "Could you please tell me how to spell fix? There was a long pause. Then I heard that familiar voice, "I guess your finger must have healed by now!"

I laughed and said, "So, it's really you, eh!" Then I said, "I wonder if you have any idea how much you meant to me during that time?" Then she responded, "I wonder if you know how much your calls meant to me. You see, I never had any children and I used to look forward to your calls."

I told her how often I had thought of her over the years and I asked if I could call her again on my next trip through. "Please do," she said, "just ask for Sally."

Three months later I was in that area again and a different voice came on the line. I asked for Sally. She said are you a friend?

I said "Yes, a very old friend."

"I am very sorry to have to tell you this," she said, "but Sally died about 5 weeks ago." But, before I hung up the operator said, "Did you say your name was Paul?" When I answered "Yes" she said, "Well, Sally left a message for you. She wrote it down in case you called. Let me read it to you." The note said, "Tell him there is another world to sing in. He'll know what I mean." I thanked her and hung up the phone. Yes, I knew what Sally meant.

So, never underestimate the impression you may make on others. Whose life have you touched today?

• •

(20) Robby – my piano student

I've always supplemented my income by teaching piano lessons. Over the years I found that children have many levels of musical ability. I've had my share of what I call 'musically challenged' students.

One such student was Robby. He was 11 years old when his mother took him to his first piano lesson. Robby said that it had always been his mother's dream to hear him play the piano.

From the beginning I thought it was hopeless. He lacked the sense of tone and basic rhythm needed to excel. But he dutifully reviewed the scales and some elementary pieces that I require all my students to learn. At the end of each weekly lesson he'd always say, "My mom's gonna hear me play someday." But it seemed hopeless. He just did not have any inborn ability

I only knew his mother from a distance as she waited in her old car to pick him up. She always waved and smiled but never stopped in. Then one day Robby stopped coming for lessons.

I thought about calling him but assumed because of his lack of ability, Robby had decided to pursue something else. I also was glad that he stopped coming. He was a bad advertisement for my teaching.

Several weeks later I mailed a flyer on an upcoming recital to the student's homes. To my surprise, Robby, who received a flyer, asked me if he could be in the recital. I told him the recital was for current students and because he had dropped out he really did not qualify. He said that his mom had been sick and unable to bring him to piano lessons but he still kept practicing at home. "I've just got to play," he insisted. I don't know why I agreed to allow him to play in the recital, but I did.

The night came and the high school gym was packed with parents, friends and relatives. I decided to place Robby last in the program. That way, I thought, I will deliver the final 'curtain closer' and cover up whatever disaster he might cause.

Well, the recital went off without a hitch; each student demonstrating their talent. Finally, it was Robby's turn. He came on stage in his usual wrinkled clothes and uncombed hair and I wondered why his mother didn't at least see that he combed his hair.

Robby pulled out the piano bench and got ready to play. I was surprised when he announced that he had chosen Mozart's Concerto #21 in C major. I was not prepared for what was to follow. His fingers were light as they danced over the ivories.

Never had I heard Mozart played so well by anyone his age. After six and one-half minutes, he ended in a grand crescendo. Everyone was on their feet in wild applause. Overcome with tears, I ran to the stage and put my arms around Robby. "How'd you do it?" I said.

Over the microphone Robby said, "Well, remember I told you my mom was sick? Well, actually, she had cancer and passed away this morning, and well...she was also born deaf so tonight was the first time she ever heard me play and I really wanted to make it special."

There wasn't a dry eye in the house that evening, as the people from the Social Services led Robby from the stage to be placed into foster care. I noticed that even their eyes were red and puffy and I thought to myself how much richer my life had been for taking Robby as my student.

That evening Robby taught me the meaning of perseverance and love, and that sometimes it's OK to take a chance on someone even when you don't know why.

This whole experience became especially meaningful to me when I discovered that Robby was killed in the senseless bombing of the Alfred P. Murray Federal Building in Oklahoma City in April 1995, where he was reportedly playing the piano.

. . . .

(21) *DOES GOD EXIST?*

A man went to a barbershop to have his hair cut and his beard trimmed. As the barber began to work, they began to have a good conversation. They talked about so many things and various subjects. When they eventually touched on the subject of God, the barber said, "I don't believe that God exists."

"Why do you say that?" asked the customer.

"Well, you just have to go out in the street to realize that God doesn't exist. Tell me, if God exists, would there be so many sick people? Would there be abandoned children? If God existed, there would be neither suffering nor pain. I can't imagine a loving God who would allow all of these things."

The customer thought for a moment, but didn't respond because he didn't want to start an argument. The barber finished his job and the customer left the shop. Just after he left the barbershop, he saw a man in the street with long, stringy, dirty hair and an untrimmed beard. He looked dirty and unkempt. The customer turned back and entered the barbershop again and he said to the barber, "You know what? Barbers do not exist."

"How can you say that?" asked the surprised barber. "I am here and I am a barber. And I just worked on you!"

"No!" the customer exclaimed. "Barbers don't exist because if they did, there would be no people with dirty long hair and untrimmed beards like that man outside."

"Ah, but barbers DO exist! That's what happens when people do not come to me."

"Exactly!" affirmed the customer. "That's the point! God, too, DOES exist!"

"That's what happens when people do not go to Him and don't look to Him for help. That's why there's so much pain and suffering in the world."

God grant me the senility to forget the people I never liked, the good fortune to run into the ones I do, and the eyesight to tell the difference.

· ·

(22) A wealthy man and his son loved to collect rare works of art. They had everything in their collection, from Picasso to Raphael. They would often sit together and admire the great works of art..

When the Vietnam conflict broke out, the son went to war. He was very courageous and died in battle while rescuing another soldier. The father was notified and grieved deeply for his only son.

About a month later, just before Christmas, there was a knock at the door. A young man stood at the door with a large package in his hands..

He said, 'Sir, you don't know me, but I am the soldier for whom your son gave his life. He saved many lives that day, and he was carrying me to safety when a bullet struck him in the heart and he died instantly... He often talked about you, and your love for art.' The young man held out this package. 'I know this isn't much. I'm not really a great artist, but I think your son would have wanted you to have this.'

The father opened the package. It was a portrait of his son, painted by the young man. He stared in awe at the way the soldier had captured the personality of his son in the painting. The father was so drawn to the eyes that his own eyes welled up with tears. He thanked the young man and offered to pay him for the picture.. 'Oh, no sir, I could never repay what your son did for me. It's a gift.'

The father hung the portrait over his mantle. Every time visitors came to his home he took them to see the portrait of his son before he showed them any of the other great works he had collected.

The man died a few months later. There was to be a great auction of his paintings. Many influential people gathered, excited over seeing the great paintings and having an opportunity to purchase one for their collection.

On the platform sat the painting of the son. The auctioneer pounded his gavel. 'We will start the bidding with this picture of the son. Who will bid for this picture?' There was silence…

Then a voice in the back of the room shouted, 'We want to see the famous paintings. Skip this one.' But the auctioneer persisted. 'Will somebody bid for this painting? Who will start the bidding? $100, $200?'

Another voice angrily. 'We didn't come to see this painting. We came to see the Van Gogh's, the Rembrandts. Get on with the Real bids!'

But still the auctioneer continued. 'The son! The son! Who'll take the son?' Finally, a voice came from the very back of the room. It was the longtime gardener of the man and his son. 'I'll give $10 for the painting...' Being a poor man, it was all he could afford. '

We have $10, who will bid $20? 'Give it to him for $10. Let's see the masters.' The crowd was becoming angry. They didn't want the picture of the son. They wanted the more worthy investments for their collections.

The auctioneer pounded the gavel.. 'Going once, twice, SOLD for $10!' A man sitting on the second row shouted, 'Now let's get on with the collection!' The auctioneer laid down his gavel. 'I'm sorry, the auction is over.'

'What about the paintings? 'I am sorry. When I was called to conduct this auction, I was told of a secret stipulation in the will... I was not allowed to reveal that stipulation until this time. Only the painting of the son would be auctioned. Whoever bought that painting would inherit the entire estate, including the paintings.

The man who took the son gets everything!' God gave His Son over 2,000 years ago to die on the Cross. Much like the auctioneer, His message today is: 'The Son, the Son, who'll take the Son?'

Because, you see, **whoever takes the Son gets everything!**

FOR GOD SO LOVED THE WORLD HE GAVE HIS ONLY BEGOTTEN SON, WHO SO EVER BELIEVETH, SHALL HAVE ETERNAL LIFE...THAT'S LOVE

(23) <u>Wrong E-mail Address</u>

A Minneapolis couple decided to go to Florida to thaw out during a particularly icy winter. They planned to stay at the same hotel where they spent their honeymoon 20 years earlier. Because of hectic schedules, it was difficult to coordinate their travel schedules. So, the husband left Minnesota and flew to Florida on Thursday, with his wife flying down the following day.

The husband checked into the hotel. There was a computer in his room, so he decided to send an email to his wife. However, he accidentally left out one letter in her email address, and without realizing his error, sent the e-mail.

Meanwhile, somewhere in Houston , a widow had just returned home from her husband's funeral. He was a Baptist minister who was called home to glory following a heart attack.

The widow decided to check her e-mail expecting messages from relatives and friends. After reading the first message, she screamed and fainted.

The widow's son rushed into the room, found his mother on the floor, and saw the computer screen which read:

To: My Loving Wife / Subject: I've Arrived / Date: March 2, 2013

I know you're surprised to hear from me. They have computers here now and you are allowed to send emails to your loved ones. I've just arrived and have been checked in.

I've seen that everything has been prepared for your arrival tomorrow. Looking forward to seeing you then! Hope your journey is as uneventful as mine was.

P. S. Sure is hot down here!!!

Chapter 23

Political stories

(1) Accounts Receivable Tax"...

Tax his land, tax his wage, and tax the bed in which he lays.

Tax his tractor, tax his mule, teach him taxes are the rule.

Tax his cow and tax his goat, tax his pants and tax his coat.

Tax his ties and tax his shirts, tax his work and tax his dirt.

Tax his bills, tax his gas, tax his notes and tax his cash.

Tax him good and let him know, that after taxes he has no dough.

If he hollers tax him more, tax him 'till he's good and sore.

Tax his coffin and tax his grave, tax the sod in which he lays.

Put these words upon his tomb, 'Taxes drove me to my doom,'

And when he's gone, we won't relax, they'll still be after the inheritance tax!

(Maybe then he'll get a refund)

NOTE: Not one of these taxes existed 100 years ago and our nation was the most prosperous in the world. We had absolutely no national debt; we had the largest middle class in the world and mom stayed home to raise kids. What happened?

. . . .

(2) From the beginning of history, **the average age of the world's greatest civilizations has been about 200 years**. During those 200 years, these nations always progressed through the following sequence:

From bondage to spiritual faith;
From spiritual faith to great courage;
From courage to liberty;
From liberty to abundance;
From abundance to complacency;
From complacency to apathy;
From apathy to dependence;
From dependence back into bondage."
The Obituary follows...

Born 1776, Died 2012
Professor Joseph Olson of Hamline University School of Law in St. Paul, Minnesota, points out some interesting facts concerning the last Presidential election:

Number of States won by: Obama: 19 McCain: 29
Square miles of land won by: Obama: 580,000 McCain: 2,427,000
Population of counties won by: Obama: 127 million McCain: 143 million

Murder rate per 100,000 residents in counties won by: Obama: 13.2 McCain: 2.1

Professor Olson adds: In aggregate, the map of the territory McCain won was mostly the land owned by the taxpaying citizens of the country. Obama territory mostly encompassed those citizens living in low income tenements and living off various forms of government welfare..." Of Professor Tyler's definition of democracy, with some forty percent of the nation's population already having reached the "governmental dependency" phase.

If Congress grants amnesty and citizenship to twenty million criminal invaders called illegals - and they vote - then we can say goodbye to the USA in fewer than five years.

This is truly scary!

. . . .

(3) <u>Samuel Thompson</u> (distinguished Professor at Penn State Law School) wrote...

I don't believe in Santa Claus but I am not going to sue somebody for singing a Ho-Ho-Ho song in December. I don't agree with Darwin but I didn't go out and hire a lawyer when my high school teacher taught the theory of evolution. Life, liberty or your pursuit of happiness will not be endangered because someone says a 30-second prayer before a football game.

So, what's the big deal? It's not like somebody is up there reading the entire Book of Acts. They're just talking to a God they believe in and asking him to grant safety to the players on the field and the fans going home after the game.

"But, it's a Christian prayer," some will argue. Yes and this is the United States of America, a country founded on Christian principles. And, we are in the *Bible Belt* and according to our very own phone book, Christian churches outnumber all others better than 200 to 1. So, what would you expect, somebody chanting Hare Krishna?

If I went to a football game in Jerusalem, I would expect to hear a Jewish prayer. If I went to a soccer game in Bagdad, I would expect to hear a Muslim prayer. If I went to a ping-pong match in China, I would expect to hear somebody pray to Buddha, *and, I wouldn't be offended. It wouldn't bother me one bit!* And, nobody is asking the atheist to be baptized. We're not going to pass the collection plate. Just humor us for 30 seconds. If that's asking too much, bring a walkman or a pair of ear plugs. Go to the bathroom. Visit the concession stand. Call your lawyer.

Unfortunately, one or two will make that call. One or two will tell thousands what they can and cannot do. I don't think a short prayer at a football game is going to shake the world's foundations.

Christians are just sick and tired of turning the other cheek while our courts strip us of all our rights. Our parents and grandparents taught us to pray before eating, to pray before we go to sleep. Our Bible tells us to pray without ceasing.

Now a handful of people and their lawyers are telling us to cease praying. May God help us! And if that sentence offends you, well…just sue me!

· ·

(4) <u>By Judge Roy Moore</u>
America the Beautiful, or so it used to be,
Land of the Pilgrims' pride I'm glad they'll never see.

Babies piled in dumpsters, abortion on demand,
Oh sweet Land of Liberty, your house is on the sand.
Our children wander aimlessly poisoned by cocaine,
Choosing to indulge their lusts when God has said abstain.

From sea to shining sea, our Nation turns away,
From the teaching of God's love, and a need to always pray.
We've kept God in our temples, how callous we have grown,
When earth is but His footstool and heaven is His throne.

We've voted in a government that's rotten to the core,
Appointing Godless judges who throw reason out the door.
How are we to face our God, from whom we cannot hide?
What then is left for us to do, but stem this evil tide?

If we who are His children, will humbly turn and pray,
Seek His Holy face, and mend our evil way.
Then God will hear in Heaven, and forgive us of our sin,
He'll heal our sickly land and those who live within.
And America the Beautiful, if you don't, then you will see,
A sad but Holy God, withdraw His hand from thee.

. . . .

(5) <u>Commander Butch O'Hare</u> – (Two stories that go together)
(Prov. 22:1 / Isa. 62:2-5)

World War II produced many heroes. One such man was Lieutenant Commander Butch O'Hare. He was a fighter pilot assigned to the aircraft carrier Lexington in the South Pacific. One day his entire squadron was sent on a mission. After he was airborne, he looked at his fuel gauge and realized that someone had forgotten to top off his fuel tank. He would not have enough fuel to complete his mission and get back to his ship. His flight leader told him to return to the carrier.

Reluctantly he dropped out of formation and headed back to the fleet. As he was returning to the mother ship, he saw something that turned his blood cold. A squadron of Japanese bombers was speeding their way towards the American fleet. The American fighters were gone and the fleet was all but defenseless. He couldn't reach his squadron and bring them back in time to save the fleet. Nor could he warn the fleet of the approaching danger.

There was only one thing to do. He must somehow divert them from the fleet. Laying aside all thoughts of personal safety, he dove into the formation of Japanese planes. Wing-mounted 50 caliber's blazed as he charged in, attacking one surprised enemy plane and then another.

Butch weaved in and out of the now broken formation and fired at as many planes as possible until finally all his ammunition was spent.

Undaunted, he continued the assault. He dove at the planes, trying to as least clip off a wing or tail, in hopes of rendering them unfit to fly. He was desperate to do anything he could to keep them from reaching the American ships.

Finally, the exasperated Japanese squadron took off in another direction. Deeply relieved, Butch O'Hare and his tattered fighter limped back to the carrier. Upon arrival, he reported in and related the event surrounding his return. The film from the camera mounted on his plane's wing told the tale. It showed the extent of Butch's daring attempt to protect his fleet. He had destroyed five enemy bombers.

That was on February 20, 1942, and for that action he became the Navy's first Ace of WW II and the first Naval Aviator to win the Congressional Medal of Honor.

A year later he was killed in aerial combat at the age of 29. His home town would not allow the memory of that heroic action die. Today, O'Hare Airport in Chicago is named in tribute to the courage of this great man.

*** The only difference between a rut and a grave is the depth ***

. . . .

(6) <u>Easy Eddy – aka AlCapone's Lawyer</u> – (See the 'Butch O'Hare story)

Some years ago, there was a man in Chicago called 'Easy Eddie.' At that time, Al Capone virtually owned the city. Capone wasn't famous for anything heroic and his exploits were anything but praise-worthy. He was, however, notorious for enmeshing the city of Chicago in everything from bootlegged booze and prostitution to murder.

'Easy Eddie' was Capone's lawyer and for a good reason. He was very good! In fact, his skill at legal maneuvering kept big Al out of jail for a long time. To show his appreciation, Capone paid him very well. Not only was the money big, but also Eddie got special dividends. For instance, he and his family occupied a gated mansion with live-in help and all the conveniences of the day. The estate was so large that it filled an entire Chicago city block. Yes, 'Easy Eddie' lived the 'high-life' of the Chicago mob and gave little consideration to the atrocity that went on around him.

'Easy Eddie' did have one soft spot however. He had a son that he loved dearly. Eddie saw to it that his young son had the best of everything - clothes, cars and a good education. Nothing was withheld and price was no object. Despite his involvement with organized crime, Eddie even tried to teach his son right from wrong. Yes, 'Easy Eddie' tried to teach his son to rise above his own sordid life. He wanted him to be a better man than he was. Yet, with all his wealth and influence there were two things that Eddie couldn't give his son. Two things that Eddie sacrificed to the Capone mob that he could not pass on to his beloved son - a good name and a good example.

One day, Easy Eddie reached a difficult decision. Offering his son a good name was far more important than all the riches he could lavish on him. He had to rectify all the wrong that he had done. He could go to the authorities and tell the truth about

"Scarface" Al Capone. He would try to clean up his tarnished name and offer his son some semblance of integrity. To do this he must testify against the mob and he knew that the cost would be great. But, more than anything, he wanted to be an example to his son. He wanted to do his best to make restoration and hopefully have a good name to leave his son. So, he testified.

Within the year, Easy Eddie's life ended in a blaze of gunfire on a lonely Chicago street. He had given his son the greatest gift he had to offer at the greatest price he could ever pay.

What do these two stories have in common, you ask? Well, Butch O'Hare was Easy Eddie's son. *And now you know ...the rest of the story!*

. . . .

(7) <u>Johnny's Not There</u> – (A personal experience while living in Georgia)

I knew a little elderly lady in Ellijay, Georgia whom I had met in church. She worked in the 'Fabric' Dept. at the local Wal-Mart store. She was aware that I played and recorded music. So at the Wal-Mart store one day she asked me if I would be available to record some songs she had written.

I told her I would be glad to do so and that if she would come over to my house some evening we would do the recording. She apologized for being so forward and kept saying, "I'm so sorry, Brother Leonard. I shouldn't be bothering you and these songs ain't that good." I assured her it was no bother to me and I loved recording.

I set up my equipment and set a mike in the middle of the living room floor. I had my back to her as I operated the recording controls and this is what I remember as the jist of her writing…

The auditorium was filled to capacity. Yellow ribbons were everywhere. The returning soldiers had just got back from *Desert Storm*. As they marched onto the platform the audience was reverent and mesmerized. The little lady standing next to me in the audience began to weep. And her weeping got increasingly more intense. I leaned over to her and said, "Ma-am, is something wrong?"

She looked up at me with the most tearful eyes you ever saw...and said, "JOHNNY'S NOT THERE." (I wish I still had a copy of that recording!)

. . . .

(8) Sack Lunches –

I put my carry-on in the luggage compartment and sat down in my assigned seat. It was going to be a long flight. 'I'm glad I have a good book to read. Perhaps I will get a short nap,' I thought. But, just before take-off, a line of soldiers came down the aisle and filled all the vacant seats, totally surrounding me. I decided to start a conversation.

"Where are you heading?" I asked the soldier seated next to me.

"Petawawa, Ontario. We'll be there for two weeks for special training, and then we're being deployed to Afghanistan."

After flying for about an hour, an announcement was made that sack lunches were available for five dollars. It would be several hours before we reached the east and I quickly decided a lunch would help pass the time. As I reached for my wallet, I overheard a soldier ask his buddy if he planned to buy a lunch.

"No, that seems like a lot of money for just a sack lunch. Probably wouldn't be worth five bucks. I'll just wait till I get to base."

His friend agreed.

I looked around at the other soldiers. None of them were buying lunch. I walked to the back of the plane and handed the flight attendant a fifty dollar bill and said, "Please take a lunch to all of those soldiers."

She grabbed my arms and squeezed tightly. Her eyes were wet with tears, and thanked me and said, "My son was a soldier in Iraq; it's almost like you are doing it for him." Picking up ten sacks, she headed up the aisle to where the soldiers were seated. She stopped at my seat and asked, "What do you like best, beef or chicken?"

I said, "Chicken" and then I wondered why she had asked.

She turned and went to the front of the plane, returning a minute later with a dinner plate from first class. "This is your thanks," she said.

After we finished eating, I went again to the back of the plane to pay a visit to the rest room. A man stopped me and said, "I saw what you did. I want to be part of it." He handed me twenty-five dollars.

Soon after I returned to my seat, I saw the Flight Captain coming down the aisle, looking at the aisle numbers. I hoped he was not looking for me.

When he got to my row, he stopped, smiled and held out his hand and said, "I just want to shake your hand."

I quickly unfastened my seat belt, stood to shake his hand. With a booming voice he said, "I was a soldier and a military pilot; once someone bought me a lunch. It was an act of kindness I never forgot."

I was embarrassed when a round of applause was heard from all of the passengers.

Later, I walked to the front of the plane so I could stretch my legs. A man who was seated about six rows in front of me reached out his hand, wanting to shake mine. He left another twenty-five dollars in my hand. When we landed I gathered my belongings and started to deplane. Waiting just inside the airplane door was a man who stopped me and put something in my shirt pocket, turned and walked away without saying a word. It was another twenty-five dollars!

Upon entering the terminal, I saw the soldiers gathering for their trip to the base. I walked over to them and handed them seventy-five dollars and said, "It will take you some time to reach the base. This will get you another sandwich. God bless you!"

That day ten young men left that flight feeling the love and respect of their fellow travelers. And as I walked briskly to my car, I whispered a prayer for their safe return. These soldiers were giving their all for our country. I could only give them a couple of meals. It seemed so little.

A veteran is someone who, at one point in his life, wrote a blank check, made payable to "The United States of America" for an amount of "up to and including my life."

<u>That is Honor. There are way too many people in this country who no longer understand it!</u>

. . . .

(9) <u>What a Legal System!</u> –

A Charlotte, N.C. man bought a box of very rare and very expensive cigars. He then insured them against fire, among other things. Within a month, he smoked all of them without having paid even the first premium on the policy. He then filed a claim against the insurance company.

In his claim, the man stated that the cigars were lost 'in a series of small fires.' The insurance company refused to pay, citing the obvious reason: that the man had consumed the cigars in the normal fashion.

Well, the man sued, and won! In delivering the ruling, the judge agreed that the claim was frivolous. He stated, nevertheless, that the man held a policy from the company in which it had warranted that the cigars were insurable and also guaranteed that it would insure against fire, without defining what is considered to be *'unacceptable fire'* and was obligated to pay the claim. Rather than endure a lengthy and costly appeals process, the insurance company accepted the ruling and paid the man $15,000 for the rare cigars he had lost in the *'fires.'*

Now, here's the best part. After the man cashed the check, the insurance company had him arrested on 24 counts of arson! By virtue of his insurance claim and testimony from the previous case being used against him, the man was convicted of intentionally burning his insured property and sentenced to 24 months in jail and a $24,000 fine.

Only in America!

. . . .

(10) YOU ARE NOT GOING TO BELIEVE THIS

At approximately 2:30 pm, September 6, 2012, I entered the Publix store on Main St. in Gainesville, FL to pick up a few items.

I gathered my items and went to the register to check-out. The person in front of me, a white female, approximate age 35-43 with fake nails, big braided hair-do, clean clothes, carrying a purse and a plastic drinking cup, put her purchase on **the check-out surface, ONE GRAPE.**

Yes, that is correct, ONE GRAPE. The cashier asked if that was all. She replied "yes." The cashier then weighed the GRAPE and told the women the cost was $.02 (TWO CENTS). The women then pulled out her Food Stamp EBT card and swiped it through the credit card machine, requesting $24.00 in cash back.

The cashier asked if she wanted the GRAPE. The woman replied no and the GRAPE was put in the garbage can. The register recorded the sale as .02, cash back $24.00. The cashier then asked if four fives would be okay because she was out of tens. The woman agreed and took the $24.00 folded it up and put it in her pocket and left the store.

As the next person in line I asked the cashier, as a tax payer, what in heck just happened here. She said she was on the clock and could not comment. I then asked if I had actually seen this person purchase and discard a GRAPE, then get cash back on her Food Stamp EBT card.

The cashier responded that it happens all day, every day in their store. She also said that if the person buying the GRAPE has it ring up over .02 she gets mad and makes her reweigh it.

My next comment was to ask the cashier if she planned to vote in November and she said she could hardly wait for 11/6/12 to get here as one tax payer to another. I paid for my groceries, in cash, and left the store madder than 10 wet hens.

∙ ∙

(11) <u>When the Music Stopped</u>...

A U.S. Chaplin in Iraq writes: "At all military base theaters, the National Anthem is played before the movie begins.

He says, "I recently attended a showing of 'Superman 3' here at LSA Anaconda. As is the custom at all military bases, we stood to attention when The National Anthem began before the main feature. All was going well until three-quarters of the way through The National Anthem, the music stopped.

Now, what would happen if this occurred with 1,000 18- to-22 year-olds back in the States? I imagine that there would be hoots, catcalls, laughter, a few rude comments and everyone would sit down and yell for the movie to begin. Of course, that is, only if they had stood for The National Anthem in the first place.

Here in Iraq 1,000 soldiers continued to stand at attention with eyes fixed forward. The music started again and the soldiers continued to quietly stand at attention. However, at the same point, the music stopped. What would you expect 1,000 soldiers standing at attention to do? Frankly, I expected some laughter and everyone would eventually sit down and wait for the movie to start.

<u>No!! You could have heard a pin drop while every soldier continued to stand at attention.</u>

Suddenly, there was a lone voice from the front of the auditorium then a dozen voices and soon the room was filled with the voices of a thousand soldiers, finishing where the recording left off: "And the rockets' red glare, the bombs bursting in air. Gave proof through the night that our flag was still there. Oh, say, does that Star Spangled Banner yet wave o'er the land of the free and the home of the brave."

It was the most inspiring moment I have had in Iraq, and I wanted you to know what kind of U.S. Soldiers are serving you! Remember them as they fight for us. Be ever in prayer for all our soldiers serving us here at home and abroad.

Written by Chaplain Jim Higgins. LSA Anaconda is at the Ballad Airport in Iraq, north of Baghdad.

. . . .

- Old People are easy to spot at sporting events; during the playing of the National Anthem. Old People remove their caps and stand at attention and sing without embarrassment. They know the words and believe in them.
- Old People remember World War II, Pearl Harbor, Guadalcanal, Normandy and Hitler. They remember the Atomic Age, the Korean War, The Cold War, the Jet Age and the Moon Landing. They remember the 50 plus Peacekeeping Missions from 1945 to 2005, not to mention Vietnam.

Chapter 24

Senior Stories

(1) <u>True Love...</u>   1 Cor. 13:13

It was a busy morning when an elderly man arrived at my clinic to have stitches removed from his thumb. He was in a hurry because he had an early appointment. I took his vitals and asked him to take a seat. I knew it would be and hour or more before someone would be able to see him. I saw him look at his watch and fidget in his chair so I decided I'd take him since I was not that busy. I talked to his doctor, got the needed supplies and called him inside.

While taking care of him we began to talk and I asked if he had another doctor's appointment this morning and why was he in such a hurry. He said there was no other doctor's appointment but he needed to go to the nursing home to eat breakfast with his wife.

When I inquired about his wife, he told me she had been there for awhile and suffered with Alzheimer's disease. As we talked and I finished dressing his wound, I asked if she would be worried if he was a bit late. He replied that she no longer knew who he was and that she had not recognized him for several years now. I was surprised and I questioned him. "And you still go every morning, even though she doesn't know who you are?"

He smiled and said, "She doesn't know me **but I still know who she is.**

I had to hold back the tears as he left. I had goose bumps on my arm and thought, "That is the kind of love I want I my life."

True love is neither physical, nor is it romantic. True love is acceptance of all that is, has been, or ever will be.

. . . .

(2) "<u>Be not deceived</u>..." (True Story) Gal. 6:7

In Campinas, Brazil, in the year 2005, a group of drunken friends went to pick up another lady friend. The mother accompanied her daughter to the car and was terribly worried about the impairment of the gang her daughter was hanging out with yet felt unable to do anything about it but pray.

As her daughter was getting into the car, the mother said, "My daughter, go with God and He will protect you."

The daughter jokingly responded, "The only place for God could squeeze into this car is if He rides in the trunk; there are so many of us!"

A few hours later the Godly mother received a call that they had been involved in a fatal accident. Everyone had died and the car had been totally demolished except for the trunk, which was still intact. The police said it was impossible for the trunk to have survived as it did. And to everyone's surprise, **<u>inside the trunk was a dozen eggs and not one of them had been broken!</u>**

. . . .

(3) <u>Christine Hewitt</u>... (a Journalist and an entertainer)... <u>Gal. 6:7</u>

...said the Bible was the "worst book ever written." In June 2006, she was found "burnt beyond recognition" in her car.

Many people have forgotten that there is no other Name, with as much as authority, as the Name of Jesus. Many have died but only Jesus died and rose again, and He is still alive!

If you bump into an Old People on the sidewalk he will apologize. If you pass an Old Person on the street, he will nod or tip his cap to a lady. Old People trust strangers and are courtly to women.

Old People hold the door for the next person and always, when walking, make certain the lady is on the inside for protection.

Old People get embarrassed if someone curses in front of women and children and they don't like any filth or dirty language on TV or in movies.

. . . .

(4) <u>Crabby Old Man</u>…

>What do you see nurses, what do you see?
>What are you thinking when you're looking at me?
>A crabby old man, not very wise,
>Uncertain of habit with faraway eyes?
>
>Who dribbles his food and makes no reply,
>When you say in a loud voice, 'I do wish you'd try.'
>Who seems not to notice, the things that you do,
>And forever is losing a sock or a shoe.
>
>Is that what you're thinking? Is that what you see?
>Then open your eyes nurse you're not looking at me.
>I once was a small boy, age ten and had a father and mother,
>And brothers and sisters who loved one another.
>
>When I was sixteen I had wings on my feet,
>Dreaming of the day when a lover I'd meet.

Leonard O'Donnell

I was a groom at twenty, had wings on my feet.
I remember the vows I promised to keep.

At twenty-five I had young of my own,
Who needed a guide and security of home.
By thirty or forty, my sons were all gone,
And the woman beside me helped me to mourn.

Now dark days are beside me, my wife is now dead.
I face the future here and spend most time in bed.
Yes, I'm an old man and nature is cruel.
Old age has come and I look like a fool.

But inside this old carcass a young boy still dwells.
And now and again my heart still swells,
When I remember the joys, the sorrow and pain,
I'm living my life all over again.

Yes I think of the years, all too few that have gone too fast.
I accept the stark fact that nothing can last.
So, nurse, open your eyes, open and see,
Not a crabby old man, look closer, see me!

· ·

(5) This is a tribute to all the Grandmas & Grandpas, Nannas & Pops, who have been fearless and learned to use the Computer.........

The computer swallowed Grandma,

Yes, honestly it's true!
She pressed 'control and 'enter'
And disappeared from view.

From 'SPAM' to BALONEY

It devoured her completely,
The thought just makes me squirm.
She must have caught a virus
Or been eaten by a worm.

I've searched through the recycle bin
And files of every kind;
I've even used the Internet,
But nothing did I find.

In desperation, I asked Mr. Google
My searches to refine.
The reply from him was negative,
Not a thing was found 'online.'

So, if inside your 'Inbox,'
My Grandma you should see,
Please 'Copy, Scan' and 'Paste' her,
And send her back to me.

CHAPTER 25

Supernatural stories

(1) <u>Angels in the Alley</u>...

Diane, a young Christian university student, was home for the summer. One evening she went to visit some friends. Time passed quickly as each shared their various experiences of the past year. She stayed longer than anticipated and had to walk home alone.

As she walked beneath the tall elm trees, Diane asked God to keep her safe from harm and danger. When she went down the alley to her house, Diane noticed a man standing at the end who appeared to be waiting for her. She became uneasy and again prayed for God's protection. Diane immediately felt a calmness and assurance that God indeed was with her. When reaching the end of the alley, she walked right past the man and arrived home safely.

The next day she read a story in the newspaper about a young girl had been raped in that same alley - just 20 minutes after she had been there. Overwhelmed by this tragedy and the fact that it could have been her, she began to weep and thanked the Lord for her safety. Compelled to help this young woman and identify the man, Diane decided to go to the police station to tell her story.

After she identified the man from the police photos, the rapist was informed of an eye-witness and he confessed to the assault. The officer thanked Diane as she was about to leave the police station. Diane asked the officer if she could ask the man one question and he agreed. Being very curious, she asked why the man did not attack her.

The rapist replied, "Because of those two big men who were with you." Diane knew no one was with her so it must've been two angels protecting her.

. . . .

(2) Thomas Jefferson

Thomas Jefferson was a very remarkable man who started learning very early in life and never stopped. At 5, began studying under his cousin's tutor. At 9, he studied Latin, Greek and French. At 14, he studied classical literature and additional languages. At 16, he entered the College of William and Mary. Also could write in Greek with one hand while writing the same in Latin with the other.

At 23, started his own law practice. At 25, was elected to the Virginia House of Burgesses. At 33, wrote the Declaration of Independence. At 46, he served as the first Secretary of State under George Washington. At 57, he was elected the third president of the United States. At 61, was elected to a second term as President. At 81, almost single-handedly created the University of Virginia and served as its first president.

At 83, he died on the 50th anniversary of the Signing of the Declaration of Independence along with John Adams.

It was Thomas Jefferson who made the following remarks: "The democracy will cease to exist when you take away from those who are willing to work and give to those who would not."

"My reading of history convinces me that most bad government results from too much government."

Thomas Jefferson said in 1802: "I believe that banking institutions are more dangerous to our liberties than standing armies.

· ·

(3) John Lennon...

During an interview, the famous singer said, "Christianity will end. It will disappear. I do not have to argue with that. Jesus was OK but His subjects were too simple and today, we (the Beatles) are more famous than Him." (1966)

A very short time later, **John Lennon was found shot six times**. Read (Gal. 6:7).

· ·

(4) A Home for Irene...

In my work at a large community hospital in Connecticut, I place patients in nursing homes. Of all my patients, the most difficult to place was Irene Manion. No one from any social welfare agency knew her. No one from a church claimed her. She had no relatives, no visitors and apparently no friends and she required a great deal of medical care. For months I made numerous phone calls to nursing homes in futile attempts to gain her admission. No one would accept her and I became obsessed with finding Irene a home. As I prayed to God each morning before work, I mentioned Irene Manion's name.

One day after a hopeful arrangement fell through, I just sat at my desk and cried. Staring at Irene's bulging file of paperwork

I said, "God, I give You Irene. Please place her where she'll get the best of care."

I then proceeded with my diligent phone work and dialed a nursing home I had called many times before. The admissions person wasn't there. Before I knew it, the operator connected me to a hallway wall phone that an evening nurse answered. In my frustration I told her about my problem.

"What's the patient's name?" the nurse asked.

"Irene Manion." To my amazement the nurse said, "Send her to us in the morning. I'll arrange for everything and I'll see that she gets the best of care." The nurse proceeded to tell me how she had been raised by a woman whom she called 'mom' when her own mother died. Now after twelve years of looking desperately for that woman, her search had ended.

Yes, Irene Manion was that nurse's 'mom.'

. . . .

(5) <u>God works in mysterious ways</u>...

One Saturday night a pastor was working late and decided to call his wife before going home. His wife didn't answer. The following Monday, the pastor received a call at the church office, on the same phone he had used on Saturday night. The man wanted to know why the pastor called on Saturday night. The pastor couldn't figure out what the man was talking about. The caller said his phone rang and rang but he hadn't answered. Then the pastor remembered he had tried calling his wife but obviously had dialed incorrectly.

The pastor apologized for disturbing the caller and explained he thought he was calling his wife. The caller said, "No, it's ok. Let me tell you my story. You see, I was planning to commit suicide on Saturday night. But before doing so, I prayed for God to give me a sign now if He didn't want me to kill myself."

The man said, "At that moment, my phone started to ring. I looked at the caller ID and it said 'Almighty God.' I became very afraid and too scared to answer the phone."

The reason why the ID showed 'Almighty God' is because the pastor's church is called '**Almighty God Tabernacle.**'

<u>God still works in mysterious ways!</u>

. . . .

(6) <u>I'll be watching over you...</u>
    A drunk man in an Oldsmobile, they said had run the light,
    That caused the six-car pile up, on Hwy 109 that night.
"A mother trapped inside her car," was heard above the noise,
Her frightened plea near split the air, "Oh God please spare my boys."

Her frightened eyes then focused, on where the back seat had been,
But all she saw was broken glass, and two children's seats crushed in.
Her twins were nowhere to be seen, she did not hear them cry.

And then she prayed they'd been thrown free. "Oh God don't let them die."
Then firemen came and cut her loose, but when they searched the back,
They did not find the little boys; the seat belts were in tact.
The policemen saw her running wild, and screaming above the noise.
"Dear God, I plead in Jesus Name, please help me find my boys."

She told the cops, "They're four years old and wear blue shirts,
Their jeans are blue to match."
One cop spoke up, "They're in my car,
And they don't have a scratch."

"They said their daddy put them there, and gave them each a cone,
Then told them both to wait for Mom to come and take them home."

The mother hugged the twins and said, while wiping at a tear,
"He could not have been at the scene, for he's been dead a year."

The cop just looked confused and asked, "Now how can that be true?"
The boys said, "Yes, Mommy, Daddy came and he left a kiss for you.
He told us not to worry, and that you would be alright,
And then he put us in this car, with the pretty flashing light."

The mother knew without a doubt, that what they spoke was true,
For she recalled their dad's last words, "I'll be watching over you."
The fireman's notes could not explain the twisted, mangled car,
And how the three of them escaped without a single scar.

But on the cop's report was scribed,
In print so very fine,
**"An angel walked the beat tonight,
On highway 109."**

. . . .

(7) <u>Man kills wife and buries children alive</u>.

A Muslim man in Egypt killed his wife because she was reading the Bible and then buried her along with their infant girl and 8-year old daughter. The girls were buried alive! He then reported to the police that an uncle killed the kids. Fifteen days later, another family member died.

When they buried him, the two little girls were found under the sand - ALIVE! The country is outraged over the incident and the man is scheduled to be executed. The older girl was asked how they survived and she said, "A man wearing shiny white clothes, with bleeding wounds in his hands, came every day to feed us. He woke up my mom so she could nurse my sister."

She was interviewed on Egyptian national TV by a veiled Muslim news anchorwoman. On public TV the girl said, "This was none other than Jesus because nobody else does things like this!" Muslims believe Isa (Jesus) would do this, but the wounds mean He really was crucified and that He is alive! But, it's also clear that the child could not make up a story like this and there's no way these children could have survived without a true miracle.

Muslim leaders will have a hard time figuring out what to do with this amazing story. The popularity of the Passion movie doesn't help either! With Egypt at the center of the media and education in the Middle East, you can be sure this story will spread. Christ is still turning the world upside down!

Please let this story be shared. The Lord says, *"I will bless the person who puts his trust in me."* Jeremiah 17

· ·

(8) <u>I heard her yell 'in English'</u>...

On one hot summer Illinois afternoon my wife and I were invited to a swimming party at the home of some friends. With our two children in the care of my grandmother, my wife and I felt as free as the breeze.

As I was standing on the diving board, I paused to look up into the beautiful serene sky. In that peaceful setting, above the party chatter, I heard a woman screaming at the far end of the pool, "The baby! He's at the bottom of the pool!"

Yet, it seemed no one was doing anything to help. People just stood and stared at her. Confused, I searched the length of the pool and saw what I thought might be a motionless form beneath the water. I dived in...and a baby was there.

I hurriedly picked him off the bottom and soon laid him on the deck. He had already turned blue and was not breathing so I quickly began CPR. "Dear God, help me do it right" I prayed.

Shortly the little guy coughed. A short breath came and then another. He was going to live! The ambulance was called for safety's sake. While we waited, I couldn't help asking the others, "Why did you ignore the woman when she said the boy was drowning?"

A friend answered, "None of us understood her, Scott."

"What do you mean?" I asked, "Even at the far end of the pool I could hear her yelling about the baby."

"But she's Mexican," her friend said. "None of us understand Spanish."

"Spanish?" Scott said, "I heard her yell in English."

"All we heard was Spanish," the others commented.

"It's true" the woman's daughter said, "Mama can't speak a word of English."

To this day, I'm still bewildered. I don't understand a word of Spanish...but I guess God does!

. . . .

(9) <u>Father, I wanted a car, not a Bible.</u>

A young man was getting ready to graduate from college. For many months he had admired a beautiful sports car in a dealers showroom, and knowing his father could well afford it, he told him that was all he wanted.

As Graduation Day approached, the young man awaited signs that his father had purchased the car. Finally, on the morning of his graduation, his father called him into his private study, told him how proud he was to have such a fine son, and how much he loved him. He handed him a beautifully wrapped gift box.

Curious, but somewhat disappointed, the young man opened the box and found a lovely, leather-bound Bible, with his name embossed in gold. Angrily, he raised his voice to his father and said, "With all your money you give me a Bible?" He stormed out of the house, leaving the Bible behind.

Many years passed and the young man was very successful in business. He had a beautiful home and wonderful family, but realized his father was very old. He thought perhaps he should go to him. He had not seen him since that graduation day. But before he could make arrangements, he received a telegram telling him his father had passed away, and willed all of his possessions to him. He needed to come home immediately and take care of things.

When he arrived at his father's house, sadness and regret filled his heart. He began to search through his father's important documents and saw the Bible, new, just as he had left it years ago. With tears, he opened the Bible and began to turn the pages. His father had carefully underlined a verse, Matt 7:11,

"And if ye, being evil, know how to give good gifts to your children, how much more shall your Heavenly Father which is in Heaven, give to those who ask Him?"

As he read those words, a car key dropped from the back of the Bible. It had a tag with the dealers name, the same dealer who had the sports car he had desired. On the tag was the date of his graduation, and the words... *"Paid In Full"* How many times do we miss God's blessings because they are not packaged as we expected?

Chapter 26

Testimonies

(1) The Dale Evans Story   1 Cor. 13:13

Dale Evans travelled many trails but not all of them happy. While she enjoyed a spectacular career that spanned over 60 years, her personal life was full of enormous heartbreak. A strong Christian faith sustained Dale Evans during the loss of three children. Her unwavering belief during such tragedies remains an inspiration to us all.

Dale Evans died at age 88 and was a gigantic star of the early days of television. At the peak of their popularity, she and her husband, Roy Rogers, had more than 2,000 fan clubs. Millions of children grew up watching Dale riding her buckskin horse 'Buttermilk' while the 'King of the Cowboys' was nearby on his beloved palomino 'Trigger.' It was a long and productive partnership, both on and off the screen. Roy and Dale were married more than 50 years and appeared together in dozens of movies.

By the time she met Roy in the mid-forties, Dale had already made several bad choices. This headstrong ambitious woman eloped at age 14 and was a single mother after divorcing within a few years. A second marriage ended in 1945. Roy's first wife died a year later after giving birth to a son. The widower, alone with three young children, married his popular co-star in 1947. Shortly afterward, Dale invited Christ into her heart. His presence in her life would carry Dale through the dark days ahead.

The couple's first child, Robin, was born with Downs Syndrome. In the challenge of caring for their daughter, God used the couple to witness His love in new ways. Afflicted by heart problems and a bout with the mumps, Robin died a few days before her second birthday. As the years went by, the Rogers family was constantly reminded that *"life is a vapor that appears for a little time and then vanishes away."* An adopted daughter, Debbie, was killed in 1964 when the church bus she was riding in collided with a car. Their adopted son, Sandy, died at age 18. Instead of growing bitter, Roy and Dale used the deaths to share their faith. Their losses made them credible as they consoled other grieving parents.

Dale Evans authored more than 30 children's records. She also wrote more than two dozen songs including the couple's theme song *'Happy Trails'* and *'The Bible Tells Me So.'* This last song was written hastily one afternoon when a producer asked her to compose a song for the end of a movie. She thought about 1 Cor. 13:13, *"And now abideth faith, hope, and charity"* and in 20 minutes the song was finished.

> Don't worry about tomorrow, just be real good today,
> The Lord is right beside you, He'll guide you all the way.
> Have faith, hope and charity, that's the way to live successfully,
> How do I know? The Bible tells me so!

(2) <u>William J. Murray</u> Gal. 5:19-21

I was born into a home of consistent rage and violence. My mother never married my father. As a result of my mother's constant angry outbursts she could not hold a job very long. My mother, brother and I lived with her parents and my unmarried uncle in a small row house in Baltimore, Md.

My grandfather had never filed any income tax return and most of what he did do was either illegal or ill advised. He had no savings. My grandfather read Tarot cards and sent out demons by burning human hair. My uncle kept hoards of pornography in his room and my mother filled the house with statues of mating animals which she worshipped.

My mother accepted the communist doctrine when I was about ten years old and from that time on there were socialists and communists study group meetings in the basement of our Baltimore home. I was taught there was no God and there was no such thing as right or wrong. My mother told me it was better to be a homosexual than to be a Christian. She taught me that the most important things in life were the physical pleasures of drink, food and sex.

For many years I lived the life I was taught. I drank a quart of vodka a day and by the time I was 30 I had been married twice. I lived only to eat, drink and have what I thought were sexual pleasures. But a time came when the women and the booze no longer gave me the happiness that my atheist mother told me they would bring. I was consuming so much alcohol that it no longer got me high. I started using marijuana and other drugs to supplement the alcohol which had betrayed me. At age 30, I began to realize how empty my life had been. There were no people in my life; my only friends were cigarettes and booze.

It was that realization that led me on my search for God. I had seen every evil in the world and now wanted to see the other side of life. I turned to the 12-step program to stop the drinking and there found my first awareness of a loving God.

Yet, that God had no name. In a novel, I read the story of the Great Physician, written by Saint Luke and I yearned to have the relationship and love of God this man had. But I did not know how to reach God.

On Jan. 25, 1980, as I was sleeping in my San Francisco apartment, the Holy Spirit came upon me and directed me to seek the truth in the Holy Bible. This was the one place I had never looked for it was the very Book that my mother had removed from our nation's schools by her lawsuit in 1963.

Now awakened by the call of God I drove to a downtown discount department store and there found a Bible under a stack of pornography. The gay check-out clerk laughed at me for buying a Bible but it was in that Bible I found the truth about Jesus Christ.

It was the Truth that sets every man free. The Truth that Jesus had paid the price for my sin so that I could be re-born and be a new person and have the gift of eternal life. I learned that this gift was mine for the asking.

Signed: William J. Murray (2 Cor. 5:17)
(son of Atheist leader Madelyn Murray O'Hair)

. . . .

(3) <u>Real Life 'Joe'</u>

Twenty years ago I started driving a taxi cab for a living. I soon found out it was a real ministry. I usually drove the night shift and my cab became a moving confessional. Passengers climbed in, sat behind me in total privacy and told me about their lives. But none touched me more than that of a woman I picked up late one night last summer.

I arrived at her run-down home at 2:30 a.m. and the building and surrounding area was quite dark and I knew the dangers. No one was waiting for me and most drivers would honk once and if no one showed up in a few seconds leave. I thought about the many impoverished people who depended upon taxis and, if at all possible, I would go knock on the door, which I did this night. I would think, "What if it were my mother, and how would I like for her to be treated?"

As I knocked I heard a frail voice say, "Just a minute." Then I heard something being dragged across the floor and soon the door opened. It was a small frail woman in her 80's wearing a print dress and a pill-box hat with a feather. At her side was a small nylon suitcase. I noticed the furniture was covered with sheets and the pictures and knick-knacks had all been put away.

"Would you carry my bag out to the car?" she asked. I graciously obliged and returned to assist the woman. She took my arm and we slowly walked to the curb. She kept thanking me for my kindness.

"Oh, it's nothing," I told her. "I just try to treat my passengers like I would want my mother to be treated."

"Oh, you're such a good boy," she said.

She gave me the address where she wanted to go and then said, "Could you drive through downtown?" I told her it was a lot longer that way and would cost quite a bit more.

"Oh, I don't mind," she said, "I'm in no hurry. I'm on my way to a hospice home."

I looked at her in the rear view mirror. I could tell she had been so pretty. Her eyes still glistened.

"I just don't have any family left," she continued, "and the doctor says I don't have very long to live." I quietly reached over and shut off the meter. For the next two hours we drove through the city. She pointed out the building where she had worked and where her and her husband used to live. For a long time we would just look out at the scenery and say nothing.

At the first hint of sunrise, she suddenly said, "I'm tired, let's go now." We drove in silence to a small convalescent home where two orderlies met us at the door. I opened the trunk and took out the small suitcase for her. As she sat in the wheelchair, ready to be escorted to another chapter of her life, she turned to me and said, "How much do I owe you?"

"Nothing," I said. Almost without thinking I bent down and gave her a hug.

She held on to me tightly and said in my ear, "You gave this old woman a bit of joy and I thank you."

I squeezed her hand and walked to my car. Behind me I heard the door shut. It was the sound of the closing chapter to another time and place.

I didn't pick up any more passengers that shift. I just drove around aimlessly and lost in thought; I could hardly talk. I thought, "What if an angry driver was called to pick up that woman? What if he had honked his horn once and drove off?" Now that it's over and I've had time to collect my thoughts, I can truthfully say, "I don't think that I have done anything more important in my life!"

In your life, people may not remember much of what you did or much of what you said. But they will always remember how you made them feel. Take a moment and appreciate the memories and the opportunities around you and make someone feel special today!

. . . .

(4) <u>Marilyn Monroe</u> was visited by Billy Graham during a presentation of a show. He said the Spirit of God had sent him to preach to her. After hearing what the preacher had to say, she said, "I don't need your Jesus."

One week later, she was found dead in her apartment.
"Be not deceived, God is not mocked."…… Gal. 6:7

(5) Pam's Story (Tebow – Story)

In a recent email, I read about a woman named Pam who knows the pain of considering abortion. More than 24 years ago, she and her husband Bob were serving as missionaries to the Philippines and praying for a fifth child. Pam contracted amoebic dysentery, an infection of the intestine caused by a parasite found in contaminated food or drink. She went into a coma and was treated with strong antibiotics before they discovered she was pregnant.

Doctors urged her to abort the baby for her own safety and told her that the medicines had caused irreversible damage to the baby. She refused the abortion and cited her Christian faith as the reason for her hope that her son would be born without the devastating disabilities physicians predicted. Pam said the doctors didn't think of it as a life but as a mass of fetal tissue.

While pregnant, Pam nearly lost their baby four times but refused to consider abortion. She recalled making a pledge to God along with her husband. Lord, if you will give us a son, we'll name him Timothy and we'll make him a preacher. Pam ultimately spent the last two months of her pregnancy in bed and eventually gave birth to a healthy baby boy August 14, 1987.

Pam's youngest son is indeed a preacher. He preaches in prisons, makes hospital visits, and serves with his father's ministry in the Philippines. He also plays football. Pam Tebow's son is Tim Tebow!

The University of Florida's star quarterback became the first sophomore in history to win college football's highest award, the Heisman Trophy. His current role as quarterback of the Denver Broncos has provided an incredible platform for Christian witness. As a result, he is being called 'The Mile-High Messiah.' Tim's notoriety and the family's inspiring story have given Pam numerous opportunities to speak on behalf of women's centers across the country. Pam Tebow believes that every little baby you save matters. I pray her tribe will increase!

May the peace of our Lord Jesus Christ be with you always!

(6) 'Make Me Like Joe'

Joe was a drunk who was miraculously converted at a Bowery mission. Prior to his conversion, he had gained the reputation of being a dirty wino for whom there was no hope, only a miserable existence in the ghetto. But following his conversion to a new life with God, everything changed. Joe became the most caring person than any one associated with the mission. Joe spent his days and nights hanging out at the mission doing whatever needed to be done.

There was never anything that he was asked to do that he considered beneath him. Whether it was cleaning up the vomit left by some violently sick alcoholic or scrubbing the toilets after the careless men left the men's room filthy, Joe did what was asked with a smile on his face and a seeming gratitude for the chance to help. He could be counted on to feed feeble men who wandered off the street and into the mission and to undress and tuck men into bed who could not take care of themselves.

One evening, when the director of the mission was delivering his evening evangelistic message, there was one man who came down the aisle to the altar. He knelt to pray and cried out for God to help him change. That repugnant drunk kept shouting, "Oh God! Make me like Joe! Make me like Joe! Make me like Joe!"

The director of the mission leaned over to the man and said, "Son, I think it would be better if you prayed, 'make me like Jesus.'"

The man looked up at the director with a quizzical expression on his face and said, "Is He like Joe?"

. . . .

(7) Billy Graham's Suit

This year (2012) Billy Graham is 93 years-old with Parkinson's disease. In January, leaders in Charlotte, North

Carolina, invited their favorite son, Billy Graham, to a luncheon in his honor. Billy initially hesitated to accept the invitation because he struggles with Parkinson's disease, but the Charlotte leaders said, "We don't expect a major address, just come and let us honor you." So he agreed.

After wonderful things were said about him, Dr. Graham stepped to the podium, looked at the crowd, and said, "I'm reminded today of Albert Einstein, the great physicist who this month has been honored by Time magazine as the Man of the Century. Einstein was once traveling from Princeton on a train when the conductor came down the aisle, punching the tickets of every passenger.

When he came to Einstein, Einstein reached in his vest pocket. He couldn't find his ticket. So he reached in his trouser pockets. It wasn't there. He looked in his briefcase, but couldn't find it. Then he looked in the seat beside him. He still couldn't find it.

The conductor said, "Dr. Einstein, I know who you are. We all know who you are. I'm sure you bought a ticket. Don't worry about it." Einstein nodded appreciatively.

The conductor continued down the aisle punching tickets. As he was ready to move to the next car, he turned around and saw the great physicist down on his hands and knees looking under his seat for his ticket.

The conductor rushed back and said, "Dr. Einstein, Dr. Einstein, don't worry, I know who you are; no problem. You don't need a ticket. I'm sure you bought one."

Einstein looked at him and said, "Young man, I too, know who I am. What I don't know is where I'm going."

Having said that, Billy Graham continued, "See the suit I'm wearing? It's a brand new suit. My children and my grandchildren are telling me I've gotten a little slovenly in my old age. I used to be a bit more fastidious. So I went out and bought a new suit for this luncheon and one more occasion. You know what that occasion is! This is the suit in which I'll be buried. But when you

hear I'm dead, I don't want you to immediately remember the suit I'm wearing. I want you to remember this:
 I not only know who I am. I also know where I'm going."

May your troubles be less, your blessings more, and may nothing but happiness, come through your door.

Life without God is like an unsharpened pencil - it has no point. Amen & Peace My Friends!

Index
(Punch-Lines)

Ch. 1 (Blonde)   p. 9-16
1. can I have my dog back?
2. follow me over to K-Mart
3. park like the rest of us do
4. wad of bread dough
5. farther away... Florida or the
6. jerk sitting on your knee.
7. cooked a pregnant bird.
8. First Class isn't going to
9. Just crap in the carburetor
10. you take away my license
11. yelled back, "It's a scarf!"
12. the first on the sun!
13. in a vacuum and someone
14. Rolex and one was named
15. send my lawn out to mowed
16. best results, put on two coats!
17. largest Re-tailer in the world!

Ch. 2 (Children)   p. 17-26
1. Where God Ain't...
2. I think I'd throw up.
3. Aspirins and keep away from
4. I just helped him cry.
5. That's all I need to know
6. Scout-leader, "And why did it
7. what is butt dust?
8. according to children
9. learned by adults
10. those crooks deducted $95.
11. truths, about growing old
12. Spurgeon, "I cannot understa
13. God keeps taking pictures
14. to have the Lamb at school
15. ain't no kin to Pappy!
16. buried at sea;
17. Parents who drugged us
18. chocolate chip cookies

Ch. 3 (Christian)   p. 27-34
1. Hawaiian good luck sign
2. chauffeur is Billy Graham.
3. Christian Like A Pumpkin
4. I guess I'd be an atheist!
5. Ketchup – hitting the bottle
6. Honey, if God gives you a cat
7. those who believe in nothing
8. my K-9 partner – what'd he do
9. tooth fairy will never believe
10. A Well Planned Life

Ch. 4 (Christmas)   p. 35-48
1. Even the church is trying
2. eat candy out of a sock!
3. Grandma Got Run Over
4. or the King James virgin?

5. Before the store opened
6. what was inside the drum.
7. pass the cranberries please
8. A lot of kneeling will
9. the dog was a shepherd
10. finding enough asses to fill
11. had to be a female reindeer
12. gold, common sense and fur
13. Christmas Mom, you'll be al
14. Christmas Scout
15. His Name at the top
16. paying their own way!"
17. should-a said something!
18. 100 points to get into heaven
19. Do-ya-patty-cake?
20. Christmas on the Ranch

Ch. 5 (Church)   p. 49-82
1. It's so dry in Texas
2. If it starts, I'm turning Catho
3. Well . . . he's there.
4. Baptizing the cat.
5. I hope I never get that way!
6. The Commode:
7. Redneck Church if...
8. can recite the entire Bible
9. Lazarus Was Dead!
10. son, but they walked
11. Robbing the Amish
12. the bridge is out?
13. Up We Go!
14. groom wearing black?
15. good care of your eyes
16. don't shove me either!
17. couldn't get a baby-sitter.
18. Thou shall not kill.
19. eight people to collect money
20. going to have a wife.
21. if we give him the money now
22. Brother, you be Jesus!
23. there's a dead seagull
24. of the poorest preachers

25. Help me preach a good sermon
26. the only feet I got!
27. hold up two fingers.
28. haven't been up to bat yet!
29. I had lunch with God,
30. short leg,... a little bit longer
31. Like talking to a wall
32. Preacher and Music Director
33. like being a pumpkin
34. Do you think Moses figured all
35. that we've ever kept them.
36. Don't worry about old age
37. carrot, an egg, and a cup
38. When you were born,
39. If it is refused, it is no pardon.
40. To make the gravy
41. the woman who cleans school
42. Mommy, if he gets loose
43. I read a quote...
44. All I really need to
45. that dash that belongs to you
46. did you do with the money?
47. No one thought they'd be seeing
48. the one Sunday I don't go
49. Asking God for ice-cream
50. Pastor Phil Blowhorn
51. Septic Tank Workers
52. Cleaning Poem
53. send the bill to my Brother-in la
54. fellow that run over Ol' Spot
55. his prayer for a new minivan
56. what happened to the flea?
57. Dead at desk for five days
58. Pls send more messengers
59. Baptist White Lie Cake
60. Baptist Dog
61. Gospel Snakes
62. where I used to go to churc
63. I'll just wait for the police.
64. A cannibal is someone
65. It was not seniors who removed
66. Now that I'm older...

67. Ch. 6 (Florida)   p. 83-88
1. higher per. of the elderly
2. Every member here is going
3. Hurricane is like Christmas
4. he may have to let her in
5. Twas the night before
6. Mr. TV moved in

Ch. 7 (Good Ole Days)   p. 89-94
1. peas porridge in the pot
2. yearly bath in May
3. Don't throw the baby out
4. raining cats and dogs.
5. called a "thresh-hold."
6. and "chew the fat."
7. the upper crust.
8. holding "a wake!"
9. was "a dead ringer."
10. Our God is Awesome!
11. God has caused the flowers
12. Fav animal; fried chicken

Ch. 8 (Jewish)   p. 95-100
1. Mama's Hanukkah Letter
2. Is anything alright?
3. "I think you're bad luck."
4. Hush up...tomorrow.
5. And so did my arthritis!
6. you want a speaking part!
7. that nice black boy
8. there are no Jews there
9. but no Chinese Jews.
10. Today they sent us you.
11. the last good meal
12. You order a baked apple

Ch. 9 (Married)   p. 101-120
1. Put your wife in the trunk
2. really good with the kids.
3. I'm going back to get her!
4. why God created Eve
5. I got the air-bag!

6. I want to stay with you guys.
7. that's Pontius, the pilot.
8. you did that yesterday!
9. poof...the husband was 90!
10. what was her maiden name?
11. I now pronounce you
12. if she finds her way home,
13. Signs in kitchens...
14. Marriage, man's perspective
15. and the neighbors listen.
16. I'll make you an offer!
17. two-lane or a four-lane?
18. 4 richer and 4 poorer.
19. keep erasing things out?
20. have to start all over again
21. Climb the walls...
22. The mood ring...
23. Monkeys in a coconut tree
24. it's 5 a.m. wake up!
25. I Miss The Old Clothesline
26. Only when he's drinking
27. Wedding dress for sale
28. P.S. Your girlfriend called!
29. Shirts for women
30. Rules for Men to follow
31. The Curtain Rods
32. Blue Silk P.J.'s
33. Happy Valentine's Day
34. you had a prescription!
35. woman's brain is used!
36. haven't eaten in three days?
37. downstream crosses bridge
38. witchcraft; today called golf
39. Men are seldom depressed
40. won't be needing this anymore
41. I-Phone / I-Hurt

Ch. 10 (Military)   p. 121-130
1. A Soldier Died Today
2. Dear Grandma and Grandpa,
3. when the train hit them.
4. The Jock Strap

5. RCMP took out his equipment
6. retrning home from Iraq!
7. he was with Marilyn Monroe!
8. My Kind Of Teacher
9. Can't wiggle out of this one
10. Mexicans in row-boat
11. Redneck Poem

Ch.11 (One-Liners)   p. 131-146
1. Will Rogers
2. Growing Older
3. But he loved her still
4. Thank God he's in bed
5. Don't take candy from strangers
6. Coincidence is when God
7. Did you know?
8. Nothing to go on!"
9. Did I see the sign right?
10. therefore I am, I think
11. On Being Thankful
12. Modern Proverbs
13. WD-40 and duct tape!
14. Bumper Stickers
15. eat crow while it's still
16. If you woke up breathing
17. need them to empty your bedpa
18. See beyond the imperfections.
19. some days you're the pigeon
20. Bill Gates – lines
21. from Ronald Reagan
22. I want to go back to
23. Rules of Life
24. More Rules of Life
25. Thoughts For Today
26. not have children after 35
27. unique. Just like everyone else.
28. say that I'm superficial,
29. old age is golden
30. Save the whales

Ch. 12 (Patriotic)   p. 147-156
1. only we see stars too!
2. experience in picking lemons?
3. to think I wasted two stamps
4. You might be a Redneck
5. Origin of Left & Right
6. four letters in American…I Can
7. The Morning Star'
8. Wal-Mart vs. The Morons
9. all 535 voting members
10. Dear Ma and Pa,
11. I Am Your Flag
12. guess Illinois already does this
13. Dad, cancel my allowance
14. $1000 Check every month
15. unplugged the life support
16. A killer whale ate them both

Ch. 13 (Redneck)   p. 157-170
1. Mule For Sale
2. to shoot my old coon dog
3. a true Red-Neck when
4. I got 5 tickets in the mail
5. somebody just stole your pick-up
6. Fine for dumping garbage.
7. nobody is gonna steal ole Henry
8. gun at you and gives you money
9. Southern Advice…
10. In need of a push…
11. Darwin Awards…
12. A Fish and Game Warden
13. wouldn't let me in without a tie!
14. The Tiny Cabin…
15. West Virginia Drivers Applicatio
16. I hope its blood…
17. Jaundice…
18. I don't know if they are afraid
19. Blessed are the cracked
20. put flares in the front and flares
21. trooper asked, "Got any ID?"
22. nobody retirin' an' movin' up North
23. Billy Bob! Did the FBI come?"

24. He makes his own lunch!
25. House Behind The House
26. And why did that upset you?
27. I'm Retired, go around me.
28. From Hawaii Pastor

Ch. 14 (School)   p. 171-178
Castor Oil and point him to
29. told me 2 plus 2 is 4 and now
30. Let me see your report card
31. The Mirror:
32. A Student's Letter to Dad
33. because he's inside your cat
34. the boy blurted out, "It's a puppy!"
35. to stay away from Aunt Karen
36. to tell people where to go.
37. to suffer without Chinese food
38. Think about all this Satan stuff?
39. There's our teacher, she's dead!
40. Cause, your feet ain't empty!
41. How much for a season pass?
42. Ant-Killer
43. Don't take life tooserious
44. Even if it's only a five or ten.

Ch. 15 (Senior)   p. 179-194
1. The Importance of Walking
2. cook & good with the kids.
3. take me out when I'm dead.
4. able to go for three weeks.
5. The $2.99 Special
6. If My body were a car!
7. the Corn Flakes back in the box
8. my Florida Driver's License!
9. Wrong Way!
10. money fell out of an armored car
11. in the wall of the crematory!
12. through me kidneys first?
13. me mother bought the ticket."
14. Will you marry me?"

15. I bought a hearing aid
16. you think I should get a bikini
17. that's prettier than freckles.
18. In My Day!
19. In The Beginning...
20. remember Monday through
21. I need a Gun – New
22. to round out a six-unit plot.
23. The Bathtub Test...
24. no nursing home in my future
25. Mint Condition... Male, 1940
26. "Crushed nuts?"
27. I haven't stolen your car.
28. one says, "Windy, isn't it?
29. and says, "Where's my toast?"
30. the name of the restaurant?
31. Think outside the box.
32. Because she can still drive!
33. a hot mama and be cheerful
34. A well planned life?
35. to pull up your zipper
36. that I don't need a license.

Ch. 16 (Sports)   p. 195-200
1. cross-country skiing
2. The Chicago Bears don't beat
3. about two minutes ago!
4. turned his head around the right way."
5. Tebow threw for exactly 316
6. St. Louis Rams and plays quarterback!
7. Mood Swings...

Ch. 17 (Travel)   p. 201-208
1. On a Kulula flight
2. are only 4 ways out of this
3. taking you for a ride.
4. To operate your seat belt,
5. one small child, pick your favorite."
6. paddle to shore and take your

7. Captain Kangaroo bounces us
8. pick your way through the wreckage
9. blasting through the skies
10. can light 'em, you smoke 'em.
11. Rough Landing
12. should see the back of mine!"
13. trying to change airlines!
14. that if someone has one short leg,
15. What are my choices?"
16. Crafty Millionaire...
17. How hot is it in Missouri?

Ch. 18 (Work)   p. 209-232
May I have large bills,
18. "its open I got that side.
19. that 1/2 was larger than 1/4.
20. just give me a dollar bill back.
21. He swallowed a quarter
22. let's look for yours!"
23. Full Body Scanner Solution
24. Be Nice To Your Nurse
25. Autopsy:
26. ever seen a little boy before?"
27. I'd call for backup.
28. awful word was "OOPS".
29. Nice Not To Know You
30. I Love my Job...
31. scoutin' out for more ground
32. Does she still have the hiccups?
33. with the engine running!"
34. 'in a series of small fires.'
35. 1000 Valentine cards
36. the broom and I'll show
37. "Peek-a-boo I.C.U!"
38. Can I get a new attorney?
39. Boots still didn't want to go on.
40. If that job was in Manhattan
41. Dear I.R.S
42. So-called Lie Detector
43. But where were you yesterday?

44. I love Baskin Robbins
45. Your IRS Rebate Check
46. Dust If You Must
47. Play your guitar with your amigos!"
48. Tators: 'Dick Tators'
49. Potatoes Have Eyes:
50. Like your coffee black?"
51. Cutting Down The Forest
52. Dumb and Dumber
53. Noah in the Year 2010
54. beat to death with a chair
55. Our God Is Awesome
56. Does God Exist?
57. Weekend shot you should go fishing!"

Ch. 19(Amazing Facts)   p.233-240
Properties of WATER
58. Properties of COKE
59. Garden Snakes Dangerous
60. Romney's Character
61. LOVE OF GOD = 101%
62. Football Players Exam

Ch. 20 (Church Stories)   p. 241-262
1. pretty pink flowers and said, I love you
2. I am grateful for...
3. How to plant your Garden
4. The Cracked Pot...
5. being smart wins out again!
6. Ben Stein: "We reap what we sow."
7. 7 wonders of the world...
8. in line to buy tickets for the circus
9. TV with Billy Graham's daughter...
10. Cheeter the Greeter...
11. Church Bulletins!

12. Petting Zoo- sacrifice-to be a blessing t
13. Taking Aim...in Seminary class
14. All I know is hearsay, Si?
15. Are You Jesus?
16. Making Pancakes...
17. Brain-the teacher must not have one!"
18. The Wicker Basket
19. Daddy's Empty Chair...
20. Allah or Jesus?
21. Our Church Needs No Money!
22. A little two-letter word 'UP'!

Ch. 21 (Holidays)   p. 263-276
1. Thanksgiving at Christmas
2. The Fourth of July
3. The folded napkin
4. I Remember Nancy... (Easter story)
5. telling me what that turkey did?
6. The 'W' in Christmas
7. Big-Wheel' Truck Stop
8. Awesome God,
9. 9.Think you are having a Bad Day?
10. If God Did Go On Strike- 'Thanksgiving
11. Good Friday in the Garden

Ch. 22 (Inspirational)   p 277-310
God's Hall of Fame (Heb. Ch. 11)
12. A Reason for Life...
13. "Are you God's wife?
14. The Bird Cage
15. My advantage was I had to try harder
16. Wesley Did you know
17. Don't quit!...
18. Things you cannot recover in life
19. The son of Sir Winston Churchill

20. Carl was a quiet man
21. Love people; use things
22. Two Heroes In Family
23. The Gingham Dress
24. A Girl With An Apple
25. The Red Umbrella
26. Packing Yo Parachute
27. Missionary Testimony
28. The Wooden Bowl
29. The Old Phone- Information please'.
30. Robby – my piano student
31. Does God exist?
32. Whoever takes the Son gets every..
33. Wrong E-Mail address

Ch. 23 (Political Stories) p. 311-324
Accounts Receivable Tax
34. great civilizations been about 200 yrs
35. Samuel Thompson wrote"...
36. By Judge Roy Moore
37. Commander Butch O'Hare
38. Easy Eddy – aka AlCapone's Lawyer
39. Johnny's Not There
40. Sack Lunches –
41. What a Legal System!
42. purchase of checkout 'one grape'
43. When the Music Stopped...

Ch. 24 (Seniors)   p. 325-332
1. but I still know who she is
2. inside the trunk was a dozen eggs
3. Christine Hewitt
4. Crabby Old Man...
5. Computer Swallowed Grandma

Ch. 25 Supernatural)   p. 331-342
1. Angels in the Alley...
2. Thomas Jefferson
3. John Lennon was found shot
4. A Home for Irene...
5. Almighty God Tabernacle".
6. angel tonight, On hwy 109
7. kills wife and buries children alive.
8. I heard her yell 'in English'
9. I wanted a car, not a Bible

Ch. 26 (Testimonies)   p. 342-351
1. The Dale Evans Story
2. William J. Murray
3. Real Life Joe – Taxi Driver
4. Marilyn Monroe
5. Pam Tebow – Story
6. Make Me Like Joe
7. Billy Graham's Suit

CPSIA information can be obtained
at www.ICGtesting.com
Printed in the USA
FFOW02n1340060718
47262946-50155FF